Praise for

never have your dog stuffed

"*Never Have Your Dog Stuffed* is a memoir by one of the most acclaimed actors of our time, who perhaps is one of the most genuinely humble. . . . What's striking about this book is not merely the scope of his accomplishments— personally as well as professionally—but the sense that the author thinks there's still so much yet to be learned."   —*Los Angeles Times Book Review*

"*Never Have Your Dog Stuffed* . . . [is] an amiable . . . amusing book. . . . Alda's path to stardom was long, narrow and twisted. The story of how he traveled is a reminder that show business is hard, uncertain work, and that breaking away from the pack is very much the exception."
                                                        —*The Washington Post Book World*

"This is no by-the-numbers memoir. . . . Alda does what a writer, even one with five Emmy Awards plus Tony and Oscar nominations, should. He tells a story, with detail, generous amounts of humor, sometimes painful honesty and insight. . . . [Alda] does what *M*A*S*H* did: He leaves you wanting more."   —*Pittsburgh Post-Gazette*

"[A] poignant, funny new memoir about growing up and finding fame."
                                                                              —*People*

"[An] entertaining autobiography tempered with humility and a depth rarely found in celebrity memoirs."   —*Publishers Weekly*

"It's hard to argue with his advice and easy to admire this revealing memoir."
                                                                    —*Houston Chronicle*

"An anomaly . . . a celebrity memoir of wit, substance and surprises. It reads like a series of stories rather than a record of his life, and while they never reveal more than you want to know, they're engaging and funny."
                                                              —*The Arizona Republic*

never have your dog stuffed

never
have your dog
stuffed

AND OTHER THINGS
I'VE LEARNED

ALAN ALDA

Random House Trade Paperbacks • New York

Never Have Your Dog Stuffed is a work of nonfiction.
Some names and identifying details have been changed.

2006 Random House Trade Paperback Edition

Published in the United States by Random House Trade Paperbacks, an imprint
of The Random House Publishing Group, a division of Random House, Inc., New York.

RANDOM HOUSE TRADE PAPERBACKS and colophon are trademarks
of Random House, Inc.

Originally published in slightly different form in hardcover in the United States
by Random House, an imprint of The Random House Publishing Group,
a division of Random House, Inc., in 2005.

LIBRARY OF CONGRESS CATALOGING-IN-PUBLICATION DATA

Alda, Alan
Never have your dog stuffed: and other things I've learned/Alan Alda.
p.   cm.
ISBN 0-8129-7440-9
1. Alda, Alan.   2. Actors—United States—Biography.   I. Title.
PN2287.A45A 3 2005   792.02′8′092—dc22   2005050135
[B]

Printed in the United States of America

www.atrandom.com

987654321

Book design by Carole Lowenstein

Act one: Get your hero up a tree.
Act two: Throw rocks at him.
Act three: Get him down again.

—*attributed to* GEORGE ABBOTT,
  on playwriting

contents

CONTENTS

act one

UP THE TREE OF THE KNOWLEDGE OF GOOD AND EVIL

chapter 1

DON'T NOTICE ANYTHING

My mother didn't try to stab my father until I was six, but she must have shown signs of oddness before that. Her detached gaze, the secret smile. Something.

We were living in a two-room apartment over the dance floor of a nightclub. My father was performing in the show that played below us every night. We could hear the musical numbers through the floorboards, and we had heard the closing number at midnight. My father should have come back from work hours ago.

My mother had asked me to stay up with her. She was lonely. We played gin rummy as the band below us played "Brazil" and couples danced through the haze of booze and cigarette smoke late into the night.

Finally, he came in. She jumped up, furious. "Where have you *been*?" she screamed. Even at the age of six, I could understand her anger. He worked with half-naked women and came home late. It wasn't crazy to be suspicious.

She told him she knew he was sleeping with someone. He denied it. "You *are*!" she screamed. He denied it again, this time impatiently.

"You son of a bitch!" she said. She picked up a paring knife and lunged at him, trying to plunge it into his face. *This* was crazy.

He caught her by the wrist. "What's the *matter* with you?"

They struggled over the knife as I pleaded with them to stop. When he forced her to drop it, I picked up the knife and rammed it point first into the table so it couldn't be used again.

A few weeks later, the three of us were at the small table by the kitchenette, eating.

I was playing with the knives and forks in the silverware tray. I found a paring knife with a bent point and I looked up at my mother: "Remember when I stuck the knife in the table?"

"When?"

"When you wanted to stab Daddy?"

She smiled. "Don't be silly. I never did that. I love Daddy. You just imagined that." She laughed a lighthearted but deliberate laugh. I looked over at my father, who looked away and said nothing.

I knew what I saw, but I wasn't supposed to speak about it. I didn't understand why. I didn't understand how this worked yet.

Gradually, I came to learn that not speaking about things is how we operated. When we would visit another family, my mother was afraid I might embarrass them by calling attention to something like dust balls or carpet stains. As we stood at the door, waiting for them to answer our knock, she would turn to me, completely serious, and say, "Don't notice anything."

We had a strange list of things you didn't notice or talk about. The night the country was voting on Roosevelt's fourth term, my father came back from the local schoolhouse and I asked him whom he'd voted for. "Well," he said with a little smile, "we have a secret ballot in this country." I didn't ask him again, because I could see it was one of the things you don't talk about, but I couldn't figure out why there was a law against telling your children how you voted.

One thing we never talked about was mental illness. The words were never spoken between my father and me. This wasn't the policy just in our own family. At that time, mental illness was more like a curse than a disease, and it was shameful for the whole family to admit it existed. Somehow it would discredit your parents, your cousins, and everyone close to you. You just kept quiet about it.

How much easier it could have been for my father and me to face her illness together; to compare notes, to figure out strategies. Instead, each of us was on his own. And I alternated between thinking her behavior was his fault and thinking it was mine. Once I learned there was such a thing as sin and I entered adolescence and came across a sin I really liked, I began to be convinced that my sins actually caused her destructive episodes. They appeared to coincide. This wasn't entirely illogical, because they both tended to occur every day. I was convinced I held a magic wand that could damage the entire household.

Like the earliest humans, I put together my observations and came up with a picture of how things worked that was as ingenious as it was cockeyed. And like the earliest people, in my early days I was full of watching and figuring. I was curious from the first moments—not as a pastime, but as a way to survive.

As I sat at the kitchen table that night, looking at the paring knife with the bent point, I was trying to figure out why I was supposed to not know what I knew. I was already wondering: Why are things like this? What's really happening here?

There was plenty about my world to stimulate my curiosity. From my earliest days, I was standing off on the side, watching, trying to understand a world that fascinated me. It was a world of coarse jokes and laughter late into the night, a world of gambling and drinking and the frequent sight of the buttocks, thighs, and breasts of naked women.

It seemed to me that the world was very interesting. How could you not want to explore a place like this?

chapter 2

NAKED LADIES

I was three years old. It was one in the morning, and I was walking down the aisle of a smoky railroad car. I liked the feel of the train as it lurched and roared under my feet. My father was in burlesque, and he and my mother and I traveled from town to town with a company of comics, straight men, chorus girls, strippers, and talking women. As I moved down the aisle, not much taller than the armrests, I watched the card playing, the dice games, the drinking and joking, late into the night.

I would fall asleep on a makeshift bed made of two train seats jammed together. A few hours later, my mother would wake me as the train pulled into Buffalo or Pittsburgh or Philly. I'd sit up groggily and gaze out the window as she pulled on my woolen coat and rubbed my face where the basket weave of the cane seat had left a pink latticework on my cheek. As the train crept slowly into the town, I could see the water towers, the factories, the freight trains jockeying across the rail yards in the gray early light. This would be the first sight I'd have of every city we'd travel to, and my heart would beat with excitement.

And then, five or six times a day—at almost every show—I would be standing in the wings, watching. There would be an opening number in which my father stood on the side of the stage and sang while chorus girls danced and showed their breasts. The person who performed this job in burlesque was called, with cheerful clarity, "the tit singer."

My father sang well, and he was a handsome man. When he walked down the street, people sometimes mistook him for Cary Grant and asked for his autograph. But when he was onstage as the tit singer, no one looked at him.

After his song, my father would be the straight man for a comic. Or, there might be a sketch with a couple of comics and a talking woman. A talking woman was a dancer or stripper who could also do lines. When a woman was new to the company, the comics would ask, "Can she talk?"

Then there would be a strip. The lights would go out, and over the loudspeaker a voice would announce: "The Casino Theater is proud to present . . . Miss Fifi."

In the pit, the drummer would beat out a rhythm while she kept time with her pelvis. She would slip off a piece of clothing and toss it into the wings. It would land a couple of feet from me, and a wardrobe mistress would pick it up and fold it carefully. The stripper would walk around the stage in time to the music and finally pull off the rest of her clothing. Except for some fringe where her underwear would go, she was naked. Blackout.

The muscle in her hip would graze my shoulder as she brushed by me. She would grab a piece of her costume and hold it against her bare chest as she walked briskly up the stairs to her dressing room.

Upstairs was where heaven was.

The chorus girls always brought me up to their dressing room. They talked with me; they patted my cheek and combed my hair. They were affectionate. I was like a pet. When they had to change costumes, they would say, "Okay, Allie, turn your back now." While they changed, I stood with my face against the wall where their costumes were hanging. My face was buried in their silk clothes, and the smell of their sweat and perfume filled my nostrils. I heard the sound of their clothing sliding on and off their bodies. All of this was far more interesting for a three-year-old than you might imagine.

But I wasn't only the dancers' pet; I was a plaything for the whole company.

When I was six months old, the comics thought it would be funny to bring me out in a high chair in a schoolroom sketch. As they told me this story later, all the great comics were in this sketch: Red Buttons, Phil Silvers, Rags Ragland. I don't know now if all these comics were actually in the same sketch; the story must have grown with each telling. They said they put a school bell in front of me on the high chair, and totally by accident, I would manage to bang on it every time one of them was getting to a punch line. "You upstaged the greatest comics in burlesque," they told me.

When I was two, the company was playing a theater in Toronto. A photographer from the *Toronto Daily Star* came backstage, and my father got the idea that if he posed me in a way that made me look as if I were smoking a pipe, the paper would be sure to print the picture and the burlesque company would get some unusual publicity. They dressed me up in my woolen suit and posed me gravely holding a pipe with tobacco in it. They seem to have invented a new name for me, too. I was born Alphonso D'Abruzzo, but that day I was Alphonse Robert Alda, "Ali" for short. The newspaper printed the picture and ran a story under it that, sixty-seven years later, is a gold mine of information on how not to raise a child.

CHILD OF TWO SMOKES PIPE
ONCE BROKE MOTHER'S NOSE

Alphonse Robert Alda, at the age of two years and three months, finds solace from worldly cares in a briar pipe.

I don't remember my mother ever telling me I had broken her nose, so this may have been invented to demonstrate how big and strong I was or maybe to account for a slight bend in her nose she wasn't fond of. As for smoking, according to the myth dreamed up by my father, I had reached up and taken the pipe out of his mouth a year earlier. My mother was quoted as saying they'd hoped I'd get sick and never smoke again but that I liked it and had continued to smoke the pipe. Then they invented a "specialist" from New York whom they said they had consulted. "He told us," my mother was quoted as saying, "provided moderation was shown, the smoking might not do Ali as much harm as the psychological aspect of denying him." This bit of invented psychology looks even stranger when, later in the article, she says: "We don't believe in pampering children. All you have to do to stop him if he starts to cry, which is seldom, is to tell him not to be a baby."

So, let's review this. You're two years old. You watch naked women shake their tits five times a day. You never get to cry or act like a baby. But denying you tobacco would be psychologically unhealthy.

At the end of the article, my mother tells the reporter how much I like to act.

"He wants to be an actor like his daddy," she said. "Watch! Ali," she asked, "what would you do if a man were chasing you with a big stick?" The little fellow spread himself against the wall, his face and eyes depicting horror and fright.

Then she changed him to a "funny man," and I switched to happy laughter; then sadness when the man fell down and hurt himself. The photographer took pictures of all of this, and they show a surprising range of emotion. The caption under them reads, "Alphonse wants to be an actor." It might just as accurately have read, "Alphonse wants to please."

A couple of days later, everyone at the theater made a fuss over me and showed me my picture in the paper. I watched my father as he proudly held up the article and showed it around. I'd been told not to lie, yet we all knew I didn't smoke (I drank a little beer with the comics, but I didn't smoke). Now here was my father, proud of the gimmick he'd come up with. The picture of me holding the pipe was a clever way to announce that the company had come to town. For him, saying I smoked was no different from coming onstage in a sketch and saying, "Well, here we are in sunny Spain." He and the audience all knew they were actually in Toronto. It was just a show, a way of *capturing attention*. And if you could capture attention, that was an accomplishment. It was *the* accomplishment.

There was a lot of ribbing in the company and practical jokes that took place right in front of the audience. Once, when I was three, a couple of comics came over to me between shows and asked if I'd like to have some fun with them. It would involve my being onstage. Would I like that? Okay, I said. Then they coached me on what to do and what to say. There was some discussion between them on my dialogue until they settled on something that made them both laugh. Then they put me where I would stay quietly until I made my entrance. My father's partner, Hank Henry, was doing a solo sketch, a pantomime of a drunken man trying to rob a safe in a bar. The band played backup music as he staggered over to the safe and pretended to steady his shaking hand by clutching one end of his necktie, which was loose around his neck, while he pulled on the other end of it as if the tie were a rope on a pulley. I remember this vividly because I was watching from a point closer than usual: As a surprise for Hank, the comics had put me onstage, *inside* the safe. I remember crouching in the wooden prop, looking through cracks and seeing the stage lights, bright as suns, and Hank lurching toward me. Under my breath, I was saying my line over and over so I wouldn't forget it. When he finally got the safe open, I stepped out, spread my arms, and said my line, one word: "Father!" For some reason, this was hilarious to the other comics. Later, they had even more fun when they told me to ask the theater manager for ten cents in wages for my performance. He wasn't amused; in fact, he acted as though ten cents were real money to him. Maybe that was their point. Anyway, I was a little confused but glad to be part of the gang.

I had my own pet in the company. One of the actors was a very short man, about my size—what used to be called a midget. He was married to a tall stripper, who loved him very much. Sometimes, when we were in the lobby late at night waiting to get into cabs and head for the train station, he would call to her across the room and say, "Honey, squeeze me with your eyes." She would squeeze her eyelids together, which utterly delighted him. While we sat in the lobby one night, on our way to the next town, I crowded him. I sat on his lap and played with his small hands, comparing my hand size to his and examining his ring. Since he was my height, I thought of him as my playmate. My mother had to pry me away from him and apologize for me.

As I think about all this now, trying to make out the beginnings of my life, I'm struck by how I grew up among people who didn't seem to know what children were, because they were children themselves. And I couldn't tell the difference between adults and children, either. We were all together in a happy, innocent, erotic Eden.

Photographs from my childhood are snapshots of dress-up and make-believe. We were in show business, and reality was what you decided it was. There was my mother in the early pictures, a beautiful woman with brown hair. She had won a beauty contest when she was twenty or so and had toured for a year with a vaudeville troupe called Fanchon and Marco, in which the entire act seems to have consisted of young women walking across the stage in bathing suits. But then, a couple of years later, the photographs begin to change. Her hair suddenly becomes blond. A slight bump on her nose goes away and the nose takes an upward turn. Around the same time, my father must have had surgery, too. His nose gets straighter and he looks even more like Cary Grant. Each time I examined the past under a microscope it seemed different, as if I were looking at it through a kaleidoscope.

Even the pictures of the miserable summer when they left me with my mother's aunts in Wilmington, Delaware, show me dressed in a series of costumes. I'm not sure how I wound up in Wilmington; maybe my parents thought the air was healthier in Delaware than in the alleys outside the burlesque theaters where I lingered with cops and their horses. But at the time, I suspected I was dumped in Wilmington because of a pig my parents loved more than me.

My father had written a sketch with his partner, Hank Henry, that involved a small pig. Midway through the sketch, Hank would say, "Get out of here and don't come back until you can bring home the bacon." My father would leave the stage, and at the end of the sketch he would come back with the pig under his arm and say, "Well, I brought home the bacon!"

Blackout.

It's hard to imagine this getting a laugh from an audience—or their playing town after town with this gag and making a living. But in order to be able to do that one blackout line, they lugged the pig from theater to theater. He rode in the back of their car. They fed him, gave him a place to sleep, and, what I was most jealous of, they took him everywhere they went, without me. For a whole summer, I was stashed in Wilmington with my mother's aunt Betty and aunt Anne, while Hank and my parents drove around the burlesque wheel with the damned pig.

I burned with anger and jealousy. On the way to Wilmington, my mother had been very cheerful, telling me what a great time I was going to have. "Aunt Anne is a very fine woman," she said. *A fine woman.* A phrase soaked in phoniness. "And Aunt Betty is so *jolly*. She's really, really funny."

Aunt Betty was not jolly. She had a nervous laugh and a couple of large warts on her nose, and she tended to wear her stockings rolled down around her ankles. She smiled at everything. You fell down, she smiled. She was peculiar—which for my mother was jolly.

Aunt Anne was skinny and stern. She had been a nurse among the

Chinese before the war. I didn't know what this meant, but I didn't like the sound of it.

My parents left me with these strange people, these *civilians* who were pretending to have something to do with our family. My parents would come by to visit me when they were playing near Wilmington, and they always brought a little suit of clothes for me, a uniform of some kind. They dressed me up in a sailor suit or a Royal Mounties outfit or a policeman's uniform, and then they took me into the yard with a box camera and took my picture, usually saluting.

On their first visit, after they took the picture, they took me over to the back of the car and showed me the pig. I could tell they expected me to be excited because he was this fat little pink animal.

I hated him. He got treated better than I did. For all I knew, he was the one going up to the chorus girls' dressing rooms now instead of me.

My parents stayed for a couple of hours, then drove off with my little brother, the pig, and I was left with these crazy civilian sisters. When the summer was over, I went back on the road with them, but it wasn't long before they had to store me away again.

When it was time for first grade, my parents realized they couldn't keep lugging me from town to town, so they signed me up at a Catholic boarding school in Manhattan. I remember the place in tones of black and white. Gray walls around an exercise yard full of screaming boys; in autumn, cold hands, smudged with city grime, holding a weekly treat of a cheap ice-cream bar, licking rivulets of fake vanilla as they ran down my fingers, tasting more of dirt than ice cream.

Once a week, I would be called to the office, where, at a wall phone, I would hold the black cylinder of a receiver to my ear and listen to my mother as she tried to cheer me up. I dreaded the calls because within a minute she would be telling me how much she missed me and sobbing.

The other children played games I didn't understand. "Come on," they said, running by me in the yard, "we're playing Nazis and Jews." I ran with them for a while before I realized they had chosen a boy at random to be the Jew. We were chasing him down, and he seemed truly terrified. I stepped out of the chase and watched as they took turns shoving him to the ground.

My parents had sent me a soccer ball, then later a second ball. This was not appreciated by the other boys. A delegation came to see me. "You have two balls," one of them said. "We'd like to borrow one." He said it with that look that goes through your eyes to the back of your head. I said yes, knowing I wouldn't see the ball again.

Then someone came and tried to take the other ball. I held on to it, and he pushed me down. I fought back instinctively. Within moments, I was in an ecstasy of rage. Somehow I had turned him facedown and I was sitting on him, pounding his back with my fists. The boys around me said, "That's enough," but I had never hit anyone before and there was no measure or thought in my fury. I kept pounding until they lifted me off him.

I was frightened by what I had done and scared by how out of control I was. I kept away from the other boys after that. I waited out the year, not knowing that I would be rescued soon from this gray place. My father had been asked to make screen tests by three movie studios and was offered a seven-year contract by Warner Bros. I traveled with them as he finished a tour in nightclubs, where we heard them playing "Brazil" every night through the floorboards and my mother expressed her discontent with a paring knife, and then we put all that behind us and headed for Hollywood and sunshine.

chapter 3

NEVER HAVE YOUR DOG STUFFED

He was a large black cocker spaniel with long flaps for ears and a fat behind that moved from side to side when he wagged his stub of a tail. He jumped onto my bed and began licking my face. I was sick with polio, and my father had brought home a dog to cheer me up. Overcome with happiness at our instantaneous friendship, I threw my seven-year-old arms around him and kissed him back.

I'd come down with polio just a week after my father had begun acting in his first movie. He was playing George Gershwin in a film biography called *Rhapsody in Blue*. So we called the dog Rhapsody.

The Gershwin biography would turn out to be one of the big pictures of the year. Having spent years in burlesque and nightclubs, my father was almost instantly a movie star. It sounds a little better than it was.

We were living in Hollywood—the real Hollywood—a block north of Hollywood Boulevard on something called Yucca Street in a dark bungalow. Its windows were covered by the leaves of overgrown banana trees. Although he was playing the lead in a big movie, my father's long-term contract paid him a salary per week that would nowadays buy dinner for two with domestic wine. If his pictures became successful, he could be loaned out to other studios for a large amount of money, which would be pocketed by Warners. This was the common practice at all the studios at the time. At that age, of course, I knew none of this. It didn't occur to me that my father was making so little money working for the Brothers Warner that we couldn't live in a drearier place if we were in a story by the Brothers Grimm. Our house was not much bigger than a cabin, but I loved it.

Our patch of tangled yard was an exotic foreign country. I had spent so much of my life in dark theaters and dim hotel rooms, where the only thing green was the peeling paint on the walls, that this seemed like nature to me. This was where I had my first bite of a mud pie; where I set up a card table and mixed household chemicals, toothpaste, and my mother's face powder, doing what I called "experiments." Now that I was sick, I wasn't allowed out of the house, but when I stood on the headboard of my bed, I could look through a high window into the backyard and see the concrete wall I used to climb over with my friends. We'd sneak under the cover of the banana trees and light matches I had stolen from my mother's kitchen. I could just reach the big box of wooden matchsticks she kept on the top shelf of the old four-legged gas stove. Sometimes my friends and I would soak paper airplanes in kerosene and pretend we were sending German fighters down in flames. For ten cents, a gas station down the block would sell us enough kerosene to blow ourselves up. It's not clear why we didn't.

But now, as I looked out through the window, there was just the gray concrete wall. No friends.

The country was in the throes of an epidemic. People were afraid to go to public swimming pools or theaters for fear of contagion. Having any contact with someone known to have polio was thought to be reckless. I'd been declared by the doctors to be out of the contagious period for weeks now, but my friends' parents had forbidden them to see me.

All except one, who sat uncomfortably for a few minutes on a wooden chair across the room and chatted with me. After he left, my mother explained that it must have been hard for his parents to allow him to come. Over the next couple of weeks, I thought about this, about how kind he was to visit me. I also noticed he didn't come back. But, after all, a plague mentality was in the air.

I had come down with polio a couple of weeks after starting second grade. My parents had enrolled me in a military academy, possibly acting once again on their weird fetish for uniforms. For the first two weeks of school, I was introduced to the fine points of drilling, marching, and standing guard. Standing guard involved walking in circles for an hour or two and being able to recite, if asked, a list of ten special orders. There were rumors among my classmates about what would happen to you if you got any of the orders wrong or in the wrong sequence. Older boys would come up to you and fire off questions, as if they were the officer of the day: What's order number three? What's order number five? This was an interesting departure from standing in the wings watching Miss Fifi take off her clothes.

At some point during this slightly stressful period, I came in contact with the virus, and a few days later on a Saturday night, we went out to the movies. We always went to the Warner Theater on Hollywood Boulevard, because after my father asked for "professional courtesy," the manager would let us in for free. We were watching, maybe, *Casablanca*. The theater was packed and we couldn't get three seats together, so I was sitting a few rows in front of my parents.

As I watched the movie, I developed a stuffy nose and I kept trying to blow into a handkerchief. I made a honking sound, even during the love scenes.

"Play it, Sam." *Honk.*

No matter how hard I blew, I couldn't clear my nose.

"We'll always have Paris." *Honk.*

"Louis, this could be the *honk* of a beautiful *honk.*"

After the movie, in the backseat of the car, I started honking again.

17

"*Was that you?*" my mother asked. "I couldn't believe it. I heard you all through the movie."

When we got home I had to throw up. They held my head as I leaned over the toilet. My knees buckled and I nearly fell into the bowl. They caught me and held me up. I could hear my mother whisper to my father. "My God, he has polio." My father whispered hoarsely, "Come on, will you? You always think the worst." But she insisted. She'd been reading about polio in magazines. She read magazines about only two subjects: crime and health. When I was about four, she took me to a nutrition lecture in Manhattan where we were encouraged to eat the peels of oranges. We went home and shared an orange peel together. She made sounds as if she were enjoying it, but we could barely choke it down, and we never ate another one. She never gave up on reading about health, though, and she knew the symptoms of the disease that was taking out thousands of children. She was sure I had polio, and she would not be talked out of it.

My father gave in, and early the next morning they called a doctor. By then my neck was stiff; I couldn't bend it to drink the pineapple juice they handed me. The doctor came and examined me and told them they had to get me to a hospital for a spinal tap. We got into the Oldsmobile and drove to the hospital. My mother was jolly—singing, telling stories to keep my spirits up. I had a feeling this was going to be another Aunt Betty.

At the hospital, they stuck a long needle into my spine and told me they were taking out some fluid. A few hours later, I saw my mother peeking through a small window that looked out onto the parking lot. She was waving and smiling cheerfully, but I saw her despair. I had polio.

I didn't really know what it meant to have polio. It didn't seem so bad. Every day, a new toy arrived in my hospital room from a Hollywood gag and gift shop: magic cards; the disappearing penny trick; the straw tube you put your fingers in and then you can't get them out again.

But eventually, when I was back home in my bedroom, lying in bed half listening to the radio and looking at the empty wooden chair where my friend had sat for a few minutes, I began to notice that my life had changed.

Rhapsody jumped onto the bed and let me scratch his belly and try to tie his ears into knots on top of his head. His appetite for affection was like his appetite for food: It didn't stop. His behind was getting heftier from scooping leftover meals off the dishes we left on the floor for him.

I don't remember his being in the room during my treatments. He may have been let out into the yard to spare him the sound of the screaming, which he wouldn't have understood.

I didn't completely understand it myself, and I was the one screaming.

Following the protocols of the Sister Kenny treatments, my parents would wrap my limbs and torso in pieces of hot wool that they had cut from blankets and folded into triangles. The blankets were heated in the dry top pot of a double boiler, so that they'd be nearly as hot as the steam under them, without the scalding wetness. But they were still plenty hot. They wrapped the hot wool around my arms, legs, chest, and belly and pinned it tightly into place. Two hours later the wraps had cooled, and it had to be done again. This was repeated all day long. In the evening, I was given a double wrap and allowed to sleep the night through.

My parents couldn't afford nursing help, and they did all this themselves. The hot packs were often too hot for them to fold into triangles without burning their fingers, and they lost control and dropped them onto my bare back. This was when I started screaming and pounding the bed with my fists to distract myself from the pain. I understood that wrapping me in packs had to be done, and I knew how hard it was for them to hear me in pain, but there was no way not to scream. If Rhapsody was in the house, he was probably hiding under the stove.

And then there were the massages. Three times a week, I was laid out on the dining room table in my Jockey shorts while a physical therapist took each of my limbs and tried to unscrew it from its socket. Sometimes she ripped an arm off and had to plug it back in again, but usually she was satisfied just to keep bending it until I agreed to turn over playmates who were members of the French underground.

The idea was to stretch the muscles that were in spasm. This and the hot packs were the discovery of Sister Elizabeth Kenny, a nurse in Australia. She was invited to teach in the United States about three years before I came down with polio, and by then the "Sister Kenny treatments" were popular throughout the country. I grew up knowing that she had saved my life, or at least had made it possible for me to walk without braces. So, it felt strange one day, as an adult, to be walking down a hospital corridor with a scientist, telling him how Sister Kenny had saved me and to hear him casually say, "Well, there's some question now about the efficacy of those treatments." I was surprised to hear there was even a question about their efficacy. This was not a thought that would have been welcome to the seven-year-old waiting for the hour to strike, as the pot on the stove bubbled under the woolen wraps.

The treatments went on for months. My eighth birthday passed. Then the skies cleared and it was spring. I could get out of bed.

The doctor said that swimming would be good for my muscles. My parents had saved enough from my father's small salary to make a down payment on a house with a pool. Amazingly, it came with a guesthouse, a barn, twenty chickens, three pigs, a horse, a cow, and a peacock—all on eleven acres of land. It also came with the owner, an eccentric German inventor, who agreed to the low monthly payments in exchange for our letting him stay on in the guesthouse.

We packed up our stuff in the Oldsmobile convertible, I held Rhapsody on my lap, and we headed for our new home in La Tuna Canyon on the other side of the San Fernando Valley. We drove for hours. La Tuna Canyon, apparently, was in Kansas.

Finally, three miles after we passed through a town called Roscoe (not so much a town as a pair of train tracks, a hardware store, and a barbershop), we made a left off the highway onto a long dusty road that turned out to be our driveway. I'd never seen anything like this—large open fields, olive trees, animals. The house was surrounded by mountains. Rhapsody and I jumped out of the car and started exploring. His tail was flicking, his behind was wagging. So was mine.

Exhausted at the end of the day, we went to sleep in our new house. On the second day, somehow in this wasteland, we found a Chinese restaurant and celebrated by eating out. We brought home the leftovers and set them out for Rhapsody, who went right into the food headfirst.

We left him in a little utility room off the kitchen. When I closed the door he had his nose in the food and was chewing industriously. A couple of minutes later, I heard yelping. It was a yelp of panic, of pain and desperation. I opened the door to the utility room, and the panic seized me as well. Rhapsody was running in circles, screaming in his dog voice, uncontrollable. The walls were spattered with excrement. With every lap, more of it flew against the white walls. I closed the door on the sight of him circling the room and went tearfully to my father. He said we should let him out of the house. He would be all right. Animals have a way of caring for themselves. We opened the back door and he ran out.

But he didn't have a way of caring for himself. He began circling the house, running as fast as he could. Once around the house, twice around, still screaming in his dog voice. Then, on the third circle of the house, on the porch, a few inches from the front door, he died.

Somehow, my dog had died from eating Chinese food. I could picture the sharp fragment of bone he must have gulped down and the damage it had done to his soft insides.

The next morning, Rhapsody was still there on the front porch. My father and I lifted him onto a blanket. There was still a stain on the brick floor where his body had been. It crossed my eight-year-old mind that he'd been there long enough for the stain of his sweat to have dried. This was more like the stain of death.

My father felt, I guess, that getting me involved would help me deal with the loss. He said, "Let's bury him together, okay, Butch?" I was choking back my tears as we each picked up a corner of the blanket and lifted Rhapsody off the porch. With shovels over our shoulders, we started walking, carrying my dead dog between us. My father had one end of the blanket, I had the other, and we walked and we walked— through the olive grove, across the field, beyond the line of eucalyptus trees, to the scruffy patch of land by the dry riverbed. We put the dog down and put our shovels into the dirt. With the first shovelful I burst into tears. And with every shovelful I cried louder and harder. We finally had an open pit in the ground, and I was uncontrollable. My father didn't know what to do. He looked away helplessly. I let the shovel drop and stood with my hands at my sides, sobbing.

After a moment, he turned to me and said, "Maybe we should have the dog stuffed."

I looked up at him. I wondered what he was talking about.

"Stuff the dog?"

"We could take him to a taxidermist and have him stuffed. You want to do that? That way you could always keep him."

If it didn't involve putting the dog in the ground and starting in with the shovels again, it sounded good to me. "Okay," I said, "let's stuff him."

So we took the dog to a taxidermist.

We entered a dark store on Hollywood Boulevard, and I walked through an eerie menagerie. There were dozens of birds—black birds, blue birds, somebody's parakeet—all dead, standing on branches. A squirrel stood on a velvet-covered board, tail at high alert, a quizzical look on his face.

The taxidermist put a studious and professional look on his own face. He wanted to know what our dog looked like. Did we have any snapshots? What kind of *expression* did he usually have?

I tried to think about this, but I couldn't remember any expression he was particularly known for. I'd never really paid attention to my dog's emotional life. I thought all dogs had pretty much the same expression—a kind of dogginess common to all of them.

My father and I launched haltingly into an effort to describe our dog's expression. We came up with vague abstractions. He was a nice dog. He had a nice expression on his face.

After a discreet pause, the taxidermist said he'd call us when the job was finished.

It took six weeks to stuff the dog. By the time he came back from the taxidermist's shop, I hadn't forgotten him completely, but he was certainly not something I thought about every day.

We pulled off the brown butcher's paper he was wrapped in and looked at him. The dog had a totally unrecognizable expression on his face. He looked as if he'd seen something loathsome that needed to be shredded. Nobody in our family knew who this was. He sat on his blue velvet board, looking up at us like something with rabies. We were kind of afraid of him.

My parents made excuses for the taxidermist. *He didn't really know the dog; he did the best he could. We'll get used to the look on his face.*

We put what now passed for our dog in the living room near the fireplace. But after a couple of days, it became difficult to walk into the room without feeling that a wild animal was going to spring at you. You were aware, out of the corner of your eye, that there was something alive but perfectly still in the room, and then you would see those glass eyes staring at you and the vicious mouth, hungry for your flesh. When guests visited, if we didn't warn them that the dog wasn't real, they'd walk into the room and stand dead still. Sometimes they would back slowly out of the room, trying to escape before it leapt at their throat.

We realized we couldn't keep him in the living room, so we put him outside on the front porch—not far, in fact, from where he'd died. The trouble now was that deliverymen were afraid to make deliveries. They would leave packages on the grass.

Losing the dog wasn't as bad as getting him back. Now that he was stuffed, he was just a hollow parody of himself. Like a bad nose job or a pair of eyes set surgically in eternal surprise, he was a reminder that things would never again be the way they were. And the longer you looked at his dead skin stretched inaccurately over a wire frame, the less well you could *remember* him as he was. As time went on, my memory of the real Rhapsody was replaced by the image of him sitting lifeless on the blue velvet board with a hideous look on his face. And anyway, it wasn't memories I wanted; I wanted the dog. I wanted him sitting at the end of our first day in the new house, patiently watching my face while I pulled foxtail burrs from the fur on his long ears.

Yet the effort to keep him had seemed to make him disappear even more. I couldn't understand why. As I did about most things in my life, starting with my mother, I kept asking the same questions: "Why is it like this? What's happening here?" But I couldn't figure it out.

I understand it a little better now, and I see now that stuffing your dog is more than what happens when you take a dead body and turn it into a souvenir. It's also what happens when you hold on to any living moment longer than it wants you to.

Memory can be a kind of mental taxidermy, trying to hold on to the present after it's become the past. I didn't know this then. Change was coming, and I was going to have to come out of my cocoon soon. But I wasn't ready for the next stage in my life, and I hung on to the early times as long as I could.

Hold off the outside, I thought. *Don't go to the edge of our world near the Land of the Civilians. Stay in Eden, where it's safe.*

But I wouldn't be able to hold off change any more than the Hollywood taxidermist could. I was headed out.

chapter 4

THE SAGE OF LA TUNA CANYON

I grew wild, like the brush in the canyon.

I spent most of my time alone. I didn't go to school because my parents thought we'd be able to go on the road when we had to if they had me tutored; our house was so isolated that I seldom saw a friend; my father worked until late at the studio, and my mother put in a long day reading nutrition pamphlets and *True Crime* detective magazines. I was free to explore. My curiosity took me on long hikes where, sweaty and smelling of sage, I climbed the mountain trails, poking into things, trying to figure out how they got that way. If I found coyote droppings on the trail, I would poke at them with a stick to see what the animal had been eating.

One morning I went up the dirt road to the henhouse to feed the chickens, and on the ground I saw the most amazing thing. A rattlesnake had tried to swallow a mouse whole and had apparently choked and died trying to get it down. *What a stupid thing for a snake to do,* I thought. *What made it think it could swallow a mouse?* Since the snake was dead and couldn't hurt me, I picked up a stick and started poking at it. And then I froze. The snake wasn't dead. He slowly backed off from the mouse's body and let his jaws locate themselves again. I was thirty inches from a rattlesnake that could jump much faster than I could. I just stood still, and for some reason he continued to back off from me and then turned and slithered away. I learned a good lesson that day: If a rattlesnake thinks he can swallow a mouse, he probably can. Don't assume you think like a snake unless you *are* one.

The snake didn't stop me from poking around, though. I couldn't resist. On our first Christmas Eve in the new house, I managed to poke my finger into an emotional light socket. Around midnight, I was in bed, excited that Santa Claus might be coming at any minute and listening for sounds on the roof. What I heard, instead, were sounds of my mother and father downstairs. I sneaked down the staircase and saw them decorating the tree and wrapping presents. Was it possible they had been lying to me for eight years about Santa? I decided to catch them in the act. When they weren't looking, I got closer and hid behind a stuffed chair. After a while, my mother, who was a terrible actress when she was trying to get away with a lie, started speaking in a strange voice. "Oh, listen, dear," she said to my father, "I think I hear Santa coming." *God,* I thought, *she's awful. Why is she so fake?* There was a knock at the door. "Oh. Here he is now," she said as she opened it. And standing in the doorway was a man in a red suit and a white beard.

"Just passing by," he said. The suit was pretty convincing, but as soon as he talked I knew it was Beetlepuss Lewis, one of my father's burlesque partners.

"Oh, come in, Santa," my mother said in an even phonier voice. "Can we get you something to drink?"

"No thanks," Santa said. "I have a bottle of wine in the sleigh."

This was what I loved about Beetlepuss and all the other comics. They couldn't let a straight line just lie there like an orphan. It was obvious that at this performance, the role of Santa was being played by

26

George Beetlepuss Lewis, and I jumped out from behind the chair and said so in a triumphant, piping voice. This was putting my finger in the emotional light socket.

My mother's face fell. She was instantly miserable, almost in tears. "You mean you don't believe in Santa anymore?" she said. She seemed despondent, as if up until now she had believed in him, too. "Can't you still believe in him?"

I explained that no matter how hard I tried, I couldn't believe that Beetlepuss Lewis was Santa Claus. "But you were so innocent when you believed. It was so sweet. Can't you try? Just a little longer?"

She was getting a good deal more mileage out of this innocence stuff than I thought it was worth. A year earlier, when I was seven, she thought I looked so cute and innocent in the bathtub, she wanted to take me into the living room and show me naked to her friends. I had to dig in my heels and pull back all the way to the bathroom door until she gave up. Now she seemed so depressed about Santa Claus that I had the feeling I had killed something in her.

There was a tug-of-war developing between her reality and mine, and she was pulling as hard as she could.

But I did love George for being funny at a critical moment in our lives. It's what made me love all the comics. There wasn't anything you couldn't be funny about. This was the group I identified with and wanted to be like, not the civilians. *Civilians are lesser creatures,* I thought. *They're not completely alive. It's true they can laugh, and that's why they make good audiences, but they don't know how to make one another laugh. Instead, they tell jokes. They recite these formulas and you go ha, ha, but they really don't know how to be funny. They're not like us. We have a secret power. We're a sacred, secret brotherhood.*

These are the crazy things I grew up thinking. The adults around me never expressed these arrogant thoughts. I worked them out for myself by watching the people who came in from the outside world.

There were my tutors, for instance. There was Miss Brown. She had a brown personality, a brown outlook. She taught me brown things in a brown way. Her brain was dry and knotted and twisted up in the bun of hair on her head. Finally, one day she just dried up completely and blew away. She was replaced by another tutor: Loraine.

Loraine was okay. She was buxom, and I liked that. And she liked to tell me stories about her boyfriends and the crazy parties they went to. She was only about ten years older than me, and she hadn't lost her playfulness, so I had a pretty good time sitting next to her, trying to figure her out. She tried to teach me about Greek myths, but we spent most of our time looking at pictures of half-naked gods and exploring my questions about whether she thought they were attractive or not. She was fun, but I was curious about a lot of things, and her answers tended to be short on facts and long on anecdotes about parties.

"What's a flame?" I wanted to know.

"It's oxidation," she said.

"No, I mean when you look at the flame, what are you actually looking at?"

"Oxidation."

This is not an answer, I thought. This is just a word. I was nine years old, and I wanted *answers*. If she had said, "You're looking at photons coming out of the atoms when they get excited," it might have sounded like something to look at and shut me up. But I kept asking her the same question, and to relieve the monotony, she launched into a supposedly hilarious story about a guy who got mad at her boyfriend and said he hoped he'd die in childbirth. This didn't seem funny to me, because since her boyfriend had been born years ago, he had already gone through childbirth. She decided not to go into detail, and I was left with the impression that sometimes civilians could have a certain kind of boisterous fun, but they really didn't know funny.

Before long, word of her stories made their way to my mother, and Loraine went off to the tutor burial ground and in came Mr. Phillips.

Mr. Phillips was in his early forties. He tutored me in the evenings. Fit and muscular, he did some kind of work during the day for the phone company. I imagined him climbing poles and coming down out of the sky at dusk, when he would sit across from me with his muscular legs crossed and a smirk on his face when I asked questions that he considered off the point. He was disciplined and expected me to be, too. He saw me doodling during one session and wanted to see what I had drawn. I wasn't inclined to show him because it was a naked woman, which I felt he would think was *way* off the point. When I refused to hand it over, he very calmly wrestled me to my knees and took it from my clutched hand. We didn't discuss the picture. He just balled it up and smirked. We went back to long division.

But after our sessions, I noticed he hung around with my mother and her friend Gail in the living room. I had seen men flirt in the burlesque company, so I knew what it was, and he was clearly doing it with Gail. Gail seemed odd to me. She was quiet and had hair that had been bleached so much it didn't have any color left. She wore too much powder and had a nose that looked as if it had been broken several times. I had long since determined from my study of the Greek gods who was attractive and who was not, and she was not someone I would have flirted with. But Mr. Phillips looked at her and wagged his tail. I wondered where all his discipline had gone. Gail was married to one of the burlesque comics who came over to our house on Sundays. She was somebody's wife. It seemed to me Mr. Phillips was definitely off the point with her.

When April Fools' Day came around, I prepared a nice little joke for Mr. Phillips. I made up a tray with a sandwich and a cup of tea and presented it to him at the start of our session. Luckily, my goldfish had just died, and I'd put him in the sandwich. The sugar bowl, of course, was filled with salt, which Mr. Phillips figured out and didn't even taste. For some reason, though, he didn't open the sandwich, so he never saw the dead goldfish. He picked it up and took a bite out of it. I was appalled. I thought *seeing* the goldfish was the joke, not eating it.

"Stop," I said. "Don't!"

He stopped midbite. "What?" he asked. The tail of the goldfish was hanging out of his mouth.

Now here, I had a decision to make. Should I tell him he had a goldfish in his mouth or let him eat it? I thought about being wrestled to the floor a couple of weeks earlier; I thought about his flirting with Gail. Finally, I thought about the smirk. There was the goldfish, right where the smirk used to be. And I thought, *Let him eat it.*

He ate it. Or at least he ate half of it, and then I wished him a Happy April Fools' Day. He took it pretty well, and he didn't get sick, but I think it wasn't long before Mr. Phillips decided to join the others in the great march of tutors heading south.

I was glad. I was more comfortable with our happy band of brothers. Every Sunday, thirty or forty of my father's old friends from burlesque would come by and my father would put dozens of ribs on the barbecue. He would stand over the fire painting the ribs with a sauce he had invented as the smoke from the charring meat swirled around his head. His pals would swim and eat and drink, and when night fell they would take turns performing their old routines. One of them was expert at the spit take. Several times during the sketch, he would be surprised by something just as he was drinking a glass of water and he would shpritz the front row. Everyone erupted in laughter and applause, not because it took them by surprise—they had seen it a hundred times. They applauded the artistry, the delicacy, of it; the ineffable meaning and utter stupidity of it.

We were arranged in rows in the living room, and the performers would be two steps up, as though onstage, on the landing of the entrance to the rumpus room. A rumpus room was a forties invention: a room where you could raise a rumpus. It had a bar decorated with decals portraying muchachos sleeping under their giant sombreros. Everyone drank Moscow mules, and the women wore peasant blouses or dresses with peplums and had pompadours made of two giant rolls of hair, as if they were carrying a pair of mice on their heads.

I was allowed to perform with the comics in some sketches. My father had a large stack of black notebooks filled with old burlesque bits. These books had been compiled and passed around like a first folio from one comic to another for decades. I read and reread them during the week, looking for sketches I could work in on Sunday. They contained the great ones: "Floogle Street," "the Crazy House," "Handful of Nickels," "Slowly I Turn." And there were dozens of short blackouts—each one a quick exchange and a punch line—like "You Will/I Won't" . . .

(Two men onstage.)
FIRST MAN: You will.
SECOND MAN: I won't.
FIRST MAN: You will!
SECOND MAN: I won't!
FIRST MAN: You will!!
SECOND MAN: I *won't!!*
(First Man takes out a gun and shoots Second Man, who falls dead.)
FIRST MAN: You *will!*

(Blackout)

. . . a brief and bizarre sketch that captured all of modern history and anticipated existentialism and theater of the absurd by forty years.

Some of the dialogue in these sketches could be tailored for whatever town you were in. While describing a despicable place or person, you would be prompted to "insert here name of local park" or "insert here name of mayor." All of it was nonsensical and impudent, and some of it was risqué enough to be completely unintelligible to me.

Sometimes I would show my father a sketch I thought I could perform in and he'd say gently, "No, that's a little rough, Bub." I had no idea what was rough about it. But his reaction would send me back to the sketch for a closer reading as I tried to piece together exactly what men and women did together that was so funny.

After the sketches, we would all get down on the living room carpet and shoot craps. I would stretch out next to Fifi, the stripper, as she pulled bunched-up dollars out of her purse and tossed them down when she was on a roll. She'd shake the dice and pitch them out with a gusto I was totally in love with. She took pleasure in her energy, and so did I.

I learned on that carpet the small but important point about gambling that you can't count on it. One day, I wanted to buy my father a radio for his birthday, and I saw how easy it was to run up a few dollars into a large pile of money. So, to raise the money for the radio I invited one of my father's friends to shoot craps with me. He said okay, and of course his experience gave him complete control of the betting. He let the session stretch out to an agonizing length as I slowly saw my few dollars disappear. Finally, I had nothing left, not even enough to buy my father a token gift. I had the broken heart of everyone who finds out for the first time that you can also lose. He looked at me very seriously and said, "You know, in gambling, when you lose, you lose. You can't get it back. But I'll make a deal with you. Just this once, I'll let you have your money back if you promise never to gamble again." There was never a promise more heartfelt or more quickly made—and mostly kept.

The carpet was where I got the best of my early education. It was where, on winter nights, I stretched out and listened to Fred Allen and Jack Benny. And I can smell now the dusty gray nap as I lay facedown listening to the recordings of Gershwin's Concerto in F and *Rhapsody in Blue*. These were the working recordings from my father's film in which he played Gershwin. Oscar Levant was at the piano in the recordings, and my father practiced for weeks to be able to play along on a dummy piano as Gershwin. This was the first music of its kind I had ever heard, and I listened to it over and over. It captivated me even more than "Pistol Packin' Mama" had the year before.

It was on that carpet that I lay with books from the shelves and, propped on my elbows, read them for hours during long afternoons. The living room shelves must have been decorated with books by the yard, chosen mainly for their bindings. I pulled down dozens of large, beautiful red leather books called the *Congressional Record*. I was delighted to see they were written in dialogue, my favorite form, and I devoured them. I especially enjoyed the sarcasm these people used against one another, even after the elaborate show of courtesy to "the distinguished gentleman from Vermont." *These* guys were funny.

And there were heavy leather-bound volumes of short stories by European writers, often about dragoons and their mistresses. I didn't know what dragoons were and I couldn't always follow what they were doing with their mistresses, but they seemed to have many of the same interests as the characters in burlesque sketches, so I felt at home. The carpet was my best school, and curiosity was my favorite teacher.

The most interesting discovery I made while I was poking around was in a little space not much bigger than a closet, off the living room. This was where my father went to write. His typewriter sat next to the stack of black books full of sketches. I went in one day and saw a sheet of paper in the typewriter. It was curled permanently around the black roller because, having had trouble getting past the first few lines of a novel he was writing, he'd left it there for weeks. But the sight of his typewritten words on the onionskin paper touched me and ignited me. I was eight years old, and for the first time I realized that writing was something you could sit down and do. Just by typing those few words, he'd opened my eyes to another world. I loved the courtroom sketches in the big black books, so I borrowed the typewriter and wrote a sketch about a judge. From then on, I knew I wanted to be a writer.

At nine, I knew I wanted to be an actor. The war was on and many lives were being changed by it, including mine.

Every Saturday night, my father drove to the Hollywood Canteen to entertain the troops passing through Los Angeles on their way to fight in the Pacific. Actors who could sing, dance, or do comedy would go onstage. The others would mingle with soldiers and sailors on the dance floor and try to boost their morale. They must have entertained hundreds of servicemen every night and fed them thousands of sandwiches a week. I could tell because my father came home late every Saturday with a huge cardboard box full of the heels of loaves of white bread, which we would feed to our three pigs the next day.

He could see how much I loved playing in the sketches with his friends, so he asked me if I'd like to go and do a routine with him one night at the Hollywood Canteen. There was no timidity on my part, and we started rehearsing on the rumpus room landing.

We worked on Abbott and Costello's "Who's on First." He was Abbott and I was Costello. Rehearsing was fun. He let me find my own way. He didn't tell me how to say the lines or even exactly what to say. It was a burlesque rehearsal, where the shape of it is laid down but there's still room for improvisation. "You might want to repeat that a few times," he said about one exchange between us. "As many times as you feel are right—usually three is good, but feel it out." Like any amateur, I tended to shift from foot to foot, and I slowly moved away from him while I talked. He put a hand on my shoulder. "Try not to drift," he said. With each rehearsal I got more confident, my energy more focused. I couldn't wait to go on.

Then, suddenly, I was standing in the dark in the wings at the Hollywood Canteen. In a few minutes, I would be going onstage. My father was at the microphone. He sang a couple of songs and did a few jokes.

A little old man is crossing the street and suddenly, out of nowhere, a truck comes by and knocks him down. *A block later,* the driver shouts out the window, "Watch out!" The little old man gets up on one elbow and says, "What's the matter, you're coming *back?*"

The audience laughed. When I heard this joke, I knew I'd be going out there in a few seconds. The laughter from the audience sent a rush of adrenaline through my body. I began shaking uncontrollably. There were *people* out there. I looked for comfort in the familiar. My fingers scanned the grain of the baseball bat I'd use as a prop, but my hands were wet and clammy on the wood. Now my father was pointing toward me and saying my name. I had to go out there. I put the bat over my shoulder and walked out to welcoming applause from the audience. This didn't relax me. The applause meant they were watching me. I was under scrutiny. A follow spot picked me up and blinded me as I met my father at the microphone. They quieted down, waiting to see what this chubby nine-year-old with buck teeth and a butch haircut would come up with. My father said his first line. I said mine, and there was a laugh. A couple of lines later, there was an even bigger laugh. The spotlight began to feel warm. I was starting to like the attention of a room full of hundreds of people. The sound of their laughter was explosive, but I could control these explosions. I could make them laugh, and if I wanted, I could stop their laughter and make them listen. The trembling was over. The laughs rolled in on waves. By the end of the sketch, I was shaking again—not with fright, but with excitement. I'd conquered them, a roomful of civilians. A roomful of civilians in *uniforms*. I had found my place on the warm side of the footlights. Now I was part of the brotherhood.

But it wasn't enough to keep out the rest of the world. Even among our gang, it turned out, there were the mirthless ones who didn't live to please and be pleased; these were the ones whose pleasure came from your not getting any. The bullies.

The first time I saw a bully in action, in fact, it was Maxie, one of the comics. Maxie had become a writer in Hollywood and now made a living stealing from the old sketches and turning them into routines for radio shows. He was married to Gail. And one night I found out how Gail's nose had been broken so many times.

I was in the backseat of the family car. My father, my mother, and Gail were in the front seat. We were in front of Gail's house, getting ready to drive off, and Maxie came over to the open window on the passenger side of the car.

"So, you're going?" he said to Gail.

"We're going for a drive," Gail said.

"You're going for a *drive*?" he said. "Really?"

"That's right," she said. "We're going for a drive."

"You bitch," Maxie said. He reached through the window and made a short, precise stab of his fist to her face. Her hand went to her nose, and Maxie aimed another short punch right where it would cause the most pain. Instinctively, my mother reached across Gail and tried to protect her.

"Stop it," my mother said, but he was already aiming a third punch at Gail's face and it caught my mother in the hand. "You've hurt me!" my mother said, and Maxie, who I suppose did not think he had a license to hit other people's wives, took a step back. Under his breath, he told Gail again that she was a bitch and we drove off.

The broken bone on the back of my mother's hand started to rise almost immediately and never returned to normal. The mark of Maxie stayed on her hand, and it never left my mind.

Maxie and Gail were strange and frightening, but I had seen other strange things and I was okay as long as I could wake up every morning and explore my world. Karl Thalhammer, who used to own the property and now lived in the guesthouse, was the inventor of something called the Thalhammer Tripod. He kept supplies of metal rods and electric motors in the garage. Rooting around in there, I found a few pieces of metal tubing and a tiny motor I lusted after. I was too timid to ask for them, but not too timid to filch them. I soldered them together into my own version of a malted-milk machine. My parents proudly showed Karl my invention one day, and he looked at it admiringly, then turned to me. "You know," he said, "if you had asked for those parts, I would have given them to you." You could measure how long I would remember that moment by the redness of my cheeks.

My father saw that I liked projects and taught me how to make lamps out of Chianti bottles. Once I started, I couldn't stop. After a while, there were Chianti bottle lamps with wine labels shellacked onto their shades all over the house. My father loved projects, too. He sent away for manuals from the Department of Agriculture in Washington and taught himself to transplant olive trees. He couldn't stop, either. Soon he had installed dozens of giant stumps of the trees up and down our driveway. He had me digging holes and cutting taproots with him, but after a while it seemed too much like work. Instead, I spent weeks raking stones, making a path around a two-acre pasture, so I could ride my horse on a track. My father was a little disappointed that I would put so much effort into my obsession and not his. "If I had asked you to work that hard, you wouldn't have done it," he said. Well, sure. Other people's obsessions are boring.

I finally gave up on the horse anyway, because he hated me. No matter where I wanted to go, he would head for the barn at a gallop and deliberately bang my leg against the fence post or head for the pasture and try to clip me in the chin with a tree branch. I rode bareback, and this would send me reeling. Once, on the way into the pasture at full gallop, I saw the branch coming, felt the thud on my chin, and woke up on the ground to the sight of him munching grass as if he were a loyal steed waiting patiently while I took a nap. I hated him as much as he hated me, and I switched to riding the donkey. He was no bargain, either. He would wait until he had carried me to a desolate spot and then start bucking. Once, beyond the eucalyptus trees, on the spot where we had tried to bury my dog, he threw me over his head, stepped on my arm, and ran away. After one of the pigs bit my little finger while I was feeding him hay, there wasn't an animal on the place I trusted, except the chickens, and they smelled.

Most of the time, though, I lived in a world of imagination. I would draw pictures of fanciful inventions, like a five-way can opener or a lazy Susan that would go inside a refrigerator and make the contents easy to reach at the touch of your hand. (I worked out the future advertising copy, too.) Sometimes I would just lie on my back for hours and watch the clouds, and sometimes I would hurl myself into impossible projects. When I was eleven, I subscribed to *Mechanix Illustrated* and read every word. I paid particular attention to the classified ads. It interested me that people could write them so cleverly that they could snare other people into sending in their money. But as much as I could see through the "get rich quick" schemes and useless products they offered, there was one ad I couldn't resist.

I saved up my allowance money and sent away for a mail-order course in taxidermy.

When the first installment arrived, I tore open the envelope excitedly and read it: detailed instructions on how to stuff a bird. This was compelling reading. Now I could do what the Hollywood taxidermist had failed to do with Rhapsody. A few days later, I found a dead owl on the property and brought him into the house. I laid him on the kitchen table next to the open pages of lesson one and started following the directions. *Make an incision from the neck to the tail and remove the innards.*

With a kitchen knife, I made the incision and split open the bird. And there were the innards. I had never seen the inside of a living thing before. There was a lot of *stuff* in there, and most of it was gooey. I read ahead in the lesson and saw that after I took care of the innards, I would have to cure the skin and make a wire frame for the body. I decided to concentrate on the frame and get back to the innards later.

The dead owl lay on the kitchen table for about a week. It began to smell, and when you passed by it, if you peeked into the chest cavity, you could see little white maggots climbing all over one another. Finally, my mother said, "Are you going to do anything more with this?"

I said I had decided to wait for the next installment, and we threw out the owl. The next installment, though, required a dead mountain lion, which I skipped as well. After that, the animals I would need to find got bigger and the stuffing of them got more complicated. The final chapter called for a moose and required tanning its immense hide and pulling it over a superstructure of metal pipes. I read the booklet twice, amazed at what people will go through to stuff something.

Meanwhile, I was trying as deftly as I could to avoid being stuffed by my mother. She tried both to hang on to a past me and to shape a future me that fit some crazy ideal. As for the past me, she would often tell me that something happened to me when I was six. I used to want to be with her wherever she went and say, "I wuv you, Momay." Then I changed. And after that I spoke differently and stopped following her into the bathroom. I don't know why, but this seemed like normal development to me. To her, it was a kind of betrayal.

As for the future me, she decided one day when I was eleven that it was time for me to learn about where babies come from and that I should learn it in such a healthy, positive way that I would be happy and well-adjusted all my life. So we sat by the pool and she opened a book and started reading aloud. Every few paragraphs she would stop and tell me how wonderful sex was. "Woooonderful," she said, looking heavenward. This was intended to make me well-adjusted; however, it didn't seem odd to her that a friend of mine, a boy a year older than me, was also there, lying on his back, listening raptly with his hand on his crotch. Didn't she see him, legs splayed, right in front of her? Didn't she think it was a strange posture to assume while attending a sex lecture by someone's mother? What *was* reality for her? Finally it was over, but it was one more step in a new direction. Little by little, I was beginning to realize I was on my own.

In the seventh grade, the supply of tutors dried up completely and I had to go to school a few miles away in a town called Tujunga. Tujunga didn't sound good, and it wasn't. I would have to travel by bus each morning to get there, which meant I would no longer be traveling with a group that played cards and drank all night. God knows what these people from the outside world did to amuse themselves. As it turned out, they amused themselves by acting like Maxie.

On my first journey into that world, my first day of school, I went down the long dirt drive to the main road. I walked past the stumps of olive trees I'd helped my father transplant. Their new shoots had sprouted and had begun to grow into trunks themselves. Out on the main road, I stood beside our large rural mailbox and waited for the school bus. The bus came by and I got on. I noticed that one of the boys on the bus seemed to be glaring at me. I made it through the first day in which people were mostly indifferent to me, but that would change soon. The next morning, when I made my way down the long driveway, the same boy who glared at me on the bus was standing by my mailbox.

"Listen, you little son of a bitch," he said by way of a greeting. "If you think I'm going to walk down here to your mailbox every day to wait for the bus, you can shove it up your ass. You wait in front of *my* mailbox, or else I'll wipe your face up and down this road. You understand that?"

I nodded that I did. Actually, he'd been exceptionally clear. His mailbox was a two-minute walk up the road, and if I thought that being some shit actor's little boy entitled me to any special favors, I could shove that up my ass, too. It couldn't be clearer. But I didn't know why he was saying this. Had someone told him to wait by my mailbox? Had he assumed he would someday be asked to wait there? I decided not to question him on this. It didn't look like he was taking questions.

The next morning, and every morning for the rest of the year, I walked the tenth of a mile to his mailbox. We stood by the bridge over the dry riverbed and waited for the bus while he explained to me what a piece of shit I was in fine detail. He seemed to enjoy talking not only about my shittiness, but about his father's temper and the beatings he got if he stepped out of line. He seemed proud to be able to endure them. And he seemed interested in looking for a way to transfer them to someone else. He was a head taller than me and spoke so effortlessly in a tone of hatred that I said nothing. I put most of my effort into not trembling, which didn't work. I trembled.

I listened quietly while he talked, partly because he terrified me and partly because I found him fascinating. He was my first in a series of bullies.

I started meeting a lot of them. My life up to this point had made me a magnet for bullies. I thought people wanted me to entertain them, to brighten up their otherwise dull lives. Wherever I went, I was ready to perform. This, I was sure, would make people like me.

I walked onto the playground that first week at school and saw hundreds of kids at recess. But to me they weren't kids. *Wow,* I thought, *look at the size of that* audience! Within a few minutes, I was up on a lunch table, performing. I did bits, impersonations, a little improvised tap dance. For some reason that I didn't understand, this made kids want to hit me.

What is this with the hitting? I thought. All I knew was funny, but they didn't know funny. We didn't even speak the same *language*. The comics were always talking about somebody *beefing* about something. To me that meant they were complaining. A kid got tired of my jokes and pushed me. I objected. He said, "You wanna beef?" *Oh, good,* I thought, *he's offering me a chance to complain.* I said yes, I *did* want to beef. But in this school beefing meant fighting. Suddenly, he was hitting me. His friend was hitting me. People who didn't know me were coming over for a free chance to hit someone.

I went home and told my parents, and the next morning my mother said she had a great solution. She went to her jewelry drawer and came back with a gigantic ring—a hefty gold thing with an ugly blue stone in it. "Here," she said, "just wear that and *hit* them with it." I wasn't so sure about this. If they didn't like jokes, how were they going to feel if I hit them with this big blue rock?

I could see that she had a fantasy in which I put the bullies in their place with one heroic sock to the puss. But I knew that the reality of the outside world didn't always match her fantasies. I had to be careful about bumping up against reality. I could break my nose on it.

I put the ring on and left for school, but as soon as I was out of the house I put it in my pocket.

When I got to school, I began trying to act like one of the sour, serious people who do only straight lines. I was out of Eden now. I had crossed the border. I had seen the snake in the garden by the chicken house, and I had discovered Beetlepuss behind Santa's beard. I was going to have to learn to live among these mirthless people who always kept their clothes on and couldn't do a spit take. But I wasn't really ready for what it was like in the Land of the Civilians.

act two

THROWING

ROCKS

chapter 5

THE BULLY PULPIT

A hulking figure in black, she carried a yardstick and looked like she wasn't afraid to use it. Sister Mary Frederick taught geometry and stood over me in the front row while she glared at the people behind me. I would look up into her nose with fascination because she had three nostrils. I often wondered if this was what attracted her to geometry or if, possibly, too much geometry could triangulate your nose.

I was twelve and I had come down out of the mountains of Tujunga to go to a Catholic school in Burbank, where the people were presumably more civilized. But there was something at this school that carried bullying to a higher level, and it caught me off guard. It was the casual but confidently reassuring suggestion that if you didn't follow the nun's orders, you would not simply be punished—your flesh would burn in hell for all of eternity. God, it seemed, was capable of both infinite love and holding a really long grudge. This was a novel suggestion for someone with my background. The wings of Gabriel had replaced the wings of burlesque, and now the women in my life wore black, not silk and satin; they smelled of wool instead of sweat and perfume—and they didn't know the odds on eight the hard way because for them there weren't any odds. Heaven and hell were sure things.

But, still, I needed to belong. So I adapted by becoming part of the system. We were asked one day to take turns giving a talk before the class, and I realized I could use my performer's instincts for this. Instead of just a talk, I gave a full-out sermon. I combined pathos, saintliness, spontaneous jokes, and animated gestures in a passionate mix. While I spoke, I could hear the nun behind me stifling a laugh, and I knew I was in. If you can make a nun laugh, can God frown? I became an enthusiastic convert to the religion I had been born into. When we went to mass, I went all the way and took Communion. I knelt at the altar and opened my mouth as the priest put the large flat wafer on my tongue. This would be the first food in my stomach since dinner the night before. My stomach would be growling, yet the taste of the thin disk made of flour and water had a special terror for me. This was, after all, not bread, but Jesus. Not a symbol of Jesus, but Jesus himself. I shut my eyes, and talked myself through it.

> *Don't chew on it. Don't even let it touch your teeth. Above all, don't let it stick to the roof of your mouth. Oh, God, you did it. You let it happen. God is stuck to the roof of your mouth. How are you going to get Him off? You have to get this off and swallow it. What if it just gets hard and stays there? You can't walk around for the rest of the day with God in your mouth. Oh, God. Melt, melt.*

Taking Communion also meant going to confession the day before, on Saturday. And that meant coming up with a string of sins that included every conceivable transgression, including some that weren't technically sins but showed my goodwill.

I didn't realize I was working my way into a corner. Along with the praise from the nuns came a catch. The catch was that if you didn't do exactly what they said, you would burn forever. If you didn't go to mass every week, you would burn. If you ate meat on Friday, you would burn.

If you didn't believe that the priest could turn bread into God, you'd burn. And if you didn't actually believe what you *believed* you believed, there was probably a way for you to burn longer than forever. It put you in a kind of desperate bind, which was not good, because the ultimate sin, the unforgivable sin, they said, was despair.

Who would choose despair? I wondered. And why would an all-knowing God pick on you for falling into a bottomless pit that you would have avoided if you could? My curiosity was making me ask dangerous questions, even as I was working on belonging.

And I did want to belong. The school slanted toward the quirky in a way that I found appealing. The monsignor who founded it had named it Bellarmine-Jefferson High School in honor of Thomas Jefferson and Saint Robert Bellarmine, whose writings, he said, were in Jefferson's library. We wore uniforms, and the patch on our shoulders showed both a crucifix and a Star of David, in recognition of Christianity's Jewish roots. As young as I was, I could appreciate the nod both to Jefferson's secularism and to Judaism. In 1948, this had a refreshing air of tolerance to it.

And I liked the monsignor. He seemed smart and decent. He was always talking to the students about tolerance, when we would fall in early in the morning to salute the flag. But the monsignor's nonconformity had its limits. My parents and I went to mass every week at his church, and one week he devoted his entire sermon to a movie playing then in theaters. It was a light comedy adapted from a Broadway play. A group of Catholic watchdogs, called the Legion of Decency, had decided that seeing this movie would corrupt everyone, including adults, because it dealt with an unmarried woman who was pregnant. To prove how disgraceful the film was, the monsignor told us one of the lines from the film. He read gravely from a sheet of paper: " 'You're pregnant?' one character says. 'A drugstore on every corner in New York, and you're *pregnant*?' "

The monsignor looked up from the page. "And they think that's funny," he said scornfully. It sounded to me like a well-constructed joke.

I wondered why he didn't think it was funny. It didn't get a laugh, of course, because he gave it a terrible reading, but that was no reason to knock the writing.

My thoughts were interrupted when I realized he was asking the congregation to stand and take the oath of the Legion of Decency. We were supposed to swear that we would never see this film or any film banned by the legion, under pain of mortal sin. The entire congregation stood. I don't know why, but I wouldn't stand. I was fourteen by now. I still wanted to fit in, but something in me wouldn't let me stand. Along with everyone else in the packed church, my father stood. I still wouldn't budge. He seemed embarrassed and gave me a nudge with his knee. I didn't move. He looked down at me and gave a jerk with his head, as if to say, "Come on. This doesn't look good."

But I wouldn't move. I shook my head from side to side. I was not going to stand. Where did I get the nerve to do this? And what principle had I heard of somewhere that I was upholding? I believed everything they told me about obedience and the teaching authority of the Church, but somehow, going to a movie didn't seem like something that should send me to hell, and I wasn't going to pretend by standing that I thought it would. I don't know exactly what that fourteen-year-old boy was thinking, sitting there on the hard pew, but as I look back, I like him.

A couple of years later, as it can in show business, our lives changed in a flash. My father's seven-year contract with Warners had run its course, and he was being offered a starring part in a Broadway musical. He couldn't leave the studio until three days before the first rehearsal, when he packed us up in the car and drove ninety miles an hour across the country. This seemed like fun, and as the nation flew by my window, I sat in the backseat reading a book about flying saucers. This was good, because when we got to New York, it was like landing on another planet. I was enrolled in a Catholic high school in White Plains. Again, I was the new kid who was a little too unguarded, a little too eager to entertain, with a laugh that was a little too loud, and most afternoons several boys in the class offered to beat me up. Unlike the school in Burbank in which we were taught by nuns and half the students were girls, this one had no women at all. The teachers were priests and brothers, and the student body was male and pimply. We were ankle deep in testosterone.

One day, I opened my desk and saw a note informing me that five of my classmates would be waiting for me in the bushes after school to beat the crap out of me. I thought it might be good to find an alternative to this.

As we jostled down the hall between classes, I noticed that next to the principal's office was a door with a sign that read, DEAN OF DISCIPLINE. I looked in and saw a tough-looking priest behind a desk. He looked like a boxer, or at least a marine. *Maybe this guy can help me,* I thought, and I made an appointment to see him.

He listened intently while I explained that five boys were planning to jump out of the bushes at me. I was hoping he wouldn't call them into the office and make me confront them face-to-face. Finally he said, "Well, that's not good . . ." *It certainly isn't,* I thought. *Thank God I've got somebody who can save me from a beating.* But then I saw he had only been pausing for effect. He went on: ". . . but, if you had to, you'd defend yourself like a man, wouldn't you?"

I realized with a sinking feeling that it was no accident he looked like a boxer. Yes, sure, I said. I would definitely defend myself—one of the first in a series of lies I made to priests.

As it does so often, this threat to my physical well-being ended in a climactic confrontation in which I punched the biggest bully in the nose and the others scattered like cowards. I love this story. Unfortunately, in my case it took place only in my head. Eventually I won out, but I did it using my brains. My fists stayed in my pockets.

I kept watching the bushes, waiting for them to jump out, but they kept postponing it. Meanwhile, I kept looking for people I could talk to. The place looked like a prison to me, with raw red bricks on the outside and shiny white subway tiles on the inside. I saw a notice taped to a wall one day announcing that the photography club was having a competition. I loved photography. When I was eleven I had gone in once a week to a camera store in Roscoe to hand over fifty cents until enough weeks had gone by to pay for the used Rolleicord they had laid away for me. And then I had spent hundreds of hours in the darkroom, developing film, making prints, until my hands smelled like a tray of hypo.

I went home from school and worked for a week on a picture. A little nervously, I brought it to the camera club and entered it, hoping I could find a place in the group. A week later I was in the hall again, and at the other end I saw Brother Jacob, the teacher who mentored the club. His face lit up, and he opened his arms and said, "You won!" My picture had won the competition. I felt flattered and excited. Then Brother Jacob was hugging me, his muscular arms wrapped around me, almost crushing me, his bony body clamped to mine, his genitals pressed against me through the thin cloth of his cassock.

This was suddenly not flattering anymore. I unlocked myself from his iron embrace and got away as soon as I could. Later, at lunch, other boys who had seen the hug in the hall laughed about it. "That's the way he operates," they said. "He's always getting guys in the darkroom and feeling them up." All the way home on the bus, I felt deflated. It was a double betrayal. It wasn't just the creepy physical advance he'd made; it was also the disregard for the work I'd done. He'd let me win just so he could get me into the darkroom. I never went back, even though he'd stop me from time to time in the hall and tell me how talented I was.

I began to think there was slightly more attention paid to sex here than there had been in the burlesque theaters. All of us were adolescent boys who were, of course, besotted with our newfound sexuality. Battalions of us were cranking away through the night, searching for salvation in pungent imaginary encounters with the goddesses found in cigarette ads. Teachers would devote hours to the subject of our hobby. Once or twice a year, we would have a three-day retreat, the first two days of which were devoted largely to what was known as "self-abuse."

They never fully explained what exactly was abusive about it, except for references to our bodies as temples. In religion class, Father Quinn told us one morning, "You know, the average adult doesn't think about sex all the time. Not at all. The normal adult thinks about sex maybe ten minutes a day." *Well,* I thought, *I don't believe this, but okay. I'll be normal. I'll get my ten minutes in right now.*" I always did what they said, and if at all possible, I took them literally.

Finally I made a few friends who were smart and, like me, were more interested in writing than fighting. We were taught English by a bright young priest named Father McMahon. My friend Joe and I had begun writing a humor column in the school paper, and Father McMahon said that if we'd write a comedy sketch for the Thanksgiving assembly, he'd let us skip a book report. This was clever of him, because I thought I was avoiding work, but I actually worked harder and learned more than if I had written a slapdash book report. Our little sketch got laughs from our classmates, and we had that feeling of immense power that comes from writing words on paper that can make other people feel something.

We got ambitious. During the summer between eleventh and twelfth grades, Joe and I and our friend Bob wrote a musical comedy— book, words, and music. The show, of course, had extremely large parts for all three of us.

As I worked on it, I sat every day at a little table, writing in longhand. Every few days, someone put a small vase of lilacs on the table. I don't remember who put the buds there, but for me the smell of creativity that summer was lilac. Day by day, I saw a play taking shape, and it was intoxicating.

When school started up again, we asked Father McMahon to read our script, and he didn't flinch; he offered to produce the play on the school stage. This meant he'd have to pay for musical arrangements, scenery, and costumes. I didn't find out until much later how much he was risking by encouraging us. He had gone into personal debt to get the play on.

The musical was called *Love's the Ticket!* and when we began rehearsals, I suddenly realized I had a solution to the bully problem. It seemed that everybody wanted to be in it: basketball players, football players, even the guys who had wanted to beat me up. Pretty soon, the bullies were up on the stage. And I had them *dancing* in a chorus line. These were guys who had left me little welcome notes in my desk that said simply "fruit" or "you faggot." Now they were working on their dance steps and hoping their makeup wouldn't run. This was very close to the perfect revenge.

Our little play was a hit. It raised money for the school, Father McMahon got his savings back, and I was no longer a fruit. I was relieved that the bully days were over.

Not quite.

chapter 6

MOM

I would hear them screaming through the night, especially the night before a matinee, when my father would angrily plead with her to let him get some sleep. Instead, when he dropped off, she would wake him by slapping him in the face with a wet towel and try to get him to admit he was seeing someone else. I was fifteen, and by this time her symptoms were in full flower. She was drinking heavily now, medicating herself with liebfraumilch. One evening, while he was out doing the show, she methodically pulled down all the curtains from the windows and turned over tables and chairs, then went to bed, telling me to leave it for him to see when he got home. Before she went upstairs, she kissed me good night.

The giant lips approached, bright red. Up close like this, you could see that her lipstick went outside the lines of her lips, covering some of the skin above them. Why would you paint lips on your skin? I wondered. Clowns do that. Thinking about this was a way of not thinking about the impending kiss.

The red lips came closer to my face, the aroma of stale white wine preceding her as she closed in on me. Then the kiss. On the mouth. With parted lips.

This was Mom. To her it was just a kiss good night. Even then I knew there was nothing erotic about this in her conscious mind; it was just that so little of her conscious mind was available to her. My job, as always, was to make the translation from what she did and said to what she would have meant by it.

A few months later, when we were living in an apartment overlooking the East River, she found an unusual way to express herself in an argument with my father by going out on the balcony and throwing her diamond wedding ring into the street below. The police came to the apartment and helped us look in the street for the ring, which we never found. Then they came back and sat on the couch to reason with her. Why did she want to do a thing like that? they asked. Didn't she want to be a good girl? She sat quietly, smiling at them with a pleasant, unfocused look, like a little girl who's just baked a perfect cake and is basking in the attention.

The crazier she got, the more I went to church. It gave me some feeling of control over a life that was at the mercy of her whim of iron. For a while, I went to mass and took Communion every day. Convinced there was a heaven, I decided to campaign for it. I smelled of incense, holy water, and unleavened wafers. Maybe inspired by my constant visits to the church down the street, my parents decided to visit with the priest in his rectory so they could be counseled on some of our family problems. The three of us went together. On a late winter afternoon, we sat in a small office with a young priest, all of us a little uncomfortable. My father was a well-known actor, they said, and asked the priest for complete confidentiality, which he assured them they had. After a half hour of a few embarrassing admissions about life in our family, there was a noise in the other room and we noticed the door was open. My mother was immediately on alert. "Someone is listening to us," she said. "Is someone spying on us?" *Here she goes again,* I thought. But then, to my surprise, the priest admitted that another priest had been listening to the entire conversation from the other room. My mother and father both felt betrayed and said so, and the priest said—lamely, I thought—that this was something he often did for "security purposes." It looked to me as if it were more for gossip purposes. We left, and they never went back for counseling.

That aborted visit, and the cops' questions the night she threw her diamond ring off the balcony, was the closest my mother ever came to therapy. Since we never spoke about mental illness, our family silence, combined with where science was at the time, left her without a lifeline.

My own lifeline came when I started college. I was young, only sixteen. The succession of tutors had had the effect of advancing me several grades while not necessarily teaching me anything, but college was where I suddenly realized there was a world of ideas. I became inflamed by them. I wanted to know how people *got* ideas. The notion that each book contained at least one original idea made them magical to me. I wanted to possess books and, if I could, to always have one in my hand.

Every day, I took an hour's ride on the elevated train that rumbled up Third Avenue past second-story bedrooms to Fordham in the Bronx. On the train, when I wasn't reading, I was writing plays I would later direct on the college radio station, and when I didn't have an idea for a script, I would listen to the people on the train and copy down bits of overheard conversation on index cards as I taught myself what real dialogue sounded like. I had a special fondness for ideas that went against the current. I was surprised to find out that the church still used an Index of Prohibited Books, so whenever I could find out what current books were on it, the Index became my unofficial reading list.

Ideas were an escape and a defense, and I holed up in my room, reading for six or eight hours at a time. My mother had never seen anyone do this before, and she became alarmed. She began looking into the books, trying to figure out what mysterious forces were taking over her son's mind. There was one in particular that worried her: a book on sociology that was popular at the time by David Riesman called *The Lonely Crowd*. She read a chapter and became disturbed. She called the college to find out if they had actually assigned this disgusting material. "What about this word that keeps appearing in here?" she wanted to know. "*Peer* groups."

Although she didn't say it aloud, "peer groups" sounded to her like people peering at one another. To the priest who answered the phone, the book, and possibly all of sociology, may have smacked of godless secularism. "*We're* concerned about that book, too," he told her. Neither one of them was fully aware of what the other meant. Two utterly different forms of paranoia had met in the dark and agreed there was something under the bed.

I really scared her one day while she was out of town for a couple of weeks with my father. I wrote them a long, rambling, adolescent letter in which I talked about my obsession with books. I said knowledge was good in itself, and it had the added advantage that knowledge was power. For some reason, this sounded to her like the note of a depressed misfit. She called me with panic in her voice. "What's the matter with you? You've got to get out and see people. What do you want power for? Are you eating? You're not taking anything, are you?" No, I said, I'm just *reading*. I had felt, mistakenly, that they would be pleased by my progress, but my new interests had separated me from them as abruptly as if I had jumped out of an airplane.

I was really still in midair, though—separated from them, but not yet grounded in anything else. I was parachuting into unfamiliar territory. One afternoon, I saw in the newspaper that the college radio station was going to play a Beethoven quartet at one o'clock. I had never heard a quartet, but I was curious and interested. I made myself a sandwich, opened a bottle of beer, and sat down to listen as they tuned up. A few minutes later, they were still tuning up. I had a drink of beer. A good five minutes went by. I couldn't understand this. How long does it take to get started with this kind of music? Then, in a stunning flash, I got it: They weren't tuning up; *this was the music*. I was used to a melody line and maybe a countermelody. Here were four voices zigging and zagging, diving under one another, playing tag with a tune I couldn't follow.

I started listening as often as I could to these strange sounds. I wanted to crack the code. I was looking everywhere for windows and doors through which I could squeeze into this new world.

Toward the end of my first year, I found out that Fordham had a program that allowed a few students to spend their junior year in Paris. This was a very appealing idea to me, because Paris was in France, where they had French girls. It sounded enormously intellectual. I asked to speak with the dean to see if I could be included.

On the appointed day, I entered a large Gothic building, complete with gargoyles, and made my way to a spacious room paneled in wood, in the corner of which was a large desk. Behind it sat a very smart Jesuit. He wasn't unkind, but he had the ability to look through you and see everything you were made of: your bones, your liver, and your ambition. He listened quietly as I waxed on about how educational it would be for me to study in Paris. Then he spoke in a measured tone.

"Yes, that's interesting," he said. "We've been watching you."

"Really?" I asked. I always assumed that someone's noticing me was a compliment.

"Yes," he said. "Frankly, I'm surprised you're still here. We all thought you'd have dropped out by Christmas."

There was less flattery here than I had thought, but I forged ahead.

"Was it the placement exams?" I asked, referring to the trivial formality of three days of testing to determine to which courses students should be assigned.

"That's right," he said, "the placement exams. We get a number of foreign students here, and we weren't sure from your results that you could actually speak English."

This was getting tricky. If I told him *why* I did so badly in the tests, he might think I wasn't a serious person. The fact was that I had decided to act like a college boy and go out drinking in the German beer houses on Eighty-sixth Street each night before the exams. I had already been accepted at the college; the placement exam seemed more of a bureaucratic exercise to me than a test. As a result, each morning I would sit at my desk and fall asleep on the exam papers.

This turned out, though, to be lucky. I was placed in a remedial English class (along with some Italian students who actually *couldn't* speak English), where, under the guidance of Mr. Memmo, I relearned my language, and I reveled in it. Mr. Memmo helped me take apart English and put it back together again in ways that let me express things that up until then I could never get out of my head and onto paper.

The dean didn't know any of this, and I didn't tell him. I let him assume that I probably possessed some native genius that allowed me to go from total incompetence to near mediocrity in only a few months.

He looked at me in silence for a moment, while I tried to look bright.

"I'll tell you what," he said. "I'll make a deal with you. If you can maintain a ninety average for your sophomore year, I'll let you go to Paris."

My heart soared. I agreed and thanked him. It was only when I got down to the ground floor of the Gothic building and out into the daylight that I wondered how I would actually be able to get an average score of ninety.

I was interested in my courses and I was reading the material, but I wasn't getting nineties. I decided to marshal my energies. If I put more effort into certain critical classes, I could raise those scores. But which ones were critical? I made some more appointments, this time with my professors. I was going to campaign for Paris the way I had campaigned for heaven. The idea was to explain to each of my teachers that I had been given the chance to go to Paris if I got a ninety average and then ask each one adroitly, "Can you tell me what I need to do to get a ninety in this class?"

This question, I thought, was extremely artful. It announced my willingness to work hard in the course . . . *if necessary*. And if the professor wanted to help out a little, he could let me know that and I wouldn't have to kill myself trying. Everyone saw through me, of course, but the way they responded helped me steer my way through the year. My history professor, a man I admired for his ability to express complex thoughts with colorful vulgarities, said, "Hey, Paris would be great for you. Sure, read as much as you can and turn in the assignments, and I'll give you a ninety." The priest who taught logic, on the other hand, was not quite as enthusiastic. He met me on a rainy day in a faculty sitting room. He came in and silently took off his coat, then methodically removed his galoshes, agonizingly slowly, and put them by the door, still not saying a word. He was a handsome man whose brother had been a movie star on the same lot with my father, but whose face had none of the willingness to please that an actor's face would have. It had long ago been made featureless by scholarly objectivity. He sat opposite me and looked at me through rimless eyeglasses. "Yes? What would you like to discuss?"

By now my mouth was dry, but I gave him my spiel. He listened with no reaction until I'd dribbled to a finish. Then, with finger and thumb he reset his glasses on his nose and spoke softly, but especially distinctly. "In order to get a ninety in my class, you'll need to do all the reading, hand in all the assignments on time, and get at least a ninety in the quizzes and the final exam. And that includes, of course, the surprise quizzes."

The surprise quizzes; he was going to lay traps for us. This was a class I'd have to be alert for. A second later, he made it explicit. "I think I should tell you—as a friend—that I don't think it would be good for you to go to Paris. I don't think you're mature enough."

As a friend? Oh, that's nice, I thought. *As a friend?*

I took the warning seriously and nearly wore out the textbook on logic. For the next few months, I was all syllogisms and predicates, universals, obverses, and inverses. The first rule of logic—that a thing cannot both be and not be at the same time and in the same respect—became my mantra. I applied it to everything. Maybe I loved it so much because it was so different from the first rule of paranoia that had been my mother's milk, where anything could be anything else. And when it came time for the movie star's brother to test me, I was ready. In the final exam, I got a hundred.

By the end of the year, with all my courses added together, my average was exactly ninety. But the path to Paris wasn't clear yet.

The year abroad was officially part of the honors program, which I had never been asked to join. Now, in order to have some control over me, I suppose, I was invited by the priest who ran the program to come to one of the meetings and think about becoming a member. I smelled a rat. The dean had said I could go to Paris. But joining the society, whose director had the final decision about the travel plans of its members, was a step backward. Maybe I was wrong, and maybe I had spent too much time listening to my mother's tortuous reasoning, but I was wary.

I couldn't be discourteous, so I went to the meeting without committing myself to join. The subject under discussion that night would be Greek comedies. I was nervous, just the way I had been standing in the wings at the Hollywood Canteen. *What if they see these enormous gaps I have in my education? What if they find out that my study of antiquity and the classics was confined to sitting on the couch next to my buxom tutor, leafing through pictures of half-naked deities?*

We sat in a dark, wood-paneled room, a half dozen honor students, a Jesuit in black robes, and me. We were each given a little glass of intellectual sherry. Disgustingly dry, it made you witty without actually being funny.

They began discussing Greek comedies, and immediately I felt swamped; I'd read the plays, but these people had read them in the ancient Greek. What could I say that wouldn't sound stupid? But as they talked, I began to have an odd feeling: *I know about this.* Greek comedy was a ribald, coarse, bacchanalian revel. So was burlesque. Pretty soon, I was regaling them with an analysis of Greek comedy as practiced by Hank Henry, Rags Ragland, and Rose LaRose. I began to realize that my education, as peculiar as it was, had been a kind of education after all. I finished my riff, and as far as I could tell, they looked dumbstruck. All of them—the priest, the students—no one knew how to react. They may have simply been appalled by my audacity, but I had the feeling I had actually come up with an idea—something I had wished for since I got to this place.

I went home feeling all right with myself. I probably hadn't said anything especially smart, but I hadn't said anything stupid, either. I left well enough alone and politely avoided ever going back. A month later, I was on a ship called the *Ile-de-France,* on my way to Le Havre.

It was a rough crossing. I stood by the railing as the ship pitched and heaved, along with a few of the passengers, and I was glad to feel the wind in my face and the roiling waves under my feet. I was eighteen and off on my own, out of the nest and headed for France, where girls were so smart they had invented a whole new way of kissing.

But, as it turned out, I wasn't on my own quite yet. At around the same time I left for Europe, my father, needing a job, agreed to do a television series about spies in World War II that was to be shot in Amsterdam. It was weak, cookie-cutter television, written by someone who told me later he was proud that he could sell script after script "without a clever line anywhere in it," but my father needed to work, and he and my mother would be in Europe at the same time that I was.

I wondered if the continent was big enough for the three of us.

chapter 7

PARIS IS THE CRUELEST MONTH

I brought a suitcase full of books to Paris. And as soon as I got there, I started filling up another suitcase with books, many of them in French, which I could barely read, and many of whose pages stayed uncut. Just *having* books was the point, and lugging a valise full of them to the train station and hoisting it up onto the metal rack made me feel like a scholar.

I sat and drank hot rum at Les Deux Magots, and that made me feel like Hemingway. If I had two rums, I felt like Sartre. Sartre liked to write in a crowded café and, amazingly, I found, so did I.

I stayed with a French couple, Pierre and Solange, three flights up at 101 rue de Charenton. Pierre was a Russian émigré with wire-rimmed eyeglasses and wiry gray hair that stood up like a porcupine's. He was an economist who was always running out of money, which I thought was an interesting specialty for an economist. Solange, younger than Pierre by ten or fifteen years, was kind and laughed easily. They seemed to make their way by taking in boarders. I slept in one bedroom, and a blind man slept in the other bedroom. Pierre and Solange slept in the living room. One day there was a knock on the door, and Pierre suddenly became panicky. "They're here!" he said in French. "They want money. I don't have it! Help me." I wasn't sure what I was supposed to do. I was eighteen, and he was a fifty-year-old economist. How could I possibly help? "Tell them I'm sick!" he said, and jumped into bed with his shoes on, pulling the covers up to his chin. *"Allez! Je suis malade!"* Then he started moaning.

Solange wasn't home, and the knock at the door was getting insistent. I opened it and saw a squat, determined man with a briefcase. Pierre called out from the other room in a voice that quavered and broke pitiably, in a way made possible only by bad acting, *"C'est . . . pour moi, Alain?"*

I led the man into the living room, where Pierre coughed and moaned his way out of a final warning. When the man left, Pierre jumped out of bed and cackled. Then he went back to work filling in thousands of numbers on a spreadsheet. He had been working for years on a study that would prove to the world that the entire Russian economy was built on sand and would eventually collapse. It was a race between his collapse and theirs.

It was a small apartment. The blind boarder got on everyone's nerves because he would often bring a prostitute up to his room at midnight and the two of them would make noise until almost dawn. And then during the day he would be cranky and irritable. I couldn't understand how, after making that kind of noise all night, he could be so cranky, pedantic, and critical.

Finally, his severity was too much for us. One evening, the four of us were eating dinner in the cramped kitchen, and I was telling a story about a trip I had taken to the countryside. By this time, my French was good enough to make a pun, and it caught Solange off guard. She burst out laughing just as she was taking a spoonful of tapioca. Unfortunately, Pierre and Solange's finances were so mismanaged that she had two bad front teeth. In fact, she had an actual hole in her teeth, through which her tapioca spurted and landed all over the blind guy. He didn't know she had sprayed him, and it seemed hard-hearted of us to find this funny, but suppressing your laughter doesn't work at a time like this, especially because the more we laughed, the more stern he looked behind his coverlet of tapioca. She reached over and wiped his lapel with a napkin. "What is it?" he asked.

"Nothing," Solange said. "You spilled a little tapioca on your suit."

The next night, he waited quietly until I made another joke, and then he turned to me and said witheringly, "You know, you're very immature."

"I am?" I said.

"Yes. I'm sorry to say. You laugh too much. Last night, you said something that was only mildly funny, and your laughter was all out of proportion to what you had said."

Well, I couldn't argue with that. I agreed with him that I needed to work on the laughing, and he seemed satisfied. Silently, Solange grinned, showing her guilty two front teeth.

I liked Solange. She was a positive person. When I translated some trite English phrase directly into French, it sounded to her like poetry. "Yesterday," she told me, "you said, 'I'm going out now to commune with nature.' You have the soul of a poet." She helped me with my French and made the best potage. I never tasted anything like it again. I guess nothing matches your first potage.

Paris was everything I'd wanted it to be and, unfortunately, more. "April is the cruellest month," Eliot said, ". . . mixing / Memory and desire." I didn't know what he meant at first, especially because I remembered it wrong. "Mixing desire with dead leaves" is what I remembered from my freshman poetry course. I repeated it to myself over and over. *Dead leaves in April? What does that mean?* Then I got it: April is cruel because the desire of youth mixes with the moldy leaves of ancient winter, still wet and slimy underfoot. As long as I was able to just be young in Paris I was okay, but the winter of my past kept showing up, and for me it was April in Paris all year long.

My parents came down to visit from Amsterdam, and we went to dinner at a fancy Parisian restaurant, where even before the main course, my mother was drunk on champagne. Suddenly, we realized one of us had said something she took as a slight as she angrily slammed the champagne bottle onto the table, spraying wine like a geyser all over my father and me. At the other tables, the French laughed. We were acutely embarrassed. She kept downing more wine and loudly accusing us both of transgressions ranging from adultery to homosexuality, while not excluding the possibility of bestiality. Then she passed out. The main course came and sat on the table uneaten as my father and I carried her out of the restaurant. He was at one end and I was at the other, much the way we had carried my dead dog to be buried. The French applauded our exit.

On the street the air revived her, but we couldn't get her back to the hotel because she thought we were trying to kill her. We tried to pull her along, but she held back, clinging to flowers in planters outside the restaurant, pulling them out by the roots. She began screaming for help. A man on a bicycle stopped to watch, trying to decide if a woman was being abused. I told him in French that she was my mother and we were taking her home. My mother screamed that we were trying to kill her. He stood, holding his bicycle, observing, trying to decide which of us was telling the truth.

As this was happening, I was thinking, *I have to remember this. I'll write about this someday. This will be a powerful scene.* I was young, and I was as drunk as she was—only I was drunk on self-dramatization.

A few weeks later, I visited my parents in Amsterdam—but I couldn't take it for long. She showed me a European radio and told me they were using it to spy on her. I didn't ask who "they" were. "Look at the word on the back of the radio," she whispered. "Telefunken. You know what that means?"

"It's the name of the company that makes the radio."

"No, it isn't. Don't try to manipulate me. I have a good mind."

I knew what was coming when she told me she had a good mind. My heart sank. "What does Telefunken mean, Mom?"

"It means they're trying to listen to your father and I having sex." She pulled the plug on the radio and hid it in a closet. "They must think I'm a fool. Look at the ceiling."

I looked at the ceiling. It had a few cracks in it. They were living in a small, charming Dutch house with flowers in the window boxes and white curtains in the window, through which you could see Dutch people bicycling down the street. I wanted to be out on the street cycling with the Dutch people, but I let her tell me about the ceiling.

"What's wrong with the ceiling?"

"You don't see the camera?"

"Where do you see a camera?"

"Right there, where the cracks come together. You think I'm stupid? You think I can't see that? They're taking pictures of me."

I couldn't take it; I left early and went back to Paris.

A month later, I was driving a car full of friends to San Sebastián in Spain, trying to get there in one night because we were all poor students and we couldn't afford even a cheap hotel. We stopped for dinner and ordered paella. While the food was on the way, I left the table to call my father in Amsterdam. Somehow, he'd gotten word to me that we needed to talk. When I reached him, he gently told me my mother had had another episode—this time very serious. She'd had to be hospitalized. My reaction was cold fury. "How could you let her be taken to a mental hospital?"

His voice got softer. He hadn't told me the whole story because he didn't want to alarm me. "They *had* to take her," he said. "She was running down the hallway of the hotel with no clothes on. She was screaming and banging on doors. They called an ambulance and a doctor sedated her and then they took her to the hospital. They don't know how long she'll have to be there."

I went back to the table and said nothing to my friends. I was too ashamed. I was still furious with my father, and with myself, because I was sure one of us had caused this. We got back in the car, and I drove. Before long, everyone in the car was asleep except me. And then, for a brief moment, we were *all* asleep. I felt a rumbling under us and woke up to see that I'd drifted off the road and was heading for a stand of trees. I stopped the car and woke them all up. "I'm a little sleepy," I said, and asked for someone else to drive.

I sat in the backseat and thought about the drama in my life until I fell asleep.

Back in Paris, I didn't go to classes. Instead, I stayed in my small room reading existential philosophers and taking long walks in the cold fall winds in the most wretchedly ugly parts of Paris. In a notebook, I wrote down my theories on what I thought would make me a good actor and what steps I would take to get to heaven. Every entry was an intellectualization, an attempt both to escape and to control my life. Meanwhile, my actual life went more and more out of control. My father, who still had no money to speak of, sent me a couple of hundred dollars a month, which ought to have been enough to live on in those days but which I spent on books and gasoline for my car as I tried to live out a crazy scheme to drive around the entire Mediterranean. Toward the end of every month, I was completely free of money. One night in Nice, I slept in my car, which for some reason I had parked on the beach. In the morning, a policeman woke me and asked me to leave. He wasn't harsh with me; in fact, his face showed concern for this boy foolish enough to bring his car out onto the sand.

I didn't know how cars worked. I didn't understand about oil, for instance. The motor began to grind slightly. Parts were wearing out and falling off. The windshield wipers stopped working, and when it rained the road looked like an impressionist painting coming at you at fifty miles an hour.

On the way into Rome, I ran out of gas. With two friends, I pushed the car into Rome. The loaf of bread on the front seat was all there was to eat until I could get to the American Express office, where next month's check would be waiting.

In Rome, my friends checked in to a hotel. I slept in the car and walked endlessly through the streets, feeling the drama, often sobbing at the thought of having a mother in an insane asylum. It wasn't that I couldn't afford a room; it was that I could suffer more this way. Living out of my car, I didn't wash or change my clothes. For two weeks, I wore the same socks. Cracks appeared on my heels, and my feet began to bleed. I was limping, able to walk only a block or two at a time. Then, just as they should in a drama, things got worse.

As I left my car one night for an evening out, I saw a man sitting on a railing, cursing me, impatient for me to leave. When I came back after dinner, I saw why. He'd broken into my car and taken my suitcase. My clothes were gone, except for a few things in the trunk.

I went to my friends' hotel and got a room.

At Christmastime in Paris, I got a call that my mother was being released from the hospital. At the same time, she'd received a letter from her mother in California: She was dying. My mother had to fly home immediately, and I was being asked to fly back with her. We took off from Copenhagen on a flight that would land just once for refueling in Reykjavík, Iceland, then take us over the North Pole to Los Angeles.

It was a long flight, during which I began to realize that we were now deep into our drama and would never get out of it. Listening to my mother's version of the last few months in the institution, I began to realize she had not so much been released from the hospital as had talked her way out of it. Every week, they'd asked her a series of questions to evaluate her. After a while, it had become clear to her that if she gave them the answers they wanted, they'd have to let her out. She was right—she did have a good mind. On the other hand, she believed her husband wanted to kill her. She'd arranged for her mother to fake a medical emergency so she could escape with her life. And *this* was why we were on the way to Los Angeles. As she talked, the relief I felt when I'd heard my mother was released from the hospital was replaced by dread. Before we landed in Reykjavík, she suddenly realized she was sitting next to an emergency exit and put two and two together. Obviously, I'd been sent on this trip to push her out of the plane. She insisted on changing seats with me, pleased at how she'd outsmarted me.

We landed in Los Angeles and went to my grandmother's small house in Burbank. Within a few hours, my mother was holding my grandmother by the hair and had her down on her knees, screaming at her. Later that night, reclining in the La-Z-Boy chair, she passed out in front of the television. The next day, I made an attempt to open up this forbidden subject with my father. I wrote him a long letter, telling him what had happened. I sealed the letter and left it on a chair while I took a shower; then I took it to the post office, bought stamps, and mailed it. A few days later, at a sidewalk café in Rome, my father opened the envelope in front of friends, happy to have a nice fat letter from his son. But paper napkins spilled out of the envelope. My mother had steamed it open while I was in the shower, read it, and short-circuited my first attempt to speak about her illness. My father, not knowing what to say to his friends, laughed and told them I was a great practical joker. For a while, he actually thought I'd sent him a wad of paper napkins.

We went back to our accustomed silence, and somehow we got by. But this silence had not made me an understanding person. There was a knot of anger that resisted untangling. Even when I was into my forties and fifties, she could still enrage me with an irrational accusation. It wasn't so much that I was impatient with her madness. I could understand that. What I resented her for was not being a mother. And I didn't just resent her; I hated her for it. She wasn't what I thought a mother was; I felt I had never *had* a mother. But what more could she have been? When we laughed together, wasn't she a mother then? And when she told me I could do anything, wasn't she the source of my confidence? She convinced me I *could* do anything. I believed it, and I went out and did things I wasn't remotely capable of. All thanks to a few words from her. Fortunately, I accomplished these things before I realized they were the words of a madwoman.

But she gave me strength. And I wanted so much to be able to love her, there were times when even the madness itself seemed to be fun. Sometimes the only way to survive living with her was to behave as though we were characters in my own private farce. Sneaking out of a hotel with her without paying the bill, rather than a harrowing experience, became a lighthearted adventure, as long as I could act as if it were happening to someone else.

I was twenty, in my last year of college, and my mother and I were staying in a hotel on Lexington Avenue. My father, unable to deal with it anymore, was divorcing her. Within a year or two, he would marry Flora Marino in Italy, and they would have a son, Antony. I would finally have a brother, even though we would be a generation apart, and for most of his childhood we would live an ocean apart.

My mother had heard somewhere that it's smart to accumulate possessions before the divorce is final. So she bought a piano, furs, jewelry, and gold place settings, but mostly things that would have little or no value as time went on. We were running up a hotel bill that was enormous. While she still had a husband, she was spending money recklessly and wiping him out financially. Finally, he cut off her funds. The hotel let us owe them for a couple of months, but eventually they got the idea that she would never pay. They informed us that on Friday night at eight o'clock we would have to be out of our rooms, and we couldn't take our baggage with us. Suddenly, this was an adventure. We decided to make repeated trips out of the hotel, wearing layers of clothing, and leave only our suitcases behind, weighted down with telephone books. I got George, my friend from school, to help me. We made trip after trip down in the elevator and through the lobby wearing our coats over four layers of clothing, which we dumped in a car around the corner. We looked extremely heavy on the way down and extremely thin on the way back up. We were proud of our straight faces. On one trip, we almost went too far. One of us tried for a sixth layer. This was pushing it. The elevator operator turned and stared at us all the way down the long descent to the lobby.

George saw him staring and after a pause said, "God, what a meal!"

"Oh, God, yes," I said. "I'm stuffed."

We thought this was hilarious. The elevator operator just stared at us. We made it out to the car, where we pulled off the clothes and headed back upstairs for more.

And she loved it. She laughed with us. She was a kid, like us.

When she laughed, she laughed from her gut, with all of herself. It made you happy to see her young and carefree like an eight-year-old. But, always, mixed in with the spring of her laughter were the dead leaves of the winter of her madness.

I needed to get to a temperate climate.

chapter 8

THE MUSE FROM THE BRONX

Bea Brown's apartment was filled with people talking and eating and drinking. I'd been invited to listen as musicians got together to play chamber music, and I was looking forward to this night because I'd been working on it and I could tell the difference now between tuning up and playing.

Four string players were getting instruments out of their cases. There was chatter and laughter, ice clinking in glasses, people going inside to throw their coats on the bed—and in the middle of all this, sitting at a music stand, was a beautiful young woman warming up on a clarinet. The musicians settled in, adjusted their stands, turned down the corners of their pages, agreed on a tempo—and started in to play the Mozart clarinet quintet.

The music washed over me: first the strings—sweet, haunting, and sad, throbbing with intensity—and out of this the clarinet emerged, softly at first, then with mounting energy, the notes rising to the ceiling, taking my heart with them. By the end of the first movement, I was in love.

She played with confidence, yet there was something about the way she listened for her entrance, the way she prepared mentally for each passage, that was endearing: She wasn't coasting. In every moment of the music, it seemed, there was something fresh she paid attention to.

Having first been aroused by the chorus girls of my childhood and then having learned to be guilty of my carnal thoughts in my teens, I was both inflamed and struck dumb in the presence of someone I desired deeply. I couldn't speak to her.

All I could manage was a mumbled, unintelligible compliment about her playing. Then the evening was over. We all went home, and I didn't even know her name.

Bea Brown was a violist and orchestra conductor I had met on the boat coming home from Europe. Bea knew I wanted to learn more about music, and I was hoping she would invite me to her apartment again. Weeks later she did, this time for dinner and then to the opera, where Bea was playing in the pit.

The clarinetist was invited, too, and this time we talked. There were twelve of us around the table, and I was thrilled to see that I could make her laugh. But what brought us together was the rum cake. Bea had made a cake for dessert and put it on top of the refrigerator to cool. It was an ancient Philco refrigerator with a sloping top—so old that it shook from the grinding of its moving parts. Slowly, during dinner, the rum cake jiggled its way to the edge of the sloping top and finally took a dive to the floor. When the guests heard the cake splat, there was laughter, but I couldn't let it rest at that. I reached for my fork and headed for the kitchen. The only other person who picked up her fork was the clarinetist. We sat down and ate rum cake off the linoleum with a flirtatious show of appetite. Was ever woman in this way wooed?

After the opera, we walked across the park. It was April 10, yet six inches of snow had fallen on Central Park. She had just come back from a year in Germany on a Fulbright, and we got lost in talk about travel, history, and art, and before long we were lost in the park as well. We had made a complete circle back to where we'd started. Then we crossed through the snow again, found the subway, and rode to the Bronx.

Before her trip to Europe, she hadn't considered the idea that talking with nonmusicians could be interesting. And fresh from Paris, I was learning how much fun civilians could be. Each of us opened a door to a new world for the other.

I left her parents' apartment, where she lived, at three in the morning. She gave me some rye bread for the ride home, because we hadn't eaten since we'd had the cake off the floor. I fell asleep on the train and woke up in Brooklyn at the end of the line. I took the train back to Manhattan, got in around five, and opened a can of beer for breakfast, with a slice of her bread from my pocket.

Her name was Arlene.

I was in love, but I couldn't pick up the phone and call her. I was so intensely shy and inexperienced, I felt I needed to ask her out on the perfect date or she might say no. Nothing was good enough, and if anything was good enough, I couldn't afford it. But it couldn't be a trivial excursion; it had to be cultural and rich with meaning.

Finally, after three agonizing weeks had gone by, I thought I had the perfect choice: an Off Broadway production of Gertrude Stein's opera, *Four Saints in Three Acts*. It's hard to know what a numbing effect this must have had on her as we sat in the last row of the balcony and listened to singers grope their way through two hours of complete and total non sequiturs. Was ever woman, I wonder, in *this* way wooed?

From then on, we were inseparable. I found out she was smart as well as talented—Phi Beta Kappa, which they don't give out for negotiating with your teachers. The clarinet was her instrument, but she could also play the piano and was studying the cello. Her parents, born in Poland and Lithuania, had an old-world eye on financial security and were sure she needed something besides music to fall back on, so she was studying for a master's degree that would allow her to teach music. Sometimes I'd meet her on a corner, where she'd be standing beside a cello almost as big as she was, having lugged it on the subway to a lesson. I was enormously attracted to this woman who could make music on a cello and hike it over a turnstile as well. We spent almost every day together, at the end of which I would ride the subway home, trying not to wake up in Brooklyn. That spring, I would often put my hand in my coat pocket and pull out a stale piece of rye bread that had been in there for a week or two.

We would meet between classes and take walks along the Bronx River where it flowed through the woods behind the university. She had spent her childhood exploring the botanical gardens on the other side of the woods, and she seemed to know the name of every flower we passed. Finally, I couldn't stand it anymore and started reeling off the names of flowers myself. Mine, of course, were in Latin double-talk, meaningless gibberish, but this only made her laugh. And that only made me love her more.

She was my muse and my salvation. "I can't believe this," she said. "You don't read the newspaper every day? How do you know what's going on?" I began reading the paper, almost every word, every day. This suggestion of Arlene's was a refreshing departure for me. I was accustomed to hearing my mother, lonely because I had been studying for hours, knocking on the door of my room and imploring me to come out and watch *What's My Line?* with her.

"I can't, I'm working," I would say.

Appalled, my mother would say, "But *What's My Line?* is on. Don't you want to know what's going on in the world?"

I lived with my mother in a penthouse she had rented on Second Avenue and Tenth Street, with a huge walled garden that ran around the perimeter of the building. Until the divorce money ran out, we stayed there during my last year of college. This was where I brought Arlene for lunch one day for her first meeting with my mother. It wasn't to get my mother's reaction to Arlene; it was more to let Arlene know what she was getting into. I didn't know how vivid a demonstration it was going to be.

My mother knew I liked her version of Swedish pancakes, with powdered sugar and cinnamon rolled up inside them, and she was making them for us. The three of us stood in the kitchen, chatting, while my mother mixed the batter. She separated the eggs, put the yolks in a bowl with flour and milk, then beat the whites into a froth and added them. This was her special touch to make the pancakes extra light, and it was at this point that she stopped chatting and looked at Arlene through squinted eyes. "You're watching this pretty carefully, aren't you." Arlene heard the suspicion in her voice but didn't react to it. She said it looked as though it were going to be delicious. My mother knew when she was being conned. "You're going to try to steal this, aren't you." Arlene tried to answer that she wasn't, but my mother could smell blood. "You think you can sell this recipe and get rich. I know what you're doing. This is mine. I invented this." There must have been at that moment about four million Swedes who knew how to make Swedish pancakes, but she was certain that beating the egg whites was a kind of culinary $E = MC^2$. I managed to change the subject, and we went into the dining room to eat. My mother feigned geniality, even though she was sitting down to a meal with a thief. Within a few minutes, her questions to Arlene became so pointed with hostility that I pushed back my chair and stood up.

"Stop it!" I said.

"Stop what?" my mother said, an innocent little girl.

"You know what you're doing. Stop it."

"How dare you speak to me that way? I'm your mother."

"Cut it out. Right now. Stop it!"

"I will not stop anything. How dare you? You bring people in here to steal from me. I have a right to defend myself. You can't do this to me. I have a good mind."

I plucked a thick candle from its holder. "Goddamn it, shut the fuck up!"

I brought the candle down on the edge of the table, smashing it. Bits of gray candle spread out across the table's surface and onto the floor, like bits of brain shotgunned across a room.

There was silence. My mother stood up and, saying nothing, left the room.

Arlene helped me clean up the scattered wax, and then we left her first lunch with me and my mother.

I thought many times after that day of the feeling that rose in me just before I grabbed the candle. What was it? Where did it come from? It felt like a kind of ecstasy. Once the impulse began, it was its own master. I welcomed it, succumbed to it. But there was really no choice. It owned me. I was trying to learn in those days how to call on my emotions on the stage, but it troubled me that I could be overtaken by anger like this without wanting it. Arlene had been calm when faced with my mother's madness, and I sensed that somehow she could help me face it, too. But by the summer, it looked for a moment as though our paths might separate.

Leopold Stokowski was conducting the Houston Symphony Orchestra in those days, and Arlene heard he was auditioning musicians in New York. Her year in Germany, studying clarinet and playing on tour, had sharpened her and given her the courage to audition for Stokowski. He hired her, at twenty-three, to play assistant first clarinet and bass clarinet. She would be away in Houston for at least the next year, maybe more. It was too long. This was a time when every male had to register for selective service. I had joined the ROTC, and after graduation I was scheduled to go on active duty for six months, where they would try to teach me how to be an infantry officer.

I called my friend George. We were both scheduled for active duty at the same base, and we got the army to let us trade his tour of duty for mine so I could be at Fort Benning in Georgia while Arlene was in Houston.

We went south, where she started playing Beethoven and I started playing soldier.

As soon as she could, Arlene visited me at Benning, and it was then she realized she was dealing with a dangerous person.

"I'm volunteering for parachute training," I told her excitedly.

"I'm sorry, what?"

"Parachute training."

"This is something you volunteer for? You don't *have* to do it?"

"Right. It sounds like fun."

"Jumping out of a plane sounds like fun?"

"Well, no. Going through the air. Doesn't that sound like fun?"

"Going through the air. You mean falling to earth. That sounds like fun?"

There was a slight pause. All she had done was ask a few questions, and I was already reconsidering the idea of leaping to my death.

Which is not to say I gave up being reckless. We were only eight hundred miles apart. On a weekend, if I drove fast enough, I could meet her sixteen hours later in Houston, spend eight hours with her, and drive back to Benning in time for reveille on Monday morning. Or we could meet halfway in New Orleans and have a few more hours together. Each weekend, I asked for permission to leave the base. Sometimes they gave it, and sometimes they didn't. Either way, I went.

Technically, I was away without leave. But when I was a boy watching war movies, going AWOL was something heroes did for love. I was the hero of my own romantic story, and the army would never know, as long as I didn't do something stupid like crash the car and call attention to myself. So, of course, I crashed the car.

We were driving in Louisiana, after a storm. The bayous had overflowed, and there was a sheet of water on the highway. Suddenly, we were hydroplaning. No matter which way I turned the wheel, the car floated on its own across the thin layer of water. We sailed to the left, into the lane of oncoming traffic, and coming straight at us was a car going about eighty miles an hour. To avoid it, I turned the wheel hard to the left and moved off the side of the road, but the highway was an inch higher than the shoulder, and that inch was enough to tip us over.

In the slow motion our brains use to tell us we may never see another day, the car started to roll. The car coming head-on curved around us and kept going as we rolled over and watched the horizon turn slowly before us. We landed back on the wheels, the door of our little Fiat flew open, and I rolled out of the car for twenty or thirty feet, scuffing my face and arms on the concrete highway. The roof had caved in and the windows had popped out, and Arlene was now in the driver's seat with a gash above her knee, where the car key had punctured her thigh.

The car wouldn't move, so we left it and hailed a passing car. A man and his ten-year-old son stopped and picked us up. As we drove, the boy could see we were hurt and shaken. Kneeling on the passenger seat, he faced us, curious and solicitous.

"Are you okay?" he asked.

"We're fine," I said.

"What's your name?" he asked.

I thought of my commanding officer back at Fort Benning, who would not be happy to find out I was more than fifty miles from the base without leave. I hesitated a moment.

"That's all right," the man said to his son. "We don't have to know their names."

I saw the boy thinking about this, trying to figure out why he shouldn't know our names. I remembered what it was like at his age being told I shouldn't know something and not knowing why.

We checked in to a motel, shaking and cold with shock. We slept a few hours, and then Arlene got on a bus for Houston and I got on one headed for Georgia. I got back before they knew I was gone. I made it. I was lucky. I would never go AWOL again.

Not until our honeymoon, three months later.

As soon as my tour of duty was up, Arlene and I got married in Houston. She was Jewish, but she said it was all right with her if we were married in the local Catholic church because I was a nervous wreck about where the pope thought you should get married.

I was less worried, though, about what the army thought of where you spent your honeymoon. I was supposed to go from Fort Benning straight to a reserve unit in New York, but I sent them a pleasant letter letting them know I'd be a little late and would be there as soon as I'd finished my wedding trip.

We could barely afford a wedding trip. We added up her savings and mine, figuring out how much we had to start life with; it came out to six hundred dollars between us. When Arlene had told Stokowski she was getting married, he'd told her she had to take time off for a honeymoon and go to Mexico. He spoke fondly about the town of Xochimilco, with its flower-laden boats. It sounded romantic beyond words.

We took half of all the money we had and got on a bus for Mexico City. It was a country bus, with people carrying live chickens. It made a winding trip through mountain roads, where we stopped in towns with exotic names like Actopan and drank gallons of *café con leche*. We climbed the pyramids and rode on the flowered boats of Xochimilco, and I had my pocket picked on a bus in Mexico City, so we stayed in the hotel room, broke, for the rest of the trip, strumming a guitar we had bought with our last few pesos. It was romantic beyond words.

Three weeks and three hundred dollars after we had been married, we made our way back to New York, where I put on my dress uniform, went down to my reserve unit in a drab building on Forty-second Street, and told the captain I was reporting for duty. He looked at me in silence for a moment. "Where were you?" he asked politely.

"I sent you a letter," I said. "I was on my honeymoon. Did you get my letter?"

"Your letter? You sent a letter? I was about to report you to the FBI."

He was a decent guy and didn't make a fuss about it, but I never quite got used to the idea that the army isn't happy just knowing what your plans are. They like to make plans for you.

Arlene and I rented a small room in Manhattan, and I started looking for work as an actor. I was confident that although I had no formal training and very little experience, I was just what they were looking for. It turned out they were looking for someone a little shorter, a little less skinny, a little more muscular, and a lot more experienced.

Arlene, again, was our salvation. When I couldn't find part-time work, she taught music at Junior High School 136 in Harlem and gave private lessons on the clarinet. But she was my salvation in more ways than helping to feed us. Eventually, she saved me from the fires of hell, and if you're going to have a muse, this is the kind of thing you'd like her to do.

When we talked about what I had read in the paper and I sounded illogical, she'd question my premises. She encouraged me to make distinctions. She helped me extend my education into the real world, and I began actually using what I had learned in logic class as I got through the day.

I was still going to mass every Sunday, because I believed that if I didn't, I would take a one-way trip to hell. I was twenty-two, and the nuns' words from my adolescence still burned in my ears. I envied people like Arlene and her father, Simon, who seemed not to need to believe what someone else told them they had to believe. Simon was a quiet man with a twinkle in his eye and a stomach that showed a strong belief in food. He had a simple rule that covered politicians, clergymen, and insurance salesmen. "They're all a bunch of fakers," he would say with a sweep of his hand that gave them the official brush-off.

I couldn't take the priests so lightly. They had a list of things you could burn for, and once you had heard the word, not believing it was at the top of the list. I didn't want to burn, and I didn't want to take the chance in believing there was no such thing as eternal fire. I kept thinking of what William James said in a gallant attempt to be pragmatic about the unprovable: "Faith is a bet you can't lose." I supposed he meant that if you get to heaven after a life of belief and you find out it isn't actually there, well, nothing lost. I turned that over and over in my mind, until I thought: *But what if you spend real time doing things you wouldn't do if there really was no afterlife? What about endless novenas and countless trips to the altar? What about meatless Fridays, and what about people who lock themselves up for life in a monastery? Is that nothing lost?*

Still, I was locked in by belief. Every exit was blocked by a sentry in black with a wimple and three nostrils, holding a yardstick.

Then one day, the heavens opened for me.

It was a sunny Sunday morning in spring. I kissed Arlene good-bye and took the train up to Fordham, where there was a little chapel I still went to for mass. There were fifty or sixty people in the pews. We knelt, we stood, we sat, we knelt. In the hundreds of masses I had been to, I never could remember when you were supposed to stand and when you were supposed to kneel. I watched and did what the others did. And when I couldn't figure out which it was they were doing, I put my behind on the seat and my knees on the kneeler and did the all-purpose half kneel.

Then the priest reached the moment when, after consecrating the host and holding it in both hands, he lifts it above his head. I looked at it. I had always looked at it. But this time I noticed that the other people in the chapel were bowing their heads. *Maybe I should be bowing my head,* I thought. *But, no. If you're not supposed to look at it, why is the priest holding it up? We're going to be swallowing it in a minute; why can't we look at it?* This led to a train of thought I had never taken before: *I wonder how many of these people bowing their heads actually believe that this is the body of Jesus? Do they realize you can't regard it as just a symbol?* And suddenly, in that moment, I remembered what the Jesuits had taught me. "No matter what," they said, "you have to follow your conscience." And I thought: *I don't know what these other people believe, but if I'm honest with myself, I do not believe the priest is holding anything but the same piece of unleavened bread that it was a few minutes ago.* I was like the boy of fourteen again, refusing to rise from the pew, holding stubbornly to his right to think for himself.

And then I remembered a second thing the Jesuits had taught me: If you don't believe in transubstantiation, you're automatically excommunicated.

I'm out, I thought. *I didn't quit; they don't want me. They let me go. I'm fired.*

A ray of sunlight fell across the chapel, just the way it did in *The Song of Bernadette.*

Arlene had never opposed what I believed. She never did anything more than ask questions. It took a while, but I began to ask questions, too, and when I did I saw that as logical as I had thought I was, it was as if there were parts of my brain operating independently, not even aware of one another. Arlene had brought me closer to facing these parts of myself. She was introducing me to a notion of reality and compassion I had never known before. She was helping me learn to live in a world that had actual people in it and not just a string of audiences. And I fought her every step of the way.

She was dragging me unwillingly into an uncomfortable side of life, the one on the other side of the footlights. Not only would I have to accept civilians as equals, I would have to become one. I knew she was smarter than I was, and she probably had some inkling I didn't have about the value of all this, but it seemed a diversion from what I really should be learning, which was acting and writing. It would be a while before I realized that these were things I'd never learn if I didn't learn her thing first.

My real education was just beginning, and it would lead to a new way of thinking of myself—as a person, and even as an actor. But first I had to be willing to be taught. Not easy for someone who at twenty-two was pretty sure he had seen it all.

chapter 9

WATCHING FROM THE WINGS

Too poor to study, and afraid I would spoil my natural genius by going to classes, I was trying to teach myself to act. I would read soliloquies from Shakespeare into a tape recorder, trying to make sense of them. I would accent one word, then another, until finally I was leaning heavily into almost every word in the sentence. It was unintelligible.

My writing wasn't going any better. Amazed that I could string words together, I wrote plays, short stories, and sketches. I wondered why writers said they had trouble filling a blank page. I filled reams of them.

But I wanted an audience for all this brilliance, and one day I saw a small classified ad in a show business trade paper asking for submissions of sketches for an Off Broadway revue. I wrote half a dozen sketches and sent them off to the post office box listed in the ad. A week later, I got a call to come down and see the producer. Would I like to have my sketches in the show? Would I like to be in the show? Would I like to direct it? Of course, I said yes; but I couldn't understand all the flattering attention until they showed me a press release that used my father's name as often as possible.

On the night of the first preview, I stood in the wings and watched the opening sketch I had written. I heard actual laughs coming from the audience. This was the first time I had heard an audience laugh at something I had written, and a cocktail of sweet, tingling hormones shot through my brain. I was suddenly aware of what an astonishing power there was in words. Once you set a thought in motion, it went on its own. You could write something on Tuesday, and they would laugh at it a week from Friday. I also began to hear what *didn't* work. And after a while, I could imagine as I wrote a line what the response would be. The wings were teaching me again.

I had watched my father from the wings since I was a baby. The wings had been my home, my spy perch, and my cocoon—my inspiration.

My father had let me stand in a magical place. From the wings, you see the actors' discipline; how even the slightest movement is both controlled and spontaneous. And the sheer physical effort: You see them spitting as they talk, sweating, giving one another energy as they toss the ball of the audience's attention back and forth between them. You see things the audience never sees.

When I was ten years old, I was standing in the wings of a vaudeville house in Baltimore. My father had become famous in the movies and was on a tour of vaudeville houses, singing and doing patter with his old partner Beetlepuss Lewis. Blackstone the Magician and Bela Lugosi were also on the bill. Lugosi didn't have a real act. A classically trained actor known in this country for horror movies, he read some poetry in a scary blue light. After the first few shows, he sat with my father and Beetlepuss in their dressing room and said he wished he had more to offer the audience. Beetlepuss thought about it and came up with an idea for him: The singer in the show, a young woman, would introduce Bela to the audience and he would come onstage and do a joke with her—a line about bats, or maybe he would ask if you can get a good glass of blood at the local diner. Then she'd laugh and say, "Oh, Bela, you kill me." And he'd look at her hungrily and say, "In due time, my dear." In those days, this was close enough to funny to seem like an act.

I watched Bela, but I *studied* Blackstone, every day, five shows a day. I loved magic. I had been inventing magic tricks for years. When I was seven, my mother was appalled when I wanted to show her a trick in which I would pretend to cut off my thumb with a kitchen knife and have it show up later in a matchbox. She wouldn't let me do it, no matter how many times I explained it was just a trick.

With a view of Blackstone from the side, I saw things from the wings the audience never saw. With elaborate gestures, he took apart a bridge table and showed them that nothing could be hidden in it. But I could see that the tabletop was thicker than the audience thought it was. I could even see the heads of a few white birds in a compartment behind it. With a flourish, he let the birds loose and the audience gasped and applauded. They were surprised, but I wasn't. This was why I liked watching actors from the wings. You could see where they hid the birds.

I watched my father, too. Knowing him so well, I could see what parts of his performance were truly him and what were layered on, just putting on a show. I was competitive, watching him critically. When he was introduced in each show, I noticed the staginess of his entrance. He walked out swiftly, making a large banana curve as he headed for the microphone so that the second half of the trip would be full face to the audience. As he scooped out a path across the stage, one hand was on his rib cage, as if he were a headwaiter holding his jacket away from a flaming dessert. I tried to figure this out. *Doesn't he realize this doesn't look like a regular person walking to a microphone?*

It didn't occur to me that he probably wasn't trying to look like a regular person. The audience expected a movie star to walk out, and that's what they got. They seemed to love it. He seemed to love it, too, and for some reason I didn't approve of his loving it.

Watching, of course, is not the same as doing. It can give you an unearned sense of accomplishment. Even at the age of ten, I was convinced I knew more about acting than my father did.

We were back in La Tuna Canyon after the vaudeville tour, and he was shooting another movie at Warners. He came into the living room where I was stretched out on the floor with the *Congressional Record* and asked if I'd like to hold the book for him while he went over his lines for the next day. I said sure, not thinking this was any special honor, and took the script. I read his first cue and he said his line. He got a word wrong and I corrected him. He said the speech again and got it right. I looked at the script for a moment, not saying anything. "Do I say more?" he asked me.

"No, that's all," I said, "but what if you said that line like this. . . ." And I read the line differently for him.

He looked at me, amused. "Are you directing me?" he asked. He was smiling, but he seemed a little amazed. I didn't know what he was amazed at.

"Don't you think it's better that way?" I asked.

"Well, let me think about it," he said. "Why don't we just do the lines for now?"

Okay, I thought, *but I'm giving you a much better reading.*

I had utter confidence. After all, look at how many performances I had *watched* by the time I was ten.

At fifteen, I would stand in the wings and watch my father and Sam Levene in *Guys and Dolls*—and I did this almost every Saturday for two years, at both shows. My father was playing a character perfectly within his range, and his own magnetism became Sky Masterson's magnetism. I was riveted by how quietly powerful he could be. In the Havana bar scene, he left a tip for the waiter, took a last sip from his whiskey glass, and plunked it down on top of the money so it wouldn't blow away. That small gesture was so strong, it became a part of me. It's how I leave a tip on the table even now; I put a glass on it, and the click it makes as it hits the tabletop is the sound of his glass hitting the table at each performance.

Watching Sam Levene was thrilling. He could ride a moment as if it were a wild animal. He went wherever it took him and stayed on its back. I'd never seen anything like this. New meanings occurred to him on the spot. Not only did he play the same lines differently every night, but the laughs rolled in from the audience in different places. How did he do it? This kind of spontaneity and this utter commitment to the moment became what I wanted to have. As good as my father was, what I was seeing as they played together a few feet away was the difference between my early life and my future life; between burlesque and theater; between performing and acting. I chose acting. I wanted to be Sam.

What I really wanted was to be both of them. But I didn't know that yet. And it would take a long time before they could both live comfortably in me.

By the time I finished high school, I'd made up my mind what I wanted to do with the rest of my life. I wanted to act. I was sixteen, and I announced it one day to my father, formally. He looked at me without saying anything for a while. "You know," he said, "it takes a lot of energy to be an actor."

"I *have* a lot of energy," I said. Of course I did. I was sixteen.

"You don't think you'd like to be a doctor?" he asked.

I knew *he* had wanted to be a doctor, but I didn't want to be one. If I did, people would come to me with problems and expect me to cure them. I would have to touch sick people and watch them die. He could see I was determined, and he let it go.

And then he gave me what was, apart from not drifting while I talked, the only advice he ever gave me about acting. "Always find a place to sit down," he said. "Your legs will get tired. Look for places to sit down. Whenever you can." I nodded as if I understood. *This is really strange advice,* I thought. What could he possibly mean? Is he so empty that he thinks this is the secret of a life on the stage? I wish I could go back now and touch his hand. Touch his hand and thank him for sharing a speck of the reality of his life with me. Not the vague generality of most people's advice, but a little bite of life: the ache in his leg on a long day. Anesthetized by youth, I missed it.

Then we talked about what my name would be. Would I use the name Alda? I was proud of being Italian, and I thought about using the name I had been born with: D'Abruzzo. But I realized that most people couldn't pronounce my name, even after I'd said it three times. Alda was a name my father had constructed by taking the first two letters of Alphonso (his own true first name) and the first two letters of D'Abruzzo. In practice, it was now our family name, so I said I would stick with Alda, which I think made him happy.

My father enjoyed being Italian, as I did, and he identified himself as an Italian even in the forties, when it wasn't especially popular to do that. The rest of the country saw Italians as somewhat foreign creatures without much class but a lot of names. When he went to Hollywood, his press releases started including the information that his real name was Alphonso Giuseppe Giovanni Roberto D'Abruzzo, about three first names more than he was born with. When he sang on *The Ed Sullivan Show,* he chose the Italian love song "Oh Marie" and dedicated it to "all my *paisans* out there." In all of this, he was trying deftly to play both sides by pointing to his Italian ancestry, but doing it in terms the American audience would accept. Italians were okay as long as they were colorful, fun-loving folks who had the good taste to know their place. He was a handsome leading man who, without making a big deal out of it, was moving the boundary a little. I knew from the experiences of my friend Joe Colangelo, though, that in places like Rye, New York, where he lived, if you were an ordinary middle-class Italian, the boundaries were not so movable.

My father, from a working-class background, dreamed of celebrating his good fortune with his family and the neighborhood he grew up in. As soon as he had saved a few dollars from the modest salary he was earning at the studio, he organized a block party in Queens for what he billed as his eight hundred cousins (another stereotype he gladly played into).

I loved going back with him to visit his family in Queens. There would be a Sunday dinner that went on for several hours at a table that took up the whole living room of my grandparents' tiny apartment. From the first steaming dish of ravioli to the chestnut shells littering the table at the end of the meal, there was laughter and loud talk. Everyone spoke at a volume that would carry across a football field. You had to do this to be heard above everyone else. A lot of the laughter was at the expense of my grandfather, a small, quiet man who had been a barber until he retired but now spent his days looking out the window and following the activities of the neighborhood. He sat quietly nursing the half glass of red wine allowed by his doctor and looking for ways to trick someone into pouring him a little more. After dinner, they played cards and I was allowed to go out with my uncle and ten cents to bring back a bucket of beer.

I was glad, as I sat with my father deciding on a new name, that "Alda" sounded Italian.

"How about your first name?" my father asked. I hadn't thought that was a problem. Everyone in school called me Al. "I don't think a nickname is good for an actor," he said. "It limits you. I called myself Buddy Alda when I started out, but it sounded too much like a kid. So I changed it to Robert." He suggested Alan, which I didn't like much, but I didn't say anything. "Alan, with one 'l,' " he said. And I liked that even less. But as we talked, I decided that he had named me the first time, and if he wanted to rename me now, I'd let him.

Then, probably to give me a chance to see what it's like to work hard, he told me he would ask a friend who ran a summer stock theater if I could work as an apprentice in his company.

When I told my friend Joe, he wanted to go, too, and my dad arranged it, maybe glad that I'd have company while I was learning to work hard.

Joe and I took a bus down to Barnesville, Pennsylvania, and began ten weeks of a daily shift that started at eight in the morning and ended around midnight. We nailed canvas to frames of fresh-smelling wood and painted the cloth with sizing to make it taut. The sizing had the clean, pale odor of glue and water, and when it dried we painted the flats and hinged them together. We set up the scenery before each show, and then sometimes I stood behind it, my face against the back of the flats, breathing in the smell of paint and sizing as I listened to the music of the speeches by Noël Coward or lyrics by Cole Porter. It wasn't the music of their songs that killed me; it was the music of the words themselves.

From the wings that first year in stock, I watched Mae West and Buster Keaton, and although I was too callow to understand what true artists I was watching, still, they impressed me. And sometimes I got to act onstage. I had talent, but it was raw talent, and I needed someone to take me through the steps that would lead to acting and not just flat-out performing. But here in Barnesville the main objective was to learn your sides, build the set, and get a new show on every week. John Kenley, the wonderful, flaming impresario of the Kenley Players, said to me, "Honey, here's my theory of acting: Shout and duck."

When I went to college that fall, I signed up for plays in the Theater Department. When my father pleaded almost wistfully with me to try a pre-med course in chemistry, I took the course halfheartedly. I was afraid if I did well in it, I'd be touching sick people for the rest of my life. It wasn't something I took naturally to. In the lab, we had to prepare for experiments by breaking glass pipettes with our hands, which left me each and every time with bloody fingers. It was a summer course in which the basic concepts were brushed past so quickly, I had no idea that we were even talking about atoms bound into molecules. In the final exam, I managed to get a score of ten.

The professor asked me into his office. I sat on the hard wooden chair while he looked over my exam paper, full of red marks. He looked up at me and stared for a moment. "Why are you here?" he asked.

"My father would like me to be a doctor," I said.

"Yes?"

"So, I was trying chemistry. To see how I would do. How it would work out."

"I see." We looked at each other for what seemed like a long time. After a while, I got up and left, leaving a world of blood, mostly my own, behind.

I was on a trajectory to become an actor. I knew I could do it, because I felt I knew more than some people who had been doing it all their lives.

My father's birthday was coming up, and I wanted to get him something meaningful. I searched New York for days, and in a small shop on the East Side, I found a tattered, leather-bound copy of Shakespeare's plays. As scuffed as it was, I could just afford it. The store owner polished it up for me and carefully covered up the scuff marks. I was proud of the gift as I presented it to my father.

He opened the wrapping and looked at the title. There was an odd expression on his face that I couldn't quite read. He thanked me, then asked in a neutral tone, "How come you got me this?"

"Well," I said, "I thought it would be something you'd enjoy reading." I didn't say what I was thinking: *It's something you* ought *to be reading*.

I was in my second year of college, and a new universe was opening up to me. I was suddenly aware of a world of ideas and galaxies of subtle shadings in language. I wanted to share that with him. Well, I didn't really want to share it. That implies acceptance on his part. I wanted to impose it on him. I was taking advantage of his gentle nature to let him know in a subtle way that I was superior to him—just one of the many wonderful, hurtful things you can do with subtlety.

He thanked me and put the book aside on a table in the living room. He let it sit, unread, thinking rightly that there was an implied criticism in the gift. I was hinting that he didn't take acting seriously enough. Somehow, I thought that all you had to do was take acting seriously to be good at it.

For several days as I moved through our apartment, I passed by the book, thinking if only he'd read it, his horizons would be extended, his acting would deepen. I was drunk with my own precocity.

Finally, the beautiful leather book I had chosen so carefully was too seductive to resist. I picked it up and opened it. I began reading *Hamlet,* and not far into the play I was stopped cold by Hamlet's speech about acting. Not the speech *to* the players ("Speak the speech, I pray you . . ."), which is technical stuff about delivery, but his lines *about* one of the players, after he's seen him play a short speech. This is a deeper version of acting than speaking words trippingly on the tongue. It gets to what theater, and in some ways life itself, is all about.

Hamlet greets the players and asks one of the actors to do a monologue for him about a character from ancient Greece called Hecuba. Almost instantly, the actor is moved to tears and the blood drains from his face as he describes Hecuba's cries of anguish on seeing her husband hacked to death by his enemy. Hamlet is stunned by how this actor can get genuinely choked up in a speech about someone with whom the actor has no connection, someone who, if she existed, lived two thousand years ago.

I was still a boy, not yet able to carry off even the technical side of acting very well, but when I read this speech of Hamlet's I was struck, as Hamlet is, by what this actor can accomplish; how emotional he can become about imaginary events. Hamlet thinks it's monstrous that the actor can do this while he, Hamlet, is unable to act with passion in the face of a real call to action—his father's murder.

> *Is it not monstrous that this player here,*
> *But in a fiction, in a dream of passion,*
> *Could force his soul so to his own conceit*
> *That from her working all his visage wann'd,*
> *Tears in his eyes, distraction in's aspect,*
> *A broken voice, and his whole function suiting*
> *With forms to his conceit? And all for nothing!*
> *For Hecuba!*
> *What's Hecuba to him, or he to Hecuba,*
> *That he should weep for her?*

As I put down the book, what was monstrous for me was that I realized that Hecuba meant nothing to me. There was no way I could weep for an offstage Hecuba who was purely imaginary. I couldn't really relate to a person who was actually there onstage, either, but I was only dimly aware of this at the time. All I wanted then was to be able to cry onstage. I wanted to care about Hecuba so much that she opened my faucets. I knew this was possible because I'd seen actors who in a scene that began casually could be so caught up that with no warning or preparation, they would choke up with tears, almost against their will. I couldn't do this, and I wanted it more than anything. I realized when I read this passage in *Hamlet* how much I craved spontaneity and how I hungered to be swept away by emotion. But in these youthful days, even if I managed to be spontaneous, when it came to emotion, all I could do was pump it up. It didn't blossom on its own. And if I started out on one emotion, I stayed there. Changes didn't come about by themselves. I was protected against change. In a way, I was imitating life, but not living it. I was stuffing the dog. If I could learn to unstuff it, maybe I'd become an actor. I didn't know it then, but maybe I'd become a better person, too.

If all that was ever going to happen, though, it was a long way off. I was going to have to stand a lot longer in the wings. Watching my words played that first night in the Off Broadway review, and listening to the audience laughing, had fueled my dream of becoming a playwright. Reading the review the next day woke me up. I opened the paper and turned to the theater section first, as I always did in those days, and there was the first review of my work as a writer. It began: "Backward children in a school for the retarded wouldn't have been proud of what happened last night." After that it got worse. There was clearly more to learn.

I tried to become more disciplined, to learn from others who had been at it longer than I had. I took a mime course with Étienne Decroux, the man who had taught Marcel Marceau. I let him teach me. I tugged on the imaginary rope and walked like a chicken and fell face forward onto the floor without flinching when he cried "Salamander!" I was taking instruction and giving my body over to another person for the first time since the physical therapist tried to take it apart when I had polio.

I went out for a beer after class one evening with a fellow student. He looked down in his beer and said, "You know, if we really want to make it, if we want to be first-class artists, we'll have to give up everything. Everything. We'll have to give up friends and movies and reading the Sunday *Times*."

I nodded and grunted in agreement. But inwardly I was thinking, *What the hell is he talking about? What kind of romantic bullshit is this?* My idea of discipline didn't include giving things up. It was supposed to be fun. I had long ago decided that the perfect regimen of a disciplined life would include a certain amount of time that was totally unaccounted for and in fact wasted. Moderation in all things, especially moderation: This was my motto, and I thought I was very clever to have thought it up.

As time went on, it was a revelation to learn, as only a few young people do, that if you looked carefully, you could find the most wonderful ways to waste time.

Of all of them, the racetrack was the best. It was there you had fresh air, a beating heart, the piercing imminence of glory, and, eventually, the rueful discovery that these massive beasts can shrug you off their backs without your ever having to get on them.

chapter 10

FUN AT
THE RACES

My career at the racetrack, brilliant as it was, had humble beginnings. It began with a search for ordinary, actual work that could support us.

I was at the dining room table, counting up our money. Our daughter Eve, one year old, was playing on the floor and swaying to a recording of Domenico Modugno's "Volare." Arlene was at the stove, making dinner. I finished counting and sat back in my chair. We had just enough to make one more month's rent.

After dinner, I went out and bought a newspaper and started looking at the classifieds. I saw that a company called Restaurant Associates was looking for a doorman. I went to the personnel office on Fifty-seventh Street and climbed the stairs, pretty confident that with a college education and an affable personality I could easily make a few dollars opening doors and hailing cabs. The personnel manager looked at me coldly. "Yes?" he said. I smiled affably and told him I was there for the doorman job. He looked at the top of my head for what seemed like quite a while; then he said, "There's a barbershop downstairs. Get a haircut and come back and then we'll talk about the doorman job." He closed the door. I went down and got a haircut for a dollar seventy-five; I thought it made me look like a geek, but it seemed to be just right for the personnel manager, because he hired me.

The Forum of the Twelve Caesars was a fancy restaurant on Forty-eighth Street, and I had to wear a coat that looked a little like a double-breasted toga, but the tips—the quarters and dollar bills I stuffed in my toga every night—paid our rent for a couple of months. And it placed me in the theater district during lunch hour. One afternoon I left the door, ran downstairs to the locker room, tore off my semitoga, put on a jacket over my striped pants, raced to the Cort Theater, and auditioned for a play. After I read for the director, I ran the two blocks to the restaurant and was back on the street before they knew I was gone. I got the part—only five lines long, but in a Broadway play, and I was able to pass on my Caesar costume to the next young artist in line.

Like most plays I got into in those days, this one closed after a couple of performances and I was back looking for a part-time job. I saw another ad in the paper. An office in Brooklyn was looking for people to sell mutual funds. I applied, was accepted, and studied to take a test for a license, which involved having to remember when the Blue Sky Laws were passed (in the 1930s) without having to know what the Blue Sky Laws *were*. More important, the manager of the office taught me how to say, "Mr. Prospect, past performance is no guarantee of future results, but if you had started ten years ago to put away ten dollars a month in the Wellington Fund, it would be worth five thousand dollars today! Only ten dollars a month. That's less than a pack of cigarettes a day." I was so convincing, I sold myself a plan.

I also was able to convince my mother's masseuse to put away a few thousand dollars that she hadn't mentioned to the IRS. But that was pretty much it. I talked to a lot of prospects, but nobody seemed all that impressed with my knowledge of the Blue Sky Laws.

Another ad in the paper took me to Queens, where they were look-ing for people to color baby pictures. This was before color film was cheap, so department stores would photograph your baby and sell you prints that were colored by hand. I had colored pictures as a boy, so I knew exactly how to do this job. The only problem was that it was piecework, and I wasn't very fast. Before I had finished the first batch of pictures, I realized I was making about ten cents an hour. I took the train back to Queens, which cost more than I had earned, gave them their photos back, and got out of the baby pictures racket.

As I walked around the city, I would scan bulletin boards for part-time jobs, and I saw a notice on one that was intriguing. A psychiatrist was looking for volunteers to be hypnotized in a study of the nervous system.

I took the train up to Albert Einstein hospital in the Bronx and was interviewed for the job. The doctor told me that if I was a good subject for hypnosis, I would get twenty-five dollars for three sessions. This was fantastic. We could live for half a week on that, and all I had to do was go into a trance.

In the first session, he told me to close my eyes and relax. He said I wouldn't lose consciousness and that my ability to go into a light trance depended not on him, but on my ability to concentrate. He said not to block out stray thoughts or sounds from the street, but to let them in and incorporate them. This seemed like good advice for all kinds of concentration, and it's how I've gone about concentrating ever since that afternoon. At first, though, I thought nothing was happening because I was fully conscious. I remembered the time I was ten years old, watching a nightclub show with my parents. A stage hypnotist asked for volunteers, and I went onstage to be hypnotized along with three other people. We all went through a comically bizarre scenario. He told us it was cold, and we shivered; he told us it was hot, and we opened our collars. But mostly we did these things because he was whispering to us, telling us what to do next, and we simply played our parts.

I decided to play along with the psychiatrist, too. I really wanted the twenty-five dollars, and if it took a little acting to get it, I would act hypnotized. Then he said, "Now I'm going to test how deep you are.

Stay in your chair and hold your legs straight out in the air. I'm going to see if I can balance this office chair on your legs." He picked up a really big swivel chair.

The chair looked as if it weighed forty or fifty pounds. *This is not going to work,* I thought. *I'm out twenty-five bucks.* He placed the chair on top of my extended legs, and to my astonishment, my legs didn't give.

He continued on with the experiment, which was designed to see if hypnosis could increase the efficiency of the autonomic nervous system. He would flash words on a screen for a fraction of a second and time how long it took for the words to become recognizable. With hypnosis, I recognized them much faster than I had without it. But what was most interesting to me was the realization that through concentration alone I could affect parts of my body that I couldn't control with conscious commands. I was sure that no amount of willpower could have allowed me to support the office chair with outstretched legs or recognize the words faster, but deep concentration *could.* I became excited by the idea that there was a way to get in touch with parts of my body that would allow me to assume the gestures of other characters and go through their emotions without the phoniness that comes from consciously forcing the body to do these things. He didn't know it, but he had given me an important way to get in touch with parts of myself, and I would use it for the rest of my life. Plus, I got the twenty-five dollars.

I went back to the classifieds, and for one ghastly night I worked in a telephone boiler room in the Bronx. At seven in the evening, I made my way down a flight of dark steps to a large basement lit by a few bulbs hanging overhead. There were dozens of phones, each in a little cubicle. Two skinny men in their thirties explained to me that I would be calling people in Riverdale. "These are good prospects. Apartments go for forty dollars a room there. These people have money. Here's the script. Stick to the script. If they hesitate, but they don't hang up, just go back to this paragraph, here."

I took the script and dialed my first prospect. "Hello," I said, reading from the paper in front of me, "this is Ed Jastrow, down here at the

Veterans of Foreign Wars." *Down here,* I thought. *That's clever. "Down here" could be anywhere.*

"Yes?" said the voice at the other end.

"We're asking people like yourself if they'd be kind enough to help us. Every Sunday we take a few paraplegic veterans out on the town. We take them on the Circle Line for a tour of Manhattan. Then we treat them to dinner at the Brass Rail Restaurant. And I have to tell you, Mr. Prospect, you should see those boys' faces at the end of that day."

"Well, I don't know how I could help. . . ."

"Well, it really doesn't take much, Mr. Prospect. All it takes is ten dollars for each veteran. Can I put you down for three boys, Mr. Prospect?"

"No, wait. I'd like to help, but don't put me down. I'm not able to."

"You know, you really should see their faces at the end of the day. It means an awful lot to them. How about if I put you down for two?"

Click.

Until this moment, I had thought there actually were veterans who were being taken on trips. But as I dialed new calls, I began mentally adding up the figures. I was supposed to be paid three dollars an hour and an extra dollar for every ten that was pledged. The phone calls cost money, too, and as dim and grungy as the room we were in was, that had to cost something. The two skinny guys were sure to be taking a cut from each ten-dollar sale, so how much did that leave for the veterans? I was starting to feel a little sick. If they gave even one dollar to help paraplegic veterans, it would be amazing. I made it through a few more phone calls, but I felt like such a shit, lying to people about wounded soldiers, I quit after about an hour. No one had donated any money, so I wasn't owed a commission, but they did owe me three dollars for my time. I didn't collect. I left and never went back.

An actor friend who was a master at part-time jobs saw I was getting desperate and offered to help. He had worked as a clown at the openings of gas stations and other businesses that were trying to draw attention to themselves. All you had to do was dance in the street for six or eight hours and hand out balloons. He was moving on to real work and offered me his clown suit. My first job was at a store on 103rd Street that sold chicken parts. I don't think they cooked the chicken parts; they just laid out the bluish legs and wings in trays and waited for people to come in and buy them, which I doubt they ever did, with or without a clown. I was handing out balloons when a group of boys about nine decided they wanted all of them.

Within a minute, I was backing up the street, smiling, joking, and reassuring them that if they were patient, there would be plenty for everyone. One of them, a chubby kid who was surprisingly strong, started twisting my wrist until I let go of a handful. Finally, I climbed a lamppost and threw the balloons as far as I could. When they ran for them, I jumped down and went home.

The next day, I was in front of a gas station in Brooklyn. Hasidic boys coming home from school in black stockings, black hats, and *payes* stood and stared at the clown with the white face and big red lips in his orange-and-black suit. I hadn't ever seen anything like them, and I guess they hadn't ever seen anything like me. They dealt with that a few minutes later by standing across the street and lobbing eggs at me.

Next, I was in the Bronx, dodging trucks and dancing in front of a Texaco station on Gun Hill Road. In fact, it wasn't exactly dancing. I leapt and twirled in the air without quite knowing how to land. The street was hot from the summer sun, and each time I came down on the ground, my foot would stick to the hot macadam while my body kept turning, and my knee would twist like a corkscrew. At the end of the day, as I limped to the men's room to wash off my clown makeup, a me-chanic who'd been watching me from underneath a car came out of the garage and stood in front of me with his hands on his hips.

"How much they pay you to jump around like that?" he asked.

"Twenty-five dollars for the day," I said.

"Shit," he said, "*you* got it easy."

I hobbled over to the toilet and washed off the clown face, but when I looked in the mirror I realized I really didn't understand the basics of makeup. All I had done at the start of the day was paint big eyes and a large mouth on my face. I hadn't applied a base. As a result, the sun had burned the outline of a huge pair of eyes and a gigantic mouth on me. I rode home on the subway with a permanent clown face that lasted a week. I was starting to feel deeply sorry for myself.

I applied for a hack license. This involved taking another quiz during which I had to convince an official of the Taxi and Limousine Commission that I knew where Penn Station was.

My first night on the job, I went down to the garage and waited for my car. You sat around for an hour or so until the driver who had your car during the day turned it in for the night shift.

We sat on long wooden benches, and while I waited, I was listening to two drivers who I could tell had been doing this for a long time. I tried to listen in on their conversation, hoping to pick up a few clues about what it would be like out on the streets. They were chatting quietly, and I could hardly hear them, so I moved a little closer, just in time to hear one of them say to the other, "Yeah, I knew it was a holdup the minute he got in the car."

"Really? How could you tell?" his friend asked.

"Well," he said, "he puts this gun to my head and he says, 'Got change of twenty?' "

I became inert. I sat with my mouth open and barely heard the dispatcher call out to me: "Alda! Your car's ready. Let's go."

Each night, I would stiffen when I heard suspicious sounds behind me, but they never turned out to be more dangerous than someone opening a package. I would come home at four in the morning and empty my pockets onto the kitchen counter of the twenty dollars or so in bills and change that I'd earned. When I woke up, Arlene would have divided it up and put it in envelopes: some for rent, some for food, and some for gas, electricity, and telephone.

Arlene's mother was discreet and warm, but you could tell she was worried about her daughter's survival. She would come over and visit for a while, and after she left we would find a piece of meat in the refrigerator. I didn't know what Arlene's father thought, but it was possible he took my unemployment in stride. He was usually out of work himself and didn't seem to mind. He visited the Lithographers Union every few weeks, but work had dried up in his field of dot etching. He seemed happy to occupy himself in other ways. He was visiting us one day and said he was going to the racetrack with his friend Singer and asked if I'd like to come along. Sure, I said. It was a welcome break from scratching for work, and I wanted to get to know Arlene's father better.

Simon was a quiet man. "Quiet" wouldn't really describe him; he was quiet when he *spoke,* which he seldom did. Once, when we asked him if he wanted a piece of cake for dessert, he didn't answer us. We thought he hadn't heard us, so we asked him again. He still stared straight ahead. So we got closer and asked him again. He looked up and said, "If I don't say no, that means yes."

Singer was even quieter, thin with sharp features. He looked like a razor blade standing sideways. He spent the day at the track without saying a word, even when he won. Simon liked to play the daily double, and occasionally he hit it, sometimes for as much as six hundred dollars. I would bet no more than two dollars a race, partly because I didn't like gambling. All around us we could see the results of gambling mania. Losing pari-mutuel tickets covered the concrete floor like dead leaves. Men whose shoes were literally down at the heels would scavenge among them, looking for uncashed winners. I went to the track with Simon and Singer a few more times, but then I had to get back to my regular way of being out of work. After a while, I heard from Simon that Singer was beginning to spend most of his days handicapping horses. He was showing signs that he thought he could beat the system. And in my way, I began to show some of the same signs. I didn't like gambling, but I liked systems. I liked looking for patterns. A system that had predictable results would not, I felt, be the same as gambling. You could lose at gambling.

I began going to the library, looking up old betting systems and trying them out against past performances of racehorses. Of the dozens of systems I studied, very rarely did one system remain successful for more than a string of twenty or so races before it began to grind its way down to chance. When you factored in the costs of going to the track in the first place, your chance of coming out ahead was zero. It reminded me of the gambler in the old joke, leaving his house in the morning and thinking, *God, I hope I break even today. I could sure use the money.*

I knew the odds were against me, but I couldn't resist the puzzle. As my eyes scanned the numbers, I saw patches of meaningful patterns and I was drawn on by each patch, looking for a longer string. I followed the numbers down an endless, winding labyrinth whose turns were marked by stretches of meaning that seductively promised order at the end of the maze. In one of the dozens of books I checked out at the Forty-second Street library, I came across a system that dated back several centuries, called the Martingale. It was one of the oldest betting systems known, and fortunes had been made with this scheme. Unfortunately, fortunes had also been lost with it. But that, I decided, was because it had always been used on even money bets, such as red or black at the roulette table. Actually, the odds are not truly even with red or black; the house makes sure of that because of the presence of the zero and double zero. And that's before they start fooling with the wheel.

But the system was simple. You make a bet, say, on red, and if you lose, you double the amount on the next bet. The idea is that since your odds are fifty-fifty, red will come up before too long; you'll win your money back and then some. I didn't realize it at the time, but later I learned, that at Monte Carlo a few people had gone thirty or forty times before seeing their color come up again. This may not sound like a long run, but the problem with doubling is that the bet gets huge very fast. If you start with only a $2 bet and keep losing, by the time you're up to the ninth bet, you have already lost $512 and have to put down another $512 to stay in the game. And your chances are still fifty-fifty that you'll lose. By the time you get to the twentieth bet, you have to fork over a million dollars, which is really an inconvenient amount of cash to carry around.

But I wouldn't have this problem because I wasn't betting on black or red. I had decided to play the favorites. If they came in often enough and paid, on average, better than black and red, the Martingale would work. The fact that it would be the first time in history that it worked didn't seem to bother me.

Since I didn't like gambling, though, I wasn't going to test the system at the track until I had it working perfectly on paper. I would take a bundle of racing results with me in a briefcase on the subway when I went to work. Once, I saw a young woman nudge her husband when she realized the papers I was studying were pages from the *Daily Racing Form. Let her nudge,* I thought. *She doesn't know I've solved the Martingale.*

I would study the columns of figures late into the night, sometimes waking up at five in the morning, having fallen asleep with my forehead on the papers, when the numbers began to dance and morph into liquid shapes.

Meanwhile, I heard from Simon that Singer had apparently become addicted to the racetrack. When he wasn't at the track, he sat at home at a little desk, facing the wall, going over issues of the *Racing Form.* He never spoke to his wife. He was immersed totally in the fantasy that he could beat the system. I shook my head in sympathy. *The poor guy,* I thought. *What a shame. His whole life disappearing into addiction.* Then I turned back to my charts.

One day I was on my way to a mutual fund appointment and heard at the last minute that the prospect had canceled. I called Arlene and told her I was near the public library and would stop in for a couple of hours for more research. She said, "Listen, why don't you get it over with? You've done enough research. Go to the track. If it works, it works. If it doesn't, forget about it." I hadn't realized how much of a strain my being submerged in numbers had been for her. She was right. I should put an end to it. I left the library, stopped at the bank, and got on the train for Aqueduct.

There had been a drizzle. The handicappers had probably spent the morning refiguring the races for the altered track conditions. But I wasn't a handicapper. I was relying purely on the probabilities of the numbers. There was no weighing of one immeasurable quality, like breeding, against another. I felt far more scientific than the handicappers.

The favorite in the first race went off at $2.10. I put $2 on him to win, which meant that if he came in first, I would get my $2 back and a profit of ten cents. But I couldn't start with more than a $2 bet because—with doubling—if I went all nine races without a winner, I'd be totally wiped out. In one of my pockets I was carrying all the money we had for that month's rent. That was okay, though, because in another pocket I had my hack license.

The first horse I bet on came in fourth. I watched the tote board between races to see which horse would go off as the favorite and went to the window and bet on the next race. And lost again.

By the seventh race, I had lost $128. My bet for the eighth race would have to be an equal amount, and if I lost that, I would have enough money to take a subway home and walk over to the taxicab company. The favorite in the eighth race went off at three to one. If he won, I'd actually make a profit.

There's something about a horse race that makes your heart beat, even if you have only a two-dollar bet on it. The entire universe is focused down to a horse's hooves, a jockey's goggles, the color of his cap. And I had a lot more than two dollars on this race. Everything we had was on it. The horses broke from the gate with the favorite trailing a couple of other horses. *Good,* I thought. *Let the others fight the wind.* Then he started pulling ahead. This didn't look good. He still had a long way to go. I had seen horses lead the pack only to fall back at the last pole. They rounded the first turn with my horse in the lead, and as they pulled toward the finish line another horse started gaining on him. He was testing the favorite. The muscles in their necks were bulging as they ran side by side. I heard myself screaming at my horse. And then he pulled away. He was out in front by a length, and it looked as though he was going to stay out. And he did. He sailed across the finish line, winning, as they say, handily.

At three to one, I won back my losses and went home with a profit of $128.

For the next month, I went to Aqueduct every day and came home with a day's winnings: twenty dollars, thirty dollars, sometimes forty. I'd come into the kitchen and lay the money on the counter, and Arlene would put it into the envelopes.

When I wasn't at the track, I'd be auditioning. Finally, one of those auditions led to an offer of a job out of town playing the leading part in a stock-company farce. I hated to abandon the system because we were raking in the dough. So I arranged with Simon to take our bankroll of $250 to the track while I was gone. I instructed him carefully in how to work the system, which by now, having lived off it for a month, I felt I could rely on if I followed the formula exactly. I went off to do the play, and Simon went off to the track.

The next day, Simon waited until the last minute to place the bet, as I had instructed him, to make sure he didn't bet on the wrong horse. It was important to be on the favorite, and sometimes at the last minute the odds can change and the favorite can become a different horse, which would throw the whole system off.

Unfortunately, I hadn't counted on a lot of other people trying to bet on the favorite at the same time, and Simon found himself in line behind ten people as last-minute bets were going down. Just as he got to the window, the bell rang and the window slammed shut. He never got to make the bet. The horse came in, but we weren't on it and we were out most of the bankroll. Simon won the daily double that day and won the bankroll back, so we were even, but I felt the chill of reality and decided to stick with a life in art.

I decided to throw out the pile of *Racing Form*s. But I couldn't make myself put them in the trash. I put them on the top shelf of a closet, where I planned never to look at them, but where I could find them again, just in case.

I wasn't addicted to gambling. I didn't like gambling. What I was obsessed with was patterns, systems. I wanted to cut out the gambling part of it, just as I had when I thought I had a sure way to get to heaven; just as William James thought faith was a bet he couldn't lose, I wanted to see a pattern in the data that would *keep* it from being gambling. It was a fascinating intellectual challenge. It surely was possible. The key was in there; order hidden among random events. I just had to find it.

I went back to working at jobs that kept us going, and from time to time I would get a real job, an acting job. And that made me know that eventually we'd be all right. We'd make a living doing this thing that gave me so much pleasure and that I knew I could be good at. Around this time, a story in an interview with Kirk Douglas caught my eye. His mother had told him, If you have to gamble, gamble on yourself. You can't lose if you work hard and gamble on yourself. *That's what I'll do,* I thought, and each job convinced me that that's the way we'd come out ahead.

But each time a job was over, I was restless. I needed something to do. I walked endlessly through New York, dropping in on agents' offices and casting directors. I would stand in line for hours to read for a nonpaying part in a hopelessly bad play. I worked on my writing. I thought up businesses I could start. But at night, when Arlene was asleep, I could hear the pile of papers in the closet calling to me. I would resist. But when I went too long without work, I reached up to the shelf and took them down for a look. I opened the yellowing pages and scanned the numbers. Past performances, times, mudders, horses pulling away by the first pole, or dropping down in class: There must be pattern in here. It can't all be random. I was looking for order. In a way, I was still looking for God, or His understudy—but in strange places. And before long, I was looking in even stranger places.

chapter 11

CONVERSATIONS
WITH THE DEAD

By the time I was twenty, I had had a lot of practice talking to dead people, if you count Jesus, Mary, and the saints, so I suppose it wasn't surprising when I began conversing with the more recently dead while experimenting with spiritualism. The difference was that I started to believe they could talk back.

It began when I went to work at the Cleveland Playhouse. In an effort to stimulate regional theater, the Ford Foundation had chosen dozens of young actors to spread around the country, and I was one of them. I had hopes that this was where I would learn Shakespeare, but they kept casting me in funny, but dopey, farces. One was a British comedy called *To Dorothy, a Son,* in which my stage wife gave birth to a baby while I dithered for two acts. The only thing that made the play memorable was that, as we approached opening night, Arlene was about to give birth to a real baby, our first. At the opening-night party, the director told her, "*Now* you can have the baby."

And about five hours later, Arlene nudged me in bed. "I'm having pains," she said. In the play, I would be running around and fainting at this news. In life, I was a little less excitable.

"You're just having cramps," I told her. "Go back to sleep." I rolled over and put my head under the pillow.

A couple of minutes later, she nudged me again. "These are *pains*," she said. "Take me to the hospital."

I did, and a couple of hours later our first daughter, Eve, was born.

No matter how I tried, I couldn't get a part in a Shakespeare play. When they did *Macbeth,* I begged to be in it. They offered me the Third Murderer, whose whole part consists of six lines, the most memorable of which is "Hark! I hear horses," but this didn't seem like a part that would give me a thorough background in handling classical language. So, as I had in college, I took things into my own hands. I had always been fascinated with the Book of Job in the Bible. I was taken by the theme of a man challenging God and the wry recognition that the guilty are not always punished in this life but often live out their lives in comfort, surrounded by their families, while the widows of their victims go hungry. On a bet with the Devil, God looks on Job, who has done no wrong, and afflicts him with boils and other disasters. He wants to show Satan how steadfast Job will be. But Job doesn't just accept his calamities. He calls out to God and challenges Him: How can God allow injustices like this? And God, a little pissed that someone would complain about the inconvenience of a few things like head-to-toe boils and the destruction of his earthly goods, answers Job out of a whirlwind, "Who are *you* to question me? I will question *you* and you will answer *me*. Where were *you* when I created heaven and earth? Where were you when I counted out the days of the behemoth?" These questions, both Job's to God and God's to Job, seemed to me to be central to our lives— or mine, anyway. How, for instance, could there be earthquakes and floods—tornadoes and plagues? How could a loving mother be so tormented by a diseased brain that she becomes afraid of her own child?

I loved it that *Job,* like the *Congressional Record,* was written in dialogue. After I made a few cuts, it actually felt like a theater piece, and when I showed it to the playhouse staff, they agreed to let me play Job. Unfortunately, opening night turned out to be the first time I nearly died while acting.

I was twenty-four years old, too young for the part, so I had decided that for the audience to believe I was Job, I would have to wear about a half pound of suppurating sores made of putty as well as a bald pate with wisps of crepe hair. I didn't really know how to keep the hair glued down, and on opening night, while I was complaining to God, a little piece of crepe hair floated off my face and wafted through the air, and when I took a deep breath to launch into another complaint, it flew into my mouth and down my windpipe. I started choking miserably. For the first minute of distress, I was sure the audience thought I was incredibly realistic. They were probably thinking, *This kid is going to die right in front of us.* I coughed and choked so long and so pathetically, they had to bring down the curtain. And this was opening night. The manager of the theater stepped over my body, parted the curtain, and went onstage. He said we would resume the play in a minute or two, but the actor has choked on a piece of crepe hair, and "as we all know, crepe hair is the work of the Devil." I was behind the curtain, dying, and he was getting laughs. I finished the play—not to especially rousing applause—and after the curtain came down, I could hear an elderly theatergoer in the front row say to his wife, "What did they put *that* on for?"

But something did get to me in that play that changed my course for a while, and it was the Devil. He was played by Mike McGuire, an actor I admired and who walked away with the evening. The Devil always has the best lines in any play, but with only two scenes, he played the part with relish and a demonic intensity that was captivating.

I watched him closely every night because I studied anyone who acted with passion and spontaneity. In fact, I studied them whether they were acting or not. After we had our first child in Cleveland, our daughter Eve became my acting teacher. For years I would sit and stare at her, hoping to understand the source of her innocent spontaneity, her sudden bursts of energy.

It's not surprising for a child to have that spontaneity, but how did Mike, playing the Devil, do it? As we talked about it, I realized that his interest in the Devil came from a strong belief in spiritualism. He told me about a man called Edgar Cayce and gave me a book on his life. At home that night, I turned the first page and entered the spirit world, where I would live for a few years in blissful self-deception.

Cayce had been active in the forties, when he supposedly had the ability, after going into a trance, to see where you'd left your sunglasses. Soon, people who had lost not only their sunglasses but their husbands and uncles were asking him to contact loved ones who were now in a very different postal zone.

I had a strange reaction reading about Cayce. My eyes would water and I would have to put down the book. There was no sadness or joy or any other emotion; I just found water coming out of my eyes. At the time, this made me wonder if I wasn't getting in touch with a higher realm. It didn't occur to me that, having spent my adolescence among the saints, I might still be nostalgic for their world; or that I was simply allergic to the paper in the book.

How could I fall into this faerie world? At fourteen, I had shaken my head and adamantly refused to let the monsignor think for me. At seventeen, I had earned a perfect score on my final in logic. But now I was reading book after book on spiritualism and extrasensory perception. At one point, I could cast a horoscope using a sidereal ephemeris, which is a kind of bus schedule of the planets. I was studiously exploring what I later came to think of as highly improbable stuff, but it headed me unexpectedly toward an interest in science. I didn't know it at the time, but I was actually working my way through the same stages of pseudoscience that humanity itself had gone through on its way to real science.

I started by exploring some of the strange things I was reading about. I hooked up an oscilloscope to a ficus plant and tried to communicate with it. In those days there were people who were sure they could talk to plants, but I never got the time of day out of mine. I tried automatic writing, where you let your hand write whatever it's inclined to put down. Some people thought if you did this you were communicating with the spirit world. *Who knows,* I thought, *maybe the spirits could predict the first race at Aqueduct.* If they could, they were keeping it to themselves.

Finally, I read a series of books about a character called Seth who was supposed to have lived two hundred years ago and could now channel himself through the body of a woman in a trance. Seth claimed to have done a lot of studying since his death and he had opinions about pretty much everything, including science. He said all matter was composed of only three basic building blocks. "Just ask any physicist," he said. We had a physicist living across the street and I asked him about it, but none of this sounded familiar to him. Since he worked with a particle accelerator every day, I thought he ought to know, and I had doubts about Seth's knowledge of science. I began reading every issue of *Scientific American.* If any of what Seth said was true, it would show up there. I was making a naïve but honest attempt to test the reality of what was in these books. In a way, it was the same way I had tested my mother's reality as a child. What I found was a whole new way of thinking. Here, in these pages, no one believed what anyone said unless it could be tested by others. An exciting world had opened up to me.

But it still hadn't answered the question that led me into this. I still longed for spontaneity. And I was trying some crazy maneuvers to achieve it.

I had a small part in Ossie Davis's play, *Purlie Victorious,* and I would stand in the wings, every night, watching Ossie deliver a ten-minute speech full of passion and anger that seemed to overtake him completely every time he did it.

I wanted to live in the moment the way he did; to have emotions well up in me and take me by surprise. I wanted to live in the now, but with all of my past ready to wash over me.

I had no idea how to do this. In order to be totally spontaneous during my opening scene in the play, I thought it would be a good idea to surprise myself with it. So instead of standing in the wings waiting to go on, I would stay in my dressing room until the very last second. When I heard over the loudspeaker that the previous scene was about to end, I'd race down the stairs to the stage and jump on the turntable that held our set just before it revolved and the lights came up on the scene, my heart beating, every molecule of me alive to the danger of being late. This would panic my scene partner, Beah Richards, who was too brilliant an actress to deserve this kind of amateur behavior. One night I made it onstage after the turntable had begun to revolve, just before the lights came up. I heard the sharpness in her whisper: "Where *were* you?" and I started hunting for some other way to be spontaneous.

I heard about an improvisational company called Compass at the Yachtsman that was going to play for the summer in Hyannisport. I had a scary audition in which I was given a name, a job, and an activity and was pushed out onstage to make a scene out of nothing. On sheer guts, I got through it and was hired.

After four weeks of rehearsal, the prospect of opening night was so frightening that one of the actors in the company tried to get out of the show by pretending to slip on a cement floor and pass out. His eyes fluttered up into his head, and we took him to the hospital with what we thought was a concussion but was actually a severe case of stage fright. The director told him we'd do the show without him, and he miraculously recovered.

John Kennedy was president that summer, and we did our show every evening in a cabaret in the basement of the hotel where he held his morning press conferences. Half of the show was made up of sketches based on improvisations we had done in rehearsal. The other half was a series of pure spot improvisations. No preparation; we just got out there and hoped for the best. One impromptu piece was a press conference in which one of the actors played Khrushchev and I played Kennedy. I read five newspapers every day to keep up with what the audience might ask me, but the reporters who covered Kennedy in the morning would come down to the cabaret that night and ask me the same questions they had asked him. None of this had been in the paper yet, and I often didn't know what they were talking about. If you weren't lucky, it could produce a state of perpetual existential nausea. I was mostly lucky. I was excited by improvising, and I was getting more spontaneous onstage. Onstage, but not off.

One Saturday night, we had a packed house and somebody high up in the government was trying to get a table. Arlene didn't like to hang around the theater, but she had come to see the show that night. After the performance, I heard that the producer of the show had panicked because the official from Washington would be turned away from a full house and had brusquely told Arlene to leave to make room for him. The producer was a decent person and I liked him, but I was furious at how Arlene had been treated. Outside the theater, I went over to him and grabbed him by the lapels. I actually saw the color blue. I saw the two of us as if I were standing off to the side, and we were both colored blue. Even the air was blue. I looked in his eyes and spoke in an unmistakably threatening voice. "If you evah, evah behave like that with my wife again, I sweah to God . . ." I heard myself saying these words and noticed there was something peculiar about the sound of them. I wasn't speaking in my own voice. I was speaking as if I were John Kennedy. I was so afraid of my rage, I had to become someone else to express it.

When I got back to New York, I was introduced to a kind of improvising that took most of the fear out of not knowing what you were doing. David Shepherd, who directed our company in Hyannisport, recommended me to Paul Sills. David and Paul had started the Compass Players in Chicago, and Compass evolved into Second City. I began working with Paul for months on a brand of improvising invented by his mother, Viola Spolin. It was an approach to improvising that changed theater in America and changed my life along with it.

Viola's theater games didn't rely on guts so much as playing by a set of rules. Concentrating on the rules kept you from concentrating on yourself, and as a result, things came out of you that were unexpectedly poignant and funny.

We were working on a scene one day when Paul Sills said, "Reach into the dark and get the answer." That stuck with me. If you had the courage not to know the answer beforehand, it would come to you. If you could trust yourself, *not knowing* was an exciting place to be.

But to trust yourself, you had to know yourself. It was hard for me to trust a stranger, and I was still a stranger to myself.

For me, reaching into the dark was a mysterious, magical process— as magical as talking to the dead, and it would still be a while before talking to living people was as easy as talking to dead ones had been.

chapter 12

YES TO
EVERYTHING

To be young, out of work, and an actor is to say yes to everything. Can you ride a horse? *Certainly.* Can you play the trumpet? *Oh, yes.* How tall are you? *How tall do you need?*

You take any acting job you can get—not just to be able to live, but also to learn how to act.

As our family grew, saying yes to everything wasn't easy, especially when Arlene was due to have our third baby. Our daughters seemed to be arriving like clockwork every year or so, and paying the doctor this time was beyond the capacity of the envelopes we kept our money in. I was offered a small part in a Broadway musical called *Anatol* that was trying out in Boston. It seemed to me from reading the script that the play would probably close out of town, but even if it did, those two weeks of work would pay the hospital bills. The hard part was that Arlene's due date fell within those two weeks. I hated owing money, and I thought I should go to Boston on the chance that she might deliver later than expected. Arlene didn't like owing money, either, but she also didn't like having a baby by herself. We agonized over it, and finally, she stayed behind while I went on the road. I tried to make the most of it. For an extra fifteen dollars a week I understudied Anatol, played by Jean-Pierre Aumont. He saw I was young and struggling and told me that actors who understudied him all became stars. Gregory Peck, he said, had understudied him. That sounded good, but I had taken on the extra responsibility of understudying knowing that I had no time to learn his songs or rehearse the dialogue. I was taking a chance that I would never have to go on for him, but I had nightmares in which I did have to go on. I would stand in the middle of the stage with the cast staring at me while I made up an entire musical comedy. Ultimately, I won that bet but lost the bet on the baby. Beatrice was born while I was in Boston, with Arlene's parents helping out. As I thought it might, the show closed out of town.

I was taking jobs that would make normal people wonder if they were perhaps not going anywhere. But actors don't think that way. We were getting by; in fact, we were happy. When money got low, I would stop drinking the single can of beer I had every night at dinner, and that would save us $1.05 a six-pack, enough to get us out of a rent crisis that month. One of us could always find a way to make a few dollars. We would take turns—one working while the other stayed home with our three daughters. In the winter, it would take an hour to diaper and bundle them up to get out of the apartment. We'd take them, two in a carriage, the third pulled by a rope on a tricycle, down the hill on 115th Street to Riverside Park, where we would spend a half hour before one of them needed a nap again, when we'd head back up the hill. Sisyphus lived just down the block.

I was in our two-room apartment, trying to see if the sun was shining by sticking my head out the window and looking up the air shaft, when the phone rang. Someone was calling from a small town in the Midwest to offer me an acting job. They had begun rehearsals for a production of *Guys and Dolls,* and their leading man had fallen sick and had to drop out. The theater, in Sullivan, Illinois, had to open the show in two and a half days. They had seen me listed in an actors' directory called *Players Guide* and wondered if I happened to know the part of Sky Masterson—since my father had played it on Broadway. I glanced over at the orange-and-black clown suit peeking out of a shopping bag in the corner of the room.

"Yes," I said, lying, "I do know the part."

"Wonderful," they said. "Can you fly right out here and do it?"

"Sure. Glad I can help out."

Somehow, standing there in our little apartment on 115th Street, talking to someone willing to hire me as an actor, I believed I *did* know the part. But I didn't. Seven years earlier, I had watched it from the wings, but I'd never learned it. And I didn't know the songs. Even if I did know the songs, I couldn't sing in tune. What was the matter with me? Was I insane? I was an actor.

I got on a plane, and as soon as the door closed, I started shaking. I shook all the way to Illinois.

I landed in Sullivan and headed for the theater, which seemed to be situated in a cornfield. The rehearsal was in progress, and I stepped in as Sky Masterson, stopping to ask for my line whenever I couldn't remember it, which meant stopping to ask whenever I *had* a line. After rehearsal, I went out with the other actors, who were mostly from there and knew the town. Apparently, this was a town in which nothing happened. Except for the summer theater, the closest thing to entertainment was driving in circles around the main square. We did that for a while, and then they decided that since I was from New York and used to more action, they would take me out to what they called Seven Hills. Fine. Whatever they wanted to do was all right with me. I just needed to get comfortable with my fellow actors.

Seven Hills was a stretch of two-lane road that had seven steep hills on it—probably the only hills for hundreds of miles. They seemed to be a natural wonder to the town's young men and a challenge to their manhood. The idea was to drive ninety miles an hour up and down these hills without crashing. The driver took off with what I would not describe as a complete discussion of what we were going to do. We went up. Down. Up. Down. At the top of each hill, the car left the ground and stayed for a moment suspended in the air. My heart was pounding. I knew I was going to die.

But this was not as bad as opening night, a day later.

I was trembling again, shaking the way I had at the Hollywood Canteen when I was nine. I came out onstage as Sky Masterson, and I got through the first scene even though one of my legs had an involuntary twitch that made my knee bang against the leg of my pants. In the second scene, I was supposed to be cocky and confident as I bantered with the ingénue, but my hands were shaking so much that I had to keep them in my pockets. Usually the first line of dialogue relaxed me, but I had a song coming up and I had to sing harmony. I was terrified, because usually, if I was lucky, harmony was what came out when I tried to sing the melody.

I was too poor to own my own suit, so they had given me a suit that had been hanging in a warehouse for six months. To calm myself, I started playing with a piece of lint in my pocket. It felt like a thick nub of lint, maybe a wad of thread. In an attempt to appear relaxed, I casually took it out of my pocket and glanced down at it. And then I saw it.

It wasn't lint. It wasn't a wad of thread. It was a cockroach.

The sight of the cockroach and the crackling sensation of its squirming between my fingers had a distinct effect on me. I was onstage in front of hundreds of people, in the middle of a play. I couldn't jump back and scream like a six-year-old girl, which was my first choice. Instead, I was focused like a laser. I looked at the actress I was playing with, and for the first time I really saw her. The cockroach had given me a reality more compelling than my fear. And the doorway to my imagination swung open. I wasn't in a little theater in a cornfield in front of an audience that might find out I didn't know the words or the melody. I was in the Save-A-Soul Mission, and I was talking to Sarah, the mission doll. I opened my mouth, and to my amazement, a song came out. And almost in tune.

ALPHONSE WANTS TO BE AN ACTOR

Alphonse Robert Alda's father and mother have spent years on the stage and now at two years he is beginning to think of acting as a career according to them. "Ali's" favorite pastime is to act little dramas with the right facial expressions. When his mother asked him what he would look like if a "funny man" was chasing him, he gave her the smile at the LEFT. "Ali's" face became a study in sorrow (RIGHT) when she suggested that the man had fallen down and hurt himself. The young actor has a whole bag of flirting tricks (CENTRE) with his eye if the need arises, his mother pointed out.

PIPE SMOKER AT TWO

For almost a year Alphonse Robert Alda of Toronto has been smoking a briar pipe, and he's only two years and three months old now. When he became curious about his father's pipe, both his parents thought they'd let him try it, hoping he'd become sick enough never to adopt the habit. But he's been smoking ever since. A New York doctor told his mother moderate smoking would not injure his health.

CHILD OF TWO SMOKES PIPE
ONCE BROKE MOTHER'S NOSE

Doctor Says Habit Will Do Less Harm Than Depriving Him of It—"Ali" Already Accomplished Actor, Like His Dad

Alphonse Robert Alda, at the age of two years and three months, finds solace from worldly cares in a briar pipe. He first smoked almost a year ago when he reached over, took his dad's pipe out of his mouth and began drawing at it. The mother and father both allowed him his first smoke hoping, they say, it might make him thoroughly sick and cure him for all time of the habit of smoking.

But little "Ali," as they call him, was made of sterner stuff. A few infantile "coos" and "ga-ga's" showed his satisfaction. Since then he has smoked.

Taken to Specialist

Fearing such a habit might be dangerous, Mrs. Alda took the child to a New York specialist. "He told us, provided moderation was shown, the smoking might not do Ali as much harm as the psychological aspect of denying him," she says.

"He likes to do everything his dad does and we take him everywhere with us. At a party he is less bother than most grown-ups and takes a great pride in being able to look after himself. He takes off his own clothes when he is told to get ready for bed. We don't believe in pampering children. All you have to do to stop him if he starts to cry, which is seldom, is to tell him not to be a baby.

"I sometimes can hardly believe how strong he is. Once when we were playing he accidentally struck my nose and broke it."

Ali Performs

Ali, who had been sitting quietly throughout the conversation, arose and started to sing to himself.

"He wants to be an actor like his daddy," she said. "Watch! Ali," she asked, "what would you do if a man were chasing you with a big stick?" The little fellow spread himself against the wall, his face and eyes depicting horror and fright.

"Suppose it were a funny man?" she said. His features changed to mirth, and laughter rang from his baby lips.

"And what if the man hurt himself?" The little head sank and the tiny face became pitifully sad.

"We have never taught him one trick. He has picked them all up from watching other people act," said Mrs. Alda.

My first appearance in a newspaper.

Learning to pretend, age two.

Early uniforms.
Upper left: On active duty with Aunt Betty in Wilmington.
Lower right: While I'm on patrol in the alley behind the burlesque theater
in Toronto, Mom and Dad stop by.

Mom, Dad, and Beetlepuss Lewis—doing a bit in a hotel room.
Every snapshot was a chance to think up a sketch. The fur coat seems to indicate
that we were out of burlesque by now and on the road in vaudeville.

There's a war on and
I'm back in uniform.
I was in the second grade,
going to military school.
One Saturday, we spent
a few hours on the boardwalk
by the ocean, taking publicity
shots. About a week later,
I came down with polio.

I remember hooking my feet under my dad's ankles when we took this picture. I adored him. This was after polio, and I was swimming eight hours a day then. The dog, a replacement for Rhapsody, was called Coffee because of his blond hair. I was told we got him from one of the Andrews Sisters. She was probably glad to have given him away. He kept biting people. We gave him away, too, and as far as I know, he was never stuffed.

In a publicity shot, my dad teaches me all about baseball. There's a certain lack of interest on my part. I may be finding out that there are no naked ladies in baseball.

I was about fifteen. My dad was in *Guys and Dolls,* and for some reason we were having our picture taken in a travel agency. My dad grabbed the palm tree off the counter and said, "Okay, we'll be dreaming about traveling to the tropics." Every shot was still a chance to write a story.

I was a sixteen-year-old apprentice in summer stock, acting in *White Cargo* with Rose LaRose, who was known mainly as a stripper in burlesque. She was playing a native seductress who, with her sexual shenanigans, drives a man so crazy he has to be carried off the island, a mental wreck. I come in to replace him, and she comes around the corner, topless, and says the immortal line: "I am Tondalayo." As she walks toward me, clearly intending to make me her next victim, the curtain comes down. But, even though the play would be over, Rose always continued walking toward me, giving me a big, lusty, naked hug, just to see me blush. The other actor in the play did fine. I was the one who went crazy.

Arlene, on tour in Germany just before we met, and *below,* clowning for my camera with my hat and coat, just after we had our first daughter. I wore this coat during my year in Europe and for the first six years of our marriage, until it was frayed and droopy. But I still wouldn't give it up. It was a Burberry, and I was sure that English people wore them until they fell apart completely. Arlene helped me get over this misconception by giving it away so I'd have to buy a new one.

Our daughters, Eve, Beatrice, and Elizabeth in Hyannisport.

Alfie the clown eats a pickle. My dressing up as Alfie and jumping around in front of gas stations kept us alive for a while so that we could eat more than pickles ourselves.

In my twenties, I finally got to act with Sam Levene in a musical about
the Yiddish theater called *Café Crown*. I was a dentist from Buffalo and he was a waiter
from Budapest. My father had just opened in *What Makes Sammy Run?* and we would be
playing on Broadway at the same time. The reviews for my father's show were mixed.
Sam was brilliant, but he was not what you would call a softie. When we rehearsed
this scene, he took almost an hour figuring out one little piece of business.
I got bored and fell asleep. When Sam saw me nodding, he yelled in that big voice of his,
"Alda, wake up! Your father's show is a flop!" As it turned out, though,
Sammy ran for 540 performances and we closed after three.

While the camera was turning, I always had the crazy idea that I couldn't get hurt because it was all make-believe. This was what I looked like moments before our nine-year-old daughter saw me slide down the hood of the car and crumple into a heap on the road. She managed to avoid running me over, and I was fine. But you'll have to read her book someday, if she writes one, to see how being an actor's daughter affected *her*.

Not as brave as it looks. They needed a shot of me skydiving for *Paper Lion,* and I figured I could fake it by jumping off a high diving board, which was scary enough. Arlene took this test shot and added the clouds in the darkroom.

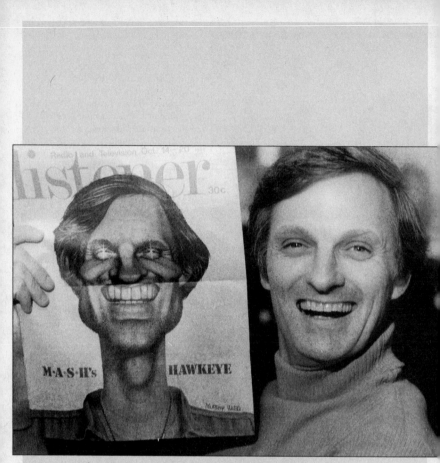

After *M·A·S·H* hit, it became clear that fame turned you into a kind of cartoon character that people could write about as if there weren't a real person behind the name. I didn't realize when I posed for Arlene's camera what a good image this picture would be of that state of dislocated identity.

There were hundreds of people from the press on our set as we shot the last scene
for M·A·S·H. Knowing it was the end, and knowing we were being watched
as we brought this part of our lives to a close, made it almost impossible to concentrate,
and we had to do many takes. Finally, we got the shot, the assistant director called a wrap,
and we were caught in the glare of the journalists' strobe flashes and the news cameras'
video lights. Naïvely, I had thought our last shot would be a quiet moment together.
Instead, we were saying goodbye in Macy's window.

Seventeen years after I had impersonated him in a cabaret, and long after he had left us, JFK and I appeared together in a tricked-up photo that was used as a prop for *The Seduction of Joe Tynan.* I played a senator, opposite Meryl Streep. It was my first script to be turned into a movie, and her first leading part in a film.

Back in New Jersey with our daughters, around the time *M*A*S*H* went on the air. From the time they were little, Arlene and I would often conduct family conferences around a picnic table like this. Everyone would get to challenge our decisions and argue her case. Then there would usually be an explanation from us that we were not a democracy. But listening, I think, made us enlightened despots.

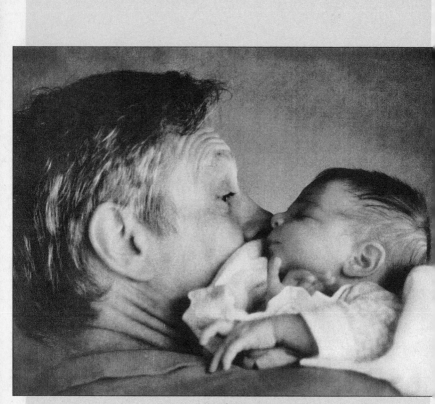

Day twelve of two new lives.

The curtain came down on a Broadway matinee of *Jake's Women*. We took our bows and then I stopped the applause. "Something happened this morning," I told the audience, "that I'm going to remember all my life. I thought I'd tell you what it is, so you can remember it all *your* life, too. My daughter just gave birth to our first grandchild, a little girl."

The audience applauded, good-naturedly. And then a woman in the first row, clearly a New Yorker, spoke up as if we were having a private conversation. "So . . . ? What else? What's her name? How much does she weigh?"

Her name was Emilia, the first of seven grandchildren. After Emilia, our daughters came up with Scott, Jake, Isabel, Olivia, Eleanor, and Matteo. I became obsessed with them, making toys out of cardboard boxes, teaching them magic tricks, making robots, figuring out how to drop an egg two stories without breaking it. (We suspended the egg on rubber bands in a box, and the egg lived.) Then I would stay up late, building websites to entertain them. They were a happy new obsession. And who could blame you for loving your grandchildren? I had found the perfect way to go nuts while staying under the radar.

Bea visits me on the set of *M*A*S*H*, dressing up in Radar's outfit.

Thirty years later, at about the same age, Bea's daughter Emi visits our house and we tap dance together in the garage.

Across the desk from Liev Schreiber in *Glengarry Glen Ross* on Broadway.
When we first moved into the theater, I thought I heard Liev going over his lines
in the dressing room upstairs from mine. But then he knocked on my door and came in.
"Can you hear that?" he said. The dialogue was coming from two stagehands arguing
in the alley. They were using Mamet's exact rhythms and the same four-letter words
for punctuation. It was an inspiring confirmation of Mamet's incredible ear. We
stayed by the window, soaking up the music of their speech, until the argument was over.
We were both nominated for a Tony, but Liev won and I didn't.
As you can see, though, I'm still young; I have plenty of time to win a Tony.

I went back to New York having learned something about concentration, but with not many opportunities to apply it.

Finally, after hundreds of auditions, I was cast as the comical young love interest in a Broadway play called *Fair Game for Lovers*. It was a good part, and in rehearsals, some of my improvised lines were thought to be funny and were kept in the play; so, on opening night I had the intoxicating pleasure again of hearing an audience laugh at something I had made up. Unfortunately, this became the *second* time I nearly died onstage. In the play, my fiancée was interested in an older man and in a moment alone onstage, I ranted impatiently about women while I smoked a cigarette. I had never quite gotten the hang of smoking. The smoke made me choke, and I often found it difficult to light a cigarette without burning the end of my nose. This night, I managed to get it lit and waved out the match, which I held at my side while I went on with my monologue. There were two important things I didn't realize: I was wearing a cheap acetate robe, and the match head was still glowing. Halfway through my comical rant, I heard a *whoosh,* like wind suddenly rushing through an open car window. I looked down and saw that the entire front of my robe was a sheet of flames. In a moment like this, a normal person might think, *How close am I to a seltzer bottle?* But not an actor. My first thought was, *Oh, God, this is going to get such a gigantic laugh.* The audience, of course, familiar with the image of people being trampled to death in a burning theater, was not laughing. There was dead silence while I furiously patted out the flames. I didn't even get a round of applause for my quick thinking. I did get a nice mention in the *New York Times* review the next day when Walter Kerr said that I was a young actor willing to do anything to get attention, including set myself on fire.

Slowly, one job led to another. Each tended to be like the previous one, or worse, but little by little, the parts got bigger; and after nine years, between small parts on television and increasingly larger ones on the stage, we were finally making a modest living from my acting and able to move to a small house in New Jersey. Our children could have a yard to play in, and instead of dragging them to a park, we could bundle them up and open the door to the yard.

The town was a mile square, the streets lined with trees that gave welcome shade in the summer. Summer was the month to enjoy the trees. In the spring, their roots pushed up the sidewalks in front of your house, and every fall they dropped three tons of leaves in your backyard. In the winter, their branches would ice up and fall on your car.

We loved it. Now we said yes to suburbia. School board meetings, town hall meetings, peace rallies, marches for fair housing; and, everywhere, I was rallying the troops. There was always a platform to get up on and make a speech that would have thrilled the nuns in Burbank.

"Mr. Mayor, you can't develop Highwood Hills. It's wilderness."

"No one *uses* Highwood Hills. No one's ever there."

"Mr. Mayor, if you're breathing, you're using it right now!"

Ah, the rhetoric, the withering reductio ad absurdum.

We came home from meetings, twenty or thirty of us, flushed with victory; we opened a gallon of cheap wine and put on a seventy-eight of Middle Eastern music. We joined hands and danced through the house, in an endless chain that snaked through the living room into the dining room, the breakfast room, the kitchen, and back to the living room.

When a foot of snow fell in winter, we walked arm in arm from house to house with a bottle of brandy in my pocket, our songs cutting the icy air. When it snowed on Easter, I ran with my friend Mike across the snow on bare feet and jumped into his backyard pool. The men were crazy and funny and they could cook, and the women could laugh and swear and raise the banner of human rights for all. Our friends loved one another, then they loved one another's neighbors, then they divorced one another. An epidemic of divorce hit the town. Just as a rash of participatory democracy had hit it a year earlier, now a plague of participatory sex was going around. Arlene and I were disturbed and saddened by the divorces, and by having to learn the trick of balancing friendships with a couple who used to be married but now felt betrayed if you stayed friends with their former partner.

On our little patch of land, I planted forsythia bushes beside the picket fence, and on New Year's Eve we stayed home and painted the living room, a bottle of champagne on the floor and Guy Lombardo on the screen. I filled my car with free scrap wood, bark left over from the milling machine in a lumberyard. I paneled the basement with it, and when you went down to the basement, you could smell the rotting wood and watch the little bugs crawling out of the walls. This was entertaining for a while, but Arlene finally asked me to take my interior decoration and decorate the dump with it.

One night I fell asleep with a book on how to do your own plumbing resting on my chest. Arlene was terrified that I might actually try to install a toilet by myself, especially because I had that manic look when I talked about how much fun it would be to learn pipe fitting. Gently, and with much talk about how clever I was, she slowly brought me to my senses.

I kept acting and trying to sell my writing, but my real life was happening in this small New Jersey town with crooked sidewalks and pompous mayors.

Our children learned about life from watching us and we learned about it from watching them. When Bea was born I'd wondered how we would manage with three children because you could only hold two on your lap at one time. But when Bea was old enough to hook a leg over yours, she was there in your lap with her two sisters. She could always find a spot for herself.

We had the children in our twenties and we were all growing up together. Once, I announced at the dinner table that I needed a new pair of pants, and that I thought I'd go out and buy them in a day or so. Our small daughters looked up at me with big eyes. *Why is he telling us this?* I was making enough money for us to live comfortably in our own small house, but in my mind I was still too poor to buy a pair of pants without talking it over with the family. Their look of innocent amazement let me know I was at a new stage in my life.

I had not wanted my children to be actors. I knew how hard the life was, especially so for women. I wanted to steer them away from the theater. But as they got older, just as my father had, I began bringing them into my world.

I decided to teach myself how to direct movies, and knowing I needed a deadline to get me started, I put up posters around town announcing that in one month, in the meeting hall of the church down the street, I would be presenting an evening of short films. *Then* I started shooting the films. One was a simple story about a nine-year-old girl who is bored and takes the keys to the family car and goes for a drive around the neighborhood. I wanted to create the illusion of danger purely with moviemaking techniques. And just as my father had brought me out onstage when I was nine, I invited our nine-year-old daughter, Eve, to act in the movie.

I wanted a shot of her appearing to drive, so I lay down on the hood of the car and shot through the windshield. She was behind the wheel and my friend Mike was beside her, out of camera range, helping steer the car. We weren't going very fast, but I had just had the car waxed so it would look good in the movie. I called out, "Slam on the brakes, Eve!" She did, and I slid like butter on a griddle down the length of the waxed hood. It was fortunate that she kept her foot on the brake, because I was lying in a heap next to the front tire.

When she was nine, our youngest daughter, Beatrice, wrote a play about Cinderella and I directed her third-grade class in it. I wanted to see what would happen if I rehearsed them using improvisation instead of asking them to learn words on a piece of paper. I never showed them the script, but with each improvisation, I brought them closer to using the words Bea had written. They never had a picture in their minds of words on a page. All they had was one another and impulses that came from inside them. When they got in front of an audience, their energy was enormous and you could hear every word at the back of the house. It made me realize how even professional actors are bound by conventional ways of working. The French call rehearsals *répétitions*, and too often that's *le mot juste*. It's better when rehearsals are a series of spontaneous little discoveries. It was becoming clear to me that life is better that way, too, instead of endless *répétitions*.

Saying yes to everything was a kind of caring without caring. I had nothing to lose, so I was free to try anything. Sometimes, until I got the hang of it, it made me more casual than I ought to have been. I got a call from Philip Rose, who had produced *Purlie Victorious*. He had a new play and wanted to have a reading for backers. Would I do the reading with Diana Sands? I said sure and gave it no more thought until the night we read it for thirty people. It was a two-character play, something any normal actor would study and analyze. I was twenty-seven, old enough to know better, yet I didn't understand that this was an audition for me as well as for the play. Diana and I had improvised together in Hyannisport, and it seemed to me we would find the play together, one way or another.

Somehow I got through the reading, at times not realizing what the scene was about until three pages after I was into it, then scrambling to make up for lost time. Phil, maybe sensing that my talent would outweigh my recklessness, hired me.

The play was *The Owl and the Pussycat*. It would show an interracial couple kissing for the first time in a romantic comedy on Broadway. Neither Diana nor I realized we were breaking ground. All we thought about as we began rehearsals was finding the heart of the play and making it work.

Elaine May, who of course is in the pantheon of improvisers, has told me she thinks improvising is a fascinating thing to do, but it doesn't teach you how to act. That may be true. I went into rehearsals for *The Owl and the Pussycat* with no idea how to break down the scenes or even how to figure out what the character was like. By chance, though, the director, Arthur Storch, had a way of working that was a perfect match for the only training I'd had in the theater aside from watching in the wings: improvisation. We had four weeks to rehearse, and for the first three of those weeks we never got on our feet. We sat at the table and read the play over and over. Then we put aside the scripts, got up from the table, and started acting out the play. If we couldn't remember what happened next, we just improvised. Where we moved on the stage was improvised, too, and almost all the staging on opening night was identical to where we had moved in those first impromptu rehearsals. Even a few stretches of dialogue that worked, but had not been written by the author, stayed in the play. Shortly before we opened, I finally figured out how to play the character, and between Diana's skill and my raw talent, we managed to run for a year.

I was entering a new phase of my professional life. I was starting to feel as though I were getting someplace. I noticed that more and more of what I improvised in rehearsal was winding up in the play, and that made me think I was a writer. As an actor, I was taking on responsibilities I had never had to face before. I had begun as an eccentric comedian. I had felt uncomfortable competing with my father, who was one of the most attractive leading men of his generation. So I had carved out an area for myself I could excel in without competing and surely losing to him. But as I got older, the parts that started coming to me were leading men, where I had to take on the responsibility of providing the drive of the play instead of standing on the sidelines, commenting wryly on the poor earnest guy who carried the story. It also meant I'd have to take the blame if the play failed. There was a lot of maturing that had to go on, and I didn't leap at it. I had to grow into it slowly. But things were changing.

I was saying yes to a little less than everything now. I had to make choices. At one point, I had to choose between playing the lead in a Neil Simon play and doing the second lead in a new musical directed by Mike Nichols. It wasn't easy to decide. The musical was *The Apple Tree,* constructed of three separate stories, the first of which was based on Mark Twain's *The Diary of Adam and Eve.* There was a speech at the end of the first act where Adam speaks at Eve's grave, and I was so moved by this speech that I wanted to be able to play that moment every night, even if it meant not being the main cheese. And that's the show I chose. It was beautiful material, but I didn't realize what a hard lesson this show would be for me.

The speech at Eve's grave was only two minutes of the first act. In the second act, I wore feathers and a breastplate in a parody of a barbarian warrior. The story was "The Lady or the Tiger," and I nearly went nuts trying to stride around the stage like a testosterone-drunk hero. I still hadn't made the transition to leading man, and suddenly I was supposed to be one of the Greek god statues I had studied as a boy beside my erotically inspirational tutor. I tried. I nearly cracked my knuckles striking my fist against the breastplate in a manly salute to the barbarian princess.

Barbara Harris played the princess, and in rehearsal I watched her carefully, especially in the third act. There was something uncanny about her ability to transform herself. On a bare wooden floor, without the help of a costume or makeup, she was singing and dancing as a chimney sweep, and I thought, *She's perfect for this part; she has these stubby fingers and pug nose and looks a little hefty. Just right for someone dreaming about being a movie star, with no chance to be one.* And then, moments later, with the help of the Devil, the chimney sweep is transformed into a beautiful, glamorous movie star. I was stunned by her transformation. With no help from makeup or costumes, her ankles had become thin, her fingers had become long and delicate, even her nose turned into a cute little movie-star nose. I wanted to be able to transform like that. I didn't know how she did it, and I don't know if she knew how she did it.

I hit the streets again. After many nights of walking up and down the hilly sidewalks of our little New Jersey town until one in the morning, talking myself into the idea that I was heroic, I was able to believe it enough to wear my feathers with pride. Then we went to Boston to try out the show, and for the *third* time I nearly died in front of an audience. I had just finished a song in act two and was heading upstage to choose one of two doors. Behind one was the Lady and behind the other was the Tiger, and certain death. Just as I turned, a huge lighting apparatus fell from the flies and, grazing the feathers of my cape, pounded against the floorboards, pinning the cape to the stage. It must have weighed a hundred pounds, and the noise was like that of a car crash. The audience gasped and so did Mike Nichols. I, of course, tugged at the feathered cape as though I were Marcel Marceau, and managed to get a laugh out of it. Mike jumped from his seat and ran backstage, where he found Jean Rosenthal, the lighting designer. Appalled and angry, he raised his voice to her. "How could that *happen*? We could have killed him!" Jean, looking very short next to Mike, but unintimidated by him, said calmly, "Mike, the theater is a dangerous place."

As exhilarating as it was to nearly have my head split open, the part of the play that got to me was in the third act where I played a parody of a rock-and-roll singer. I had a big entrance: Standing on a platform ten feet high, I was rolled onstage wearing tights, a leather jacket, and a giant wig with hair that stood out about a foot from my head.

A large silk cloth was draped over me, and once I was onstage a couple of dancers would whip off the cloth and I would be revealed to the audience with a dumb look on my face. This would get a laugh. Then I'd climb down from my perch and sing a parody of a folk-rock song. Sheldon Harnick kept honing the lyric, and by the sixth performance he had written six versions of it. When I was given the seventh version, Mike Nichols said, "Look, you don't have to put the song in tonight. Get used to it first." But no, I was an improviser; I could handle changes like this. I decided to go on with all seven versions dancing around in my head. Just before the show, I tried to run through the song and realized I couldn't tell if I was in version three, five, or seven. So I took a pen and wrote the lyric on the back of my hand.

The dancers wheeled me onstage and pulled off my shroud, and I started to sing. The fear of forgetting prodded my sweat glands. After the first few lines, I went completely blank. Not a single version of the song presented itself. At a moment like this, of course, the orchestra goes on playing. Something has to come out of your mouth. I looked down at my hand, only to see it glistening with sweat. The words of the song were running down my arm and dripping onto the floor. In a blind panic, I made up my own lyric and got through the song with words that had little to do with one another other than that they rhymed. I spent the next day learning the words.

That night I remembered the song, but I fell apart anyway. As I waited to go on and do that number, I felt a blackness come over me. The strain of being out of town with a musical was compounded by the realization that I was thirty and my life still wasn't where I'd thought it would be at this point. I had thought that by now I'd be playing Oedipus, and instead I was standing on a platform under a shroud, ready to be dragged onstage so I could look stupid in tights and a fright wig. As they rolled me out, under the cloth tears were streaming down my face. I was in despair. I managed to dry my face with a swipe of my hand just before they whipped off the silk. I looked stupidly at the audience, and they laughed. I did the song and finished the show. Then I took another long walk through the streets of Boston, thinking about where I was in my life. That moment under the silk shroud was a turning point for me. I realized that I was never going to have things the way I wanted them, no matter how vivid they seemed in my imagination. In a way, life itself was an improvisation in which I was going to have to deal with what came to me and not think about what should have come. I went back to the show the next night with more energy than I'd ever had.

But I still was pulled by forces I didn't feel good about. I left the show for a couple of months to do a movie in Mexico that was terrible, starting with the title—*The Extraordinary Seaman*—and got worse with each page. My agents told me I should do it because I would be playing the young lead in a picture with David Niven, Faye Dunaway, and Mickey Rooney. But the casting didn't improve the words on the paper. And filming it was a disaster from the first moment. We shot it outside a town called Coatzocoalcos, on a river that wound through a thick jungle. Members of the crew were carried out on stretchers with typhoid.

The river was so full of unfamiliar microbes that a nick on my shin turned into a major infection. John Frankenheimer, the director, set me and three other actors adrift in a rowboat in the Gulf of Mexico while he and the camera crew flew off in a helicopter to get a shot of us bouncing helplessly in the water. While they were gone, the waves grew to ten-feet-high surges. We knew there were sharks in these waters because every morning we'd see them prowling around the support boat. When we pointed to them, Frankenheimer said, "No, no, they're dolphins." Right. Dolphins.

As the little wooden boat careened with the waves, one of the actors, a Polynesian prince named Manu Tupou, told us confidently how to take care of a shark. "Just punch him in the nose and he'll go away," he said. "We do it all the time at home."

This was fine for a Polynesian prince to talk like that, but the rest of us had reservations, which we expressed in various ways. I started screaming, "Are you crazy? Are you crazy?" And every time the boat rose on a ten-foot wave, Mickey Rooney would say, "I'm out of here. Taxi!" The first few times you could tell he was kidding, but after a while it became clear that he was actually trying to hail a taxi in the Gulf of Mexico. The other actor in the boat, Jack Carter, just kept looking up at heaven with his arms out, saying, "Why me, God? Why me?" It sounded like a joke, because Carter couldn't say anything that wasn't funny, but it was actually a prayer before dying.

We finished the picture, and it was released directly into obscurity. I heard that it played on an airplane over Pittsburgh, and I imagined people strapping on parachutes and jumping to get away from it.

This was what happened anytime I did a movie I had no respect for. It was as though it had never happened. I was never able to make a cynical choice I could profit from.

I flew back from Mexico and finished the run of *The Apple Tree*. Closing nights always have a sense of finality. But not like this. I packed up my things in my dressing room, stuffing them into a brown paper bag, and said good-bye to the doorman. Arlene had seen our closing show, and we were the last ones to leave. We walked past stagehands striking the set and workers taking down signs outside the theater. We passed the front of the building, and Arlene suddenly pulled me out of the way as a bunch of letters with electric bulbs screwed into them came crashing down on the end of a rope. The letters hung in the air beside me, swaying on the rope, and in the gloom of the darkened Shubert Alley I could just make out what they spelled. A . . . L . . . A . . . I had nearly been hit on the head by my own name in lights.

But at least I knew what my next job was. As the run was coming to a close, I had been practicing throwing a football backstage with the stagehands because I was getting ready to do a movie about football, called *Paper Lion,* another part I was totally unqualified for. I was going to play George Plimpton, who had researched a book about the Detroit Lions by becoming a member of the team. My only experience with this game had been football practice in high school for two weeks. My mother, seeing I was going to be seriously killed by my teammates, put an end to it by telling the school that my orthodontist had forbidden me to play. I was embarrassed that I was avoiding getting tackled with a note from my dentist, but before long the embarrassment, along with the purple splotch on my hip, faded.

Now I was going to be on the field with actual Detroit Lions, who felt that hitting people was a calling from God. In one scene, eleven of them piled on top of me, and when I finally got up, I had been kicked in the ankle so many times, my left foot was asleep, and it stayed that way for half an hour. I learned to throw a football fifty yards, but every time I did it, I had to ice my elbow all through the night to be able to work again the next day.

Plimpton had also boxed once with Archie Moore, so I had to play a scene where I boxed with Sugar Ray Robinson. Sugar Ray was an extremely kind and gentle person. He spent the morning patiently showing me how to throw a punch and how to bob and weave to avoid his punches. Then we spent the afternoon filming a fake fight in the ring. I immediately forgot everything he had taught me that morning and stepped into his left hand. I felt the blunt pain as blood started pouring out of my nose. Sugar Ray was upset and blamed himself, but I had walked into the stone wall of his left all on my own.

I tried to throw myself into everything I did, but my aim wasn't always that good. There was too much I needed to learn. I was still on a knife edge between talent and skill, between a willingness to take chances and an ability to make the chance pay off. Sometimes the chances I took were bizarre.

I went to the Bahamas to shoot a movie with Blythe Danner and the Canadian actor Heath Lamberts. The director decided the script should be put aside and that the film should be totally improvised. A friend of mine, Chuck Rapoport, had written the script, and I knew what it felt like to have even a word of what you've written changed, but I was so in love with improvising that I went along with it and we completely mangled Chuck's script. This would become another movie shot from a cannon, straight into obscurity.

One night during the shoot, intoxicated with improvising and cheap cognac, Heath and I went to a nightclub where a few dozen sailors were sitting at tables, bored, drunk, and noisy in several different languages. We were in Freeport, where ships docked from all over the world. I looked at the sailors and the small, empty stage. I looked at Heath.

"Why don't we put on a show?" I said.

"A show? How can we do that? None of these guys speaks English."

"We'll do it in gibberish. They'll all think it's a language they don't know."

The logic of this, along with the buzz from the cognac, appealed to Heath. We got up onstage and introduced ourselves in complete gibberish. The sailors understood that a show was starting and gave us polite applause. We began improvising a sketch that made no sense whatever, in gibberish or any other language. There were scattered laughs, which encouraged us. I introduced the next act, which, through elaborate gestures, they understood would be a belly dancer. Heath came out wearing some silk scarves he had found backstage and began dancing. He was pretty good, and the veil over his face made him look like a kind of plump, virginal seductress.

The sailors, not realizing they were watching a guy, started getting rowdy—whooping and whistling. A couple of them reached over their tables, trying to grab at his veils.

The more he twirled and wiggled, the more excited they got. Then he took a bow, taking the veil off his face, and their excitement turned to fury. They felt we had insulted them because we had let them become aroused by a man. Several of them got up and started for the stage. Smiling and bowing, we backed off the stage with all deliberate speed. We left the club, as I remember, through a window in the men's room, just as if we were Hope and Crosby in *The Road to Freeport*.

I hadn't seen my mother in a couple of years, partly because we lived in New Jersey and she lived in Los Angeles and partly because I was avoiding her, hardly even talking to her on the phone. I couldn't handle the anger I felt at hearing her scrambled reality. I couldn't go near the dark place in which she lived. It was a black hole I was afraid I'd never escape.

On a trip to California to act in a movie called *The Moonshine War*, I stopped off to visit her. She was in a rented apartment in Glendale. She lived in darkness. Bedsheets covered the windows. Outside her apartment was a bright California afternoon, but I had to strain to see her in the shadows. Physically, she had changed. She still had wide red lips painted on her face, but her once blond hair was thin now and colored orange. She was obese, dressed in a muumuu that covered her like a tent. There were piles of junk everywhere. She lived like someone with her belongings in a shopping cart, their meaning and value known only to her. She smiled nervously when I came in but looked at me suspiciously and listened for the threat in everything I had to say. As we talked, I realized that even this hovel was more than she could handle. Although I had been sending her money, she hadn't known how to manage it, and now she was about to be evicted. I felt guilty and panicky. I had to rescue her from this, but in three days I had to be working in another city.

I left her apartment and found a real estate broker who handled houses in Burbank, where my grandmother had lived. Homes were less expensive there, and I thought she might find some comfort in a familiar town. I was shown a house that was clean and airy and, with no time for bargaining, agreed to the asking price, which was about half of what I'd be getting paid to do the movie. Then I went to a department store and in three hours bought a houseful of inexpensive furniture. I arranged for her to be moved and flew up to Stockton. A few days later, she called me.

"This is the most unhappy day of my life," she said. I was dumbfounded. Why? I had just moved her out of a dark hole. "Why didn't you sign the house over to me?" she asked, hurt and angry. Sign it over to her? She couldn't even manage to pay the rent on the hovel. How could she handle ownership of a house?

"You could take it away from me any time you want," she said. "How can you do this to me?"

She still thought I wanted to push her out of the plane. I tried to reason with her, but my anger and frustration were not a good match for her madness. I realized with a burn of embarrassment that my impulse to rescue her was one part actual rescue and one part a wish for gratitude. I had to settle, grudgingly, for simply doing the right thing.

After the shoot was done, I went back to our small town. My life was changing. It wasn't the same as when I was starting out and could say yes to everything. Now I had something to lose, and in spite of my resolve under the shroud in Boston, I was hesitant in my decisions. Nothing seemed good enough. I was turning things down because they weren't classy enough.

I stayed home more and more. I was playing tennis with friends, playing softball with my children, teaching our oldest daughter, Eve, how to count in base six using the new math. I was trying to write—sometimes sinking into narcissistic despair at the frigid whiteness of the blank page. But I wasn't acting. I had gone from saying yes to everything to saying yes to practically nothing. Instead of leaping into the unknown, I was inert. After a year and a half of turning things down, my caution had turned me into a stuffed dog.

I took another walk around our town. *You're an actor. You've got to act,* I thought. *It doesn't matter what it is. You've got to jump in. No matter what comes up next. Take it and make the best of it.*

Could I do this? Would I actually take the next thing that came along, no matter *what* it was?

A few weeks later, I was sent a script for a movie that was going to be shot in Utah State Prison, using real inmates as extras and actors in smaller parts. I thought it was a good script, and in any case, I was going to stick to the deal I had made with myself.

I got on a plane and headed for prison.

chapter 13

MY LIFE IN
PRISON

I landed in Salt Lake City in a big basin of salt surrounded by towering mountains. I wanted to learn as much as I could about prison life, so I had arrived in time to see a show put on by the inmates inside the prison walls.

I got to Utah State Prison after dark and went through two or three checkpoints before I could get into the auditorium. It was packed. *Who are all these people?* I wondered. Relatives? People from a Mormon town with no other entertainment? The show turned out to be an evening of dreadful morbidity. Someone sang, "If I had the wings of an angel, over these prison walls I would fly." Then there was a comedy sketch in which we saw shadows cast against a white sheet while an inmate pretended to take sausages out of another inmate's belly. Maybe this was prison humor, but I found it depressing, and I left at the intermission. When I got to my car, though, I found that the parking lot was locked until after the show, and so was the door back into the auditorium. For some reason, it was surprising to me that you couldn't come and go as you like. I sat in the car and listened to the radio while I thought about the job ahead of me. I'd be playing a college professor who, enraged because his wife and child have been run over by a reckless driver, slams the driver against his car, killing him accidentally. The young professor goes to jail, and we see prison through the eyes of an ordinary citizen. I looked through the car window at the hulking cement building, and I hoped we'd be able to show the place as it really was.

The next day, when we were in the prison rehearsing, I asked if I could spend the night in a cell so I could see what it was like to sleep in a prison. The warden looked at me in grim silence. Finally he said, "We'll think about it." By the end of the day, I got word that there was no way I'd be allowed to sleep in the prison. *Gee,* I thought, *what a shame. I'll miss the noises at night, the talk exchanged from cell to cell.*

I was thinking, in other words, like a lunatic.

The next day, we arrived early in the morning to begin the shoot. In the raw, early light, the prison was a clear statement of no escape and no compromises. Big and gray, it was surrounded by rings of fences dotted with gun turrets. It was planted on low-lying land with a magnificent view from the exercise yard of the snowcapped Wasatch Mountains. But the view was the only thing magnificent about this place. Mostly you felt a heaviness in your chest just looking at it. You do notice the door clank behind you when you walk in. You also notice the overbearing feeling of being inside a lot of concrete.

During the first day, curious at having outsiders among them, a long stream of inmates came over and talked with me. Remarkably, according to what they told me, nearly every inmate in the prison didn't do it. Several thousand people had been locked up unjustly and, by an incredible coincidence, all in the same prison.

On the other hand, they knew an awful lot about how to knife somebody.

We were shooting a scene in the exercise yard, where an inmate was to stab another prisoner. It was staged so that he would walk by the victim, stab him quickly, and walk on, disappearing into a crowd. After we did the first take, one of the inmates came over to Tom Gries, the director.

"Listen," he said, "anybody stabs a guy like that, he's a dead man. This looks stupid."

We stopped shooting, and Tom conferred with the inmate, who was suddenly our technical adviser.

"You want to kill somebody, you don't stab him once," he said. "You stab him repeatedly, until you're sure he's dead. You just stab him once and he lives, forget it, you're dead."

"Won't somebody see you do it?" Tom asked.

The inmate smiled and demonstrated how to do it. He pumped his hand quickly over and over into the man's stomach. It took just a second or two.

Tom decided to restage the scene. After watching the new staging, the inmate went over to him again. "That's a crappy-looking weapon you got there," he said. He took a homemade knife out of his pocket and handed it to the director. "Use this," he said.

"Where'd you get that?"

"I made it in the shop." It was a spoon that had been sharpened to a point.

We were all surprised that he was walking around with this thing in his pocket. The inmate chuckled. "Everybody's got a weapon in his cell. Maybe two or three."

These were the people who would have been my roommates had I slept over the night before.

One man who had been there for a couple of decades came over and taught me about prison etiquette. If you accidentally bump into someone in the hall, you look him in the eye and apologize immediately and sincerely. Otherwise the next time you're walking in the hall, you may get the edge of a dining hall tray smashed into your teeth.

After a day of this, I was exhausted. I started trying to look busy when they came up to me, but if they wanted to talk, they did. You couldn't stop them. A very tall, very muscular man in his thirties called

Nick came over. Nick had a small, shaved head and an enormous neck. He started giving me instructions on how to commit an armed robbery. He didn't bother with the usual claims of innocence; he got right down to business. "First of all," he said, "you gotta take a gun with you, and you gotta be willing to use it. Because, I mean, they're gonna use theirs."

I didn't challenge the logic of this because I was fixated on the size of his neck. It seemed to have a larger circumference than his head. *How did he get a neck like that?* I wondered.

Suddenly, I was aware he was saying something to me that I should be paying attention to.

". . . going to have to kill you."

"I'm sorry—what?"

"I said if I'm ever holding up, like, a drugstore and you're there at the counter, I'm going to have to kill you."

"Why would that be?"

"Because you'll tell on me. I've already been sent up twice. If I come back, they'll keep me here. I'm not coming back. So, I'm going to kill you."

I noticed the slight shift in his grammar from "I'm going to *have* to kill you" to "I'm going to kill you."

I realized the chances were slim that I'd ever be in the same store while he was holding it up; on the other hand, it seemed like something I ought to take care of while we were still in the discussion stage. "Why don't we just work this out?" I said. "We could figure this out right now. I won't tell them—how's that? Then you won't have to, you know, kill me."

"No, no," he said. "They can make you talk. I'm going to kill you."

He smiled. He seemed to enjoy telling someone he was going to kill him. It cheered him up immensely.

He faded back into the crowd, but he managed to reappear every couple of days, always just before I shot a scene, to remind me that he was going to kill me if I ever shopped in the wrong drugstore. You knew he was doing it purely for the sadistic pleasure it gave him, but it was the kind of thing that made you wonder how much you really needed aspirin in your life.

Even when Nick left me alone, I was finding out about prison life in ways I hadn't expected. We were going to shoot in an inmate's cell one day, and when we entered it I saw a woman sitting on his bed. I was confused. There were no women in this prison. She looked up at me languidly and a little defensively, as if to say, "What are *you* looking at?" And then I realized she was a man. She was dressed like a woman, with a woman's body language, and from the possessive look on the face of the guy next to her on the bed, she was clearly *his* woman, his punk. I knew there was sex in prison, but I hadn't realized how much. The inmates told us there was plenty for everyone, whether through mutual understanding, financial arrangements, intimidation, or rape.

The administration of the prison, I learned from the inmates, was really two-tiered. The warden and the guards were the top tier, the official tier. They could inflict a range of punishments, including the greatest threat: max. Maximum security is where you're placed alone in the innermost box of the prison's Chinese boxes in a totally dark cell for anywhere from days to weeks. This was where people sometimes went crazy, and because of this, when an inmate returned from max he was often given some leeway by the other prisoners.

The inmates—the next tier in the administration of the prison—had their own set of rules, their own enforcers, and their own leaders. Their punishments ranged anywhere from beatings to sudden death. There were competing hierarchies among the inmates. Blacks and whites, for instance, were separate groups. And there were subdivisions among these groups. Some kind of invisible quantum mechanics usually held these different kinds of energy apart and kept them from annihilating one another, but not always.

And then there were the nutcases. A short guy, called Tiny, with a manic personality came up to me while I was on my way to play a scene. They always got me while I was trying to remember my lines. I didn't want to stop and talk; I kept moving, but he was beside me, sometimes in front of me, walking backward to face me, talking so fast that the pitch of his voice got higher as he spoke.

"You know that stunt they have in this movie where the guy jumps off the fifth floor?" Tiny asked.

"Yeah, I do." There was a scene in which a young inmate has been brutally gang-raped and he commits suicide by jumping from the fifth tier of cells.

Tiny said, "I'm going to do that stunt."

"Well," I said, "I think they have a stunt man for that."

Tiny put a hand on my chest and stopped me. "If a stunt man does that stunt, he's going out of here feet first. *I'm* doing the stunt."

"Tiny, it's the fifth floor. You could get killed. You have to know how to do it."

"Hey, that's easy for me," Tiny said. "I was a second-story man. When the cops came, I used to jump out the window. This one time, I landed on my head on cement. Two floors, and I landed on my head—and that didn't bother me at all."

I wished him luck—sure that Tom, our director, would not be dumb enough to let him do the stunt. And then a week later, I found myself up on the fifth tier with Tiny, who'd been allowed to do the fall. He put one leg over the railing, and sweat started to bead on his head. He clung to a metal railing and stayed that way for a moment: one foot on the floor, the other suspended over a space five stories high. Piled on the deck below him were cardboard boxes that were intended to break his fall. From where we were standing, they didn't look as though they'd be much help. And they looked easy to miss.

"Tiny, you don't have to do it," I whispered to him. "Tell them you changed your mind."

"No, I'm doing it," he said. But he didn't move. Now he was drenched with sweat.

Then the catcalls started. Hundreds of other inmates were standing around the boxes waiting for the jump. His hands were welded solid to the railing. He couldn't let himself go. They called him pussy and punk. They whistled and made falsetto girlie sounds. Still, he was paralyzed with fear. Finally, Tom couldn't wait any longer. "Jump or get down," the crew told him. After another agonizing minute, he swung his leg over the railing and got back on safe ground, next to me. The stunt man took his place and jumped.

As he walked down the stairs, Tiny was jeered. His humiliation was complete. His status was downgraded to pussy, and he stood little chance of standing up to anyone who wanted access to anything he had, from his cigarettes to his body. I wondered why Tom had allowed Tiny to put himself in this position.

Tom, it turned out, had an odd sense of humor. A few days later, we were in the exercise yard, waiting for the sun to come out. A group of inmates was standing nearby, waiting for something interesting to happen. To pass the time, Tom said to them, "You know, if you want to get out of here, you ought to make Alda a hostage." The blood drained from my face. He saw this and turned back to the inmates, who were listening with what I would call genuine interest. "Really," he said. "Nobody will stop you if you have an actor with you."

I said nothing, knowing he couldn't be stupid enough to say it again. And a couple of days later, he said it again. "Seriously, guys, you ought to think about taking Alda hostage." I couldn't believe what I was hearing. By now, he thought he had a hilarious running gag with the inmates. I wondered how he could think that getting out of prison was a subject for comedy with these men. But whenever we had a group of them together, he said, "Don't forget—he's your return ticket."

I took him aside. "Tom, don't joke like this. These people are in here for a reason. They're dangerous people. And they have knives." He just smiled at me and went to set up the next shot.

Finally, we were shooting the last scene. Three weeks in Utah State Prison were coming to an end. In a few hours, I'd be on a plane home.

Tiny, the second-story man, was in the final shot with me, and so was Nick, the armed robber with the size ninety-two neck who had such a good time telling me he was going to kill me in a drugstore someday. We were about ten feet from the door that led to the outside world. We got the final shot, and the assistant director called a wrap. Nick and Tiny came over to me.

"Is that it? The movie's over?" Nick asked.

"Yeah," I said. "We're done."

"That's it?" Tiny asked. "No more shooting?"

"No, we're done," I said.

Each put a hand on one of my arms. These were strong guys, even Tiny. They held me in a viselike grip while Nick took out a box cutter with a razor in it and held it to my throat.

"We're taking you hostage," he said.

I didn't say anything. They walked me across the corridor, and we stood with my back to the wall.

"You think we're kidding, don't you," Tiny said.

"We're not kidding," Nick said. "We're getting out and you're coming with us."

Time did that thing where it slows to a crawl. Every moment seemed to take fifteen minutes. I had long, internal dialogues with myself during each tick of the clock.

"Teach us to care and not to care," T. S. Eliot said. As usual, I had remembered it a little differently. "Teach us to care without caring" was what stuck in my head, and it sounded like the perfect Zen solution to the need for both action and repose, trying hard while not trying at all. But I had never known how to achieve it.

As I stood against the wall with a razor to my throat, caring without caring came over me like a cool breeze. Calmly, I stood and waited.

"You think we're kidding, don't you," they said again. "We're not. We're getting out of here."

This may be a joke, I thought. *On the other hand, we're only a few feet from the exit. What if they find that the joke is working and decide to go ahead with it? What if they have someone waiting outside with a car?* You get to consider a lot of possibilities when time slows down.

One of the guards walked over to us. He spoke to Nick and Tiny in a reasoning tone.

"Come on, boys," he said. "You don't want to go to max for this, do you? This isn't worth it."

The guard was only eighteen inches from me, and I could see that he was trembling. His voice was shaking. If this was a joke, the guard didn't know about it.

I looked down and saw that the guard was wearing a gun. If they decided to go ahead with this, all they had to do was grab the gun, and then somebody would get hurt.

"Why don't you let him go, boys?"

"No, we're getting out of here. We're taking him with us."

I watched and listened for what seemed like hours but was probably only seconds.

Finally, Nick lowered the box cutter and showed me he'd retracted the blade. "It's a joke," he said. Clearly relieved, the guard took the box cutter from him, and Nick and Tiny moved off. As far as I know, they didn't get in trouble for this incident—not for having a weapon and not for holding it to someone's throat. At least not while the movie crew was there. Maybe everyone was glad there was no real crisis, and they were willing to let it pass. I walked over to Tom Gries. Speechless, I looked at him, waiting for an explanation. He just smiled. "I don't think the guard was in on it," he said.

A few minutes later, I walked through the door to the outside world, unaccompanied by Nick and Tiny. I left and they stayed.

While we were shooting in prison, I had read a script for another job, a television pilot. It was extraordinarily well written, but it sat on the night table in my hotel room for days. I didn't know what to do. If the pilot sold, I would be committing myself for years. I called Arlene and told her I had been offered a terrific script, but of course I couldn't do it because it had to be shot in California. Our family was settled in New Jersey, and we didn't want to uproot our children, who were entering their teens or just about to. It didn't seem possible to do the series. "This thing could run for a year or two," I told her.

The next day, she called me back and said, "Look, if you really think it's that good, why don't you do it? We can probably work something out. We could travel back and forth or something."

I knew she was right, but still I hesitated. The story dealt with some harsh realities of human behavior. What if the producers wanted to sanitize it and just go for laughs? I held off on my decision until I could get out of prison and talk to them face-to-face in Los Angeles. I wouldn't be able to get to Los Angeles until the night before the first rehearsal was to begin.

I got on a plane and headed for Beverly Hills, where I had to decide in the next few hours if I would do a television series about a bunch of doctors and nurses in Korea.

GETTING DOWN
FROM UP A TREE

At last, I make sense of life,
understand the universe,
and defeat death.

chapter 14

ME AND HECUBA

We sat in the coffee shop of the Beverly Hilton until two in the morning. Gene Reynolds, who was producing the show, and Larry Gelbart, who was writing it, were genial and patient, but they must have been at least a little anxious. Rehearsals were to start the next day, and they still didn't know who was going to be playing Hawkeye. I told them I was afraid the show might become nothing more than high jinks at the front, that under the pressure to entertain, it might make war look like a fun place to be. They said they didn't want that, either. They seemed sincere, but I had learned from an expert not to trust a stranger, even if he was your son. And for better or worse, I was reluctant to defer to their experience or the positions they held. I could have said, *Okay, they're in charge; let them do it their way*—but the boy in the church pew who shook his head no wouldn't let me. Finally, I could see they were as committed as I was to what I hoped for the show. We talked for a few more minutes, having the sincere but requisite conversation about how excited we were to be working together, and we went home, only to get up after a few hours' sleep and begin rehearsals for M*A*S*H.

Ten days later, I was standing in an aluminum shed in the mountains of Malibu, staring at the sandy floor, not sure what to do. I was waiting for my cue for the first shot of the show, and I was surprised to see how nervous I was. I didn't feel I knew the character; I felt naked and awkward. Imagination escaped me. I didn't know who I was. It was a simple shot, without dialogue. All I had to do was open the door and walk across the compound, but something important was missing. I felt a tingle of excitement that could pass for utter fear. Even after the days of rehearsal, as I waited for my cue, I was still wondering: *How am I supposed to be this guy who seems totally unlike me? He drinks, he chases women, he's a smart aleck. And what's he thinking, what does he want? God,* I thought, *I'm thirty-five. I've been acting for almost twenty years. How can I have reached this point in my life and still be uncertain about this?* Thoughts like this didn't help. I only became more inert.

I heard them call for quiet on the set.

I looked down at my boots for inspiration. Actors often say they don't really know the character until they put on the shoes. The wardrobe master had told me these boots, scuffed gray with wear, were once worn by a real soldier. I wiggled my toes against the leather, soft with use. These boots must have been full of stories. They did make me feel as though I were in the army—but they didn't make me feel I was Hawkeye.

Outside I heard, "Take one," and the snap of the clapper board.

Any second now the director would call, "Action!" I put my hand on the doorknob. . . .

M*A*S*H would be a turning point in my life. My life would change when I stepped through this door—more than I could imagine as I stood there. But first, I had to get out of this damn shed. *Look,* I thought, *how different am I from him? We're all human, right? We all have these same impulses. . . .*

"Action!"

No more time to think. *Jump in,* I told myself.

I opened the door and walked out across the compound. So far, I was still me. *If I get all the way across this patch of dirt without transforming into him,* I thought, *I'm sunk. Jump, for God's sake.*

Extras playing nurses and aides were crisscrossing the compound. Ahead of me, a nurse's path began to cross mine. Without thinking, I reached out and grabbed her around the waist and pulled her over to me. She smiled and patted me on the cheek. All of a sudden, I was Hawkeye. Even before the shot was over, I was walking with a lighter step. *Gee,* I thought, *that wasn't so hard.*

Clutching at a nurse was not a major artistic achievement, but it got me started on finding an answer to a question that had been nagging at me, even tormenting me, since I first began to act: How can I be so captured by my own imagination that I can truly connect both to the person I'm playing and to the person I'm playing with?

This is not a question that bothered me when I was living in Eden with the burlesque comics and straight men and talking women. They were performers, and as disciplined as they were, *performing* was a simpler thing than this mysterious transformation I hoped for now that would somehow bring me into contact with other people's lives. I didn't know it, but what I was really looking for was compassion. Not consciously, of course. I didn't consciously want to become compassionate. Who in his right mind would give up his place at the center of the universe? Compassion is scary. If you open up too much to people, they have power over you and make you *do* things for them. Better to keep them at a distance, keep them on the other side of the footlights. Learn to juggle—learn to fall down in funny ways. Keep them as an audience where *you* can be in control. Keep the curtain up, keep the play going. It holds off judgment. *See me up here? You love me, right? I'm the best, right?* But if I wanted really to act, I was going to have to find the doorway to compassion, and that would be an even harder one to walk through than the door of the shed.

First days are almost always difficult. Going onstage for the first time in a play was usually for me a cycle of fear followed by exhilaration at taming the beast, the audience. Once I was out there, the stage felt like home, but for years while I was waiting for the play to begin on an opening night, just the sound of the audience on the other side of the curtain could make my heart race. They had the sound of a mob. And that sound could return me to the anxiety of the chubby little boy clutching his bat with moist hands as he waited to go onstage at the Hollywood Canteen.

But something simple happened that first day of M*A*S*H that made it easy for us: It got very cold. December in the mountains of Malibu can be uncomfortable, especially if you're pretending it's summer in Korea and wearing a Hawaiian shirt. We were freezing. So we made a fire in a large, rusty oil drum, and between shots we all stood around it, hugging one another. We'd met only a few days before, but the cold let us drop our inhibitions and throw our arms around one another. Without even trying, by the end of the week there was an unusual level of comfort and trust. And we kept on huddling when we moved to the sound stage. We drew up a circle of chairs and never left them between shots. At first, it was so we could go over our lines. Then, after a while, it was just to be together.

We ribbed one another; we told stories and looked for ways to make one another laugh. This wasn't that hard, because like the characters we played, we had distinct personalities. Bill Christopher, who played Father Mulcahy, was studious, translating ancient Greek during his breaks. For one scene, he had to spend a long time at the bottom of a car in which about twelve nurses were piled on top of him. When he finally crawled out, someone asked him if he was all right, having spent two hours under all those women. "Yes, fine," he said. "Fortunately, I had my copy of the *Iliad* with me." When he joined the show, David Ogden Stiers could so disappear into the character of the aristocratic Winchester that audiences who have seen him since in movies probably don't recognize him. He also could disappear into such elaborate practical jokes that sometimes they became the basis for stories on the show.

Between shots, McLean Stevenson would go off on riffs that were so bizarre, there was no way you could keep your knees from buckling. When Harry Morgan joined the show, he kept us laughing in a way only he could. He'd say something that had no discernible humor in it but was delivered with such deadpan sincerity, you were helpless. He'd see you getting pissed about something, look at you gravely, and say, "Give us a little kiss," and you'd fall over.

Wayne Rogers's little quirk was that he didn't like to drive, and I'd give him a lift when we went out to location. My quirk was that on the way I would tell him my dreams and let him interpret them for me. No matter what he told me they meant, I believed him.

In one dream, I was acting in a scene on the show and the director had me say one of my lines while perched on top of an armoire. I told Wayne what a nightmare it was for me. "This is very important," Wayne said. "Directors are always asking us to do these unbelievable things to make it easier to shoot. Your dream is telling you to resist them. Don't give up reality. Don't do an armoire." From then on, we'd be rehearsing a scene and one of us would be asked to do something completely improbable for the convenience of the camera, and the other one would whisper, "Don't do an armoire."

When Wayne left the show, Mike Farrell took his place in the tent and as someone I confided in. We had a physical rivalry as well, competing to see who could learn to stand on his hands first. He had studied judo in the army, and as a pastime, every time I was called to the set, he would walk behind me and see if he could trip me and make me fall down.

The actors were resourceful, making the most of what was given them, and I admired them for it. Larry Gelbart had heard a story about Lenny Bruce that inspired a short scene involving a soldier who was trying to get out of the army by dressing as a woman. Jamie Farr was able to turn that sight gag into one of the most memorable characters on the show. Gary Burghoff, who had been in the original movie, had the ability to appear completely genuine and yet more innocent and naïve than he really was, which was something I had thought no actor could do. Loretta Swit and Larry Linville were able to play scenes of comic passion in so many ways that I wondered how they did it without repeating themselves. And Loretta never stopped looking for ways to make her character a three-dimensional person; by the end of the series, her character was known as Margaret instead of Hot Lips.

We made the most of everything because we knew that this was a chance we might never have again. We gave ourselves over to the work and to one another. We spent more time together than we did with our families, and we reached that point in closeness where you become aware of the other person's imperfections as they become aware of yours, and you either stick it out with them or walk the other way. We stuck it out. And, often, we stayed in the chairs long after we had finished the shooting day to listen to one another's heartfelt, sometimes bitter, gripes and looked for compromises. But mostly we made one another laugh. And it was the laughing, even more than the compromises, that led to trust. This was good, because trust is where the gold is. It's what lets you come out of the wings and go onstage.

I had learned a lot by watching, but now on M*A*S*H I had the most intense chance I'd ever had to learn by *doing*. In the hurried schedule of television, there was a blizzard of doing. A couple of dozen pages came at you every day, sometimes at the last minute. You had to learn them and find out what was under them, and sometimes it didn't all come together until you were under the lights and the camera was turning. We were strict about saying the lines as written, but there was still a little of the thrill of improvisation.

As if this weren't enough, I still wanted with all my heart to write and to direct. I followed the directors around, making notes on how they worked. When I was on an airplane, I spent my time writing. I was on airplanes a lot, because Arlene and I solved the problem of living in New Jersey while I worked in California by her flying out with our children to spend summers in Los Angeles and my flying home on weekends during the fall and winter when the children went back to school.

Anytime I had two days off, I'd fly home. There was one week when I flew home three times. I got a lot of writing in, but each day blended into the next in a perpetual buzz of jet lag.

Finally, stimulated by the brilliance of Larry Gelbart's writing, but a little awed by him as well, I got up the nerve to show him a few scenes I had written. He was always generous with new writers and encouraged me to come back when I had a story idea. The advantage for a young writer on a show like this is that you don't have to create everything from scratch. Rich characters and the world they inhabit already exist. I made it even easier on myself by borrowing the structure for my first story from *La Ronde*. In my version, the object that's passed from couple to couple is a pair of long johns during a cold spell in the Korean winter. It makes the rounds in a series of two-handed scenes of love, bartering, extortion, and losing at poker. As I was writing it, I began to have that feeling that writers get once in a while—a thrill that shoots through you and says, *This is going to work.* You don't think it's great or wonderful or brilliant, you just know it's going to work. I jumped out of my chair and started dancing around the room.

By the time we were done I had written nineteen episodes for *M*A*S*H* and had helped rewrite some others. I was so excited to be writing I started pitching ideas for series to the networks. I wrote two or three pilots and even had a show on the air about a family. It was called *We'll Get By*, although it didn't quite get by and lasted only thirteen episodes. Those thirteen shows took six months of writing—all while I was working full-time on *M*A*S*H*. I had never had so many opportunities come my way, and now I was saying yes to way too much. I would come into my dressing room between shots as Hawkeye, lie down on the floor, and try to think up lines for *We'll Get By* with Allan Katz and Don Reo, who were writing that series with me. Once, they had to wake me up because I had fallen asleep while I was talking. To stay awake, Katz and Reo and I would throw balled-up sheets of paper at one another or pitch lines while walking around the room on the backs of furniture without setting foot on the floor. Once during a Saturday session at my house, we got in the pool and tried a technique I don't believe is used in most collaborations. We'd all duck under the water, and the rule was you couldn't come up for air until you had thought up the next line of dialogue.

One night, after finishing a pilot for something that never made it on the air, I was so excited to have it over with, I went into the editing room with a bottle of champagne from which I kept taking celebratory swigs. A few hours later, I was in my fatigues, acting on the *M*A*S*H* set. By chance, it was a scene in which Hawkeye has a miserable hangover, which was lucky because that's exactly what the actor playing him had. At one point, I left the Swamp and walked over to the huge cyclorama painted with mountains and threw up on Korea. Reflecting on this barrage of writing and producing I was doing outside our own show, Larry turned to Gene and said, "We've created a monster."

But they were generous to the monster. They were letting me learn to direct, too. Gene Reynolds was an exceptionally good director, and I didn't want to let him down when I directed for the first time. His advice was simple: "Don't forget to count the shots on your shot list." That implied I'd better have a shot list, and it had better not go on forever. The first story I was given to direct ended in a camp picnic that needed eighty extras and three cameras to shoot. The final scene was a tug-of-war in which half of us got pulled into a mudhole. We'd be able to do it only once before the sun went down. And we just made it. As the scene ended, I dragged the last person out of the mud and we walked off to the tents while the sun dipped behind the mountain, giving us an automatic fade to black and an end to the episode.

That night, I was at the airport on my way back to New Jersey, and as I walked down the long sidewalk to my terminal, I remembered my day, shot by shot. For the first time, I had been able to tell a story on film. My step quickened and I began to skip, with long strides, like a kid. "I can do it!" I kept saying. "I can do it!"

None of these little voyages of discovery would have been possible for me or for any of us if we weren't floating on the frothy sea of Gelbart's writing. The words we spoke on *M*A*S*H,* especially when Larry wrote them, were like poetry of the funny bone. We'd all been trained in the theater, and we never changed a line without asking permission. If in rehearsal the scene failed to take off, Larry would come right over on his bicycle, take out his wrench, and reach into the speech to tighten a word here or knock a phrase sideways there, and pretty soon it was sailing again. One day, Wayne and I were out on location in the mountains and we were going over our lines together. Wayne stopped me in the middle of a speech. "Why do you suppose you say that?" he asked me.

I looked at the script. "I don't know," I said. "It doesn't make sense, does it."

The line made no sense at all. We couldn't call Larry and ask him what it meant because this was before cell phones and the studio hadn't wanted to spend money on putting in a phone line for us in the mountains. We decided that this bit of dialogue was simply an example of Gelbart's wit at such a high level that we didn't get it, and I said it the way it was written. The next day at the rushes, I was sitting next to Larry when the scene came on screen. He turned to me, appalled. He looked stricken, even hurt.

"Why did you say that?" he asked me.

"Why did I *say* it? It's what you wrote."

"That was a *typo!*"

"Ah," I said. "A typo. I thought it . . . you know . . . meant something." The next day, we reshot the scene. And not long after that, they put in a phone.

I hated it when they called us a sitcom. We were a comedy, sometimes a drama, but we always told a story with strong characters and often explored a theme that had something to do with people's lives. We began the show during the Vietnam War, and some people felt it was really about *that* war. I know Vietnam was certainly on Larry's mind when he wrote the pilot, but I thought of the show as about *all* war, and especially about Korea. We certainly tried to be as accurate as possible about the Korean War and the state of medicine at the time. Larry and

Gene and Burt Metcalfe, who took over producing the show when they left, all spent hundreds of hours interviewing doctors and nurses who had lived through the actual MASH experience in Korea. All of us who wrote for the show would sift through these transcripts looking for any scrap of a story or insight into their lives that would give our script authenticity. Sometimes whole stories could be written from a chance remark by a nurse. Sometimes an interview would give us one memorable line, like when the surgeon told how moving it had been to be operating in such cold conditions that steam would rise out of their patients' open bodies and sometimes the doctors would warm their hands over them.

There were more emotional demands made by the show than any sitcom would ask of you. One day, as we were finishing up an episode, I was handed a script for the following week. I read through it, and when I got to a scene toward the end, I put down the script and stared into space. The scene started with joking and laughter, and then suddenly, without warning, the character broke down crying. It was the thing I both dreaded and hungered after. How was I going to do this?

In the scene, I had to tell about a childhood boating accident in which a younger brother (called Harry or something) almost died. And that memory was supposed to trigger a cathartic breakdown. How? What was Harry to me or me to Harry? The night before we shot, I asked the director to stay late on the set with me while I looked for things that would get me worked up about this imaginary little brother. I thought about various dead dogs in my life; fantasy plane crashes in which friends and family die horrible deaths. Nothing. Hours passed.

Finally, at midnight, I pictured the physical layout of the imaginary accident in detail: the sound of the water against the boat, the dripping oars, the coiled mooring rope. When I saw cracked green paint on the inside of the boat, for some reason it triggered emotion in me, and it did it time after time. I had no idea why this happened, but I was relieved, and we quit for the night.

The next day, when I saw the cracked green paint in my imagination, I burst into tears. I was immensely satisfied with myself. *At last,* I thought—*Hecuba!* I had always thought that if I could do this, I would finally be an actor.

Not quite. Crying, and doing it copiously, may have been my holy grail, but it turns out that some things are even harder. Conveying a lot by doing little is much harder. We always do more than we need to. I've heard of a director who was so frustrated with an overactive actor, he threw up his hands and yelled, "Don't just *do* something—stand there!"

I *wasn't* at the end of my search for Hecuba. I was only just beginning. As the years went by on *M*∗*A*∗*S*∗*H,* I was surprised by how much more there was to learn.

Like concentration. The *M*∗*A*∗*S*∗*H* set was the place to learn it; it was a collection of anticoncentration hurdles. First there was the problem of time. Like a pilot going a thousand miles an hour, you had to learn to be precise but quick. Burt Metcalfe and I once wrote the entire second act of an episode during a long dinner in an Italian restaurant—and it turned out to be one we were proud of.

Then there was the sound stage itself. The show had not been expected to be a hit, and we'd been put in Stage Nine, one of the oldest and smallest sound stages on the lot. It was drafty and cold in the winter and sweltering in the summer. Exhausted from fourteen-hour days, we took naps on the cots in the tents between scenes—until we realized the cots had fleas.

Gary Burghoff had asked for a place where we could escape the hubbub of the sound stage and go over our lines together, so the carpenters knocked together a little shed for us. When Mike Farrell wasn't tripping me, we relaxed there between shots, playing chess. We shared the shed with stacks of bedpans and bloody dummies that were used on stretchers during triage. After a while, the place seemed a little depressing, so I had fresh flowers delivered every week. But apparently we shared the shed with more than dummies. Every night the mice would come in, eat the chrysanthemums, and pee on our chessboard.

Sometimes the lights were so hot in the tiny plywood set for the colonel's office that they ate up all the oxygen. After twelve hours in there, we had Silly Putty for brains. Giggling would break out like a contagious disease. Everything seemed funny, especially anyone's attempt to be serious. We staggered against the walls in uncontrollable fits of laughter. Directors hate giggling fits, and they sit there, solemnly immune to the hilarity, which of course is even funnier to those infected with it. I think we all felt, though, that this little bit of anarchy was helpful to the show in the long run. There's something about sharing the helplessness of a laughing jag that brings you closer together. From that first week in the mountains, standing in a group hug around the fiery oil drum, we knew the value of relating, of being focused on one another. And relating, really listening, was at the heart of what made us an ensemble.

At first, onstage and in life, I didn't really know what relating was. And *listening* was more a kind of waiting than anything else. *I* talk and then *you* talk. And then I listen for when *I* get to talk again. But relating, I came to understand, happens not just while I'm talking; it also happens while you're talking, and in between.

During rehearsals for *The Apple Tree,* Mike Nichols got frustrated as Barbara Harris and I played a scene, and he yelled out something from the darkened house I would never forget: "You kids think relating is the icing on the cake. It isn't. It's the cake." I never forgot it, but it was years before I understood what it meant.

When I started out as an actor, I thought, *Here's what I have to say; how shall I say it?* On M*A*S*H, I began to understand that what *I* do in the scene is not as important as what happens between me and the other person. And listening is what lets it happen. It's almost always the other person who causes you to say what you say next. You don't have to figure out how you'll say it. You have to listen so simply, so innocently, that the other person brings about a change in you that *makes* you say it and informs the way you say it.

The difference between listening and pretending to listen, I discovered, is enormous. One is fluid, the other is rigid. One is alive, the other is stuffed. Eventually, I found a radical way of thinking about listening. Real listening is a willingness to let the other person change you. When I'm willing to let them change me, something happens between us that's more interesting than a pair of dueling monologues. Like so much of what I learned in the theater, this turned out to be how life works, too.

Sitting in our circle of chairs, I became closer to these people than I ever had with other actors.

As time went on, our concentration took a strange shape. In the beginning, we were quiet and attentive before every shot. After three or four years, though, someone observing us would have thought we had no sense of discipline. We were telling stories and laughing while the crew was lighting the set. Then, called in to do the scene, we'd still be kidding, and loudly. Somewhere in our heads, we knew where we were in the process, but on the surface it wasn't always apparent. The assistant director would call for quiet and the noise level would go down a few decibels, but not many. The third assistant on the camera would hold the clapper board up to the lens and announce the scene number. You could sometimes still hear us talking. The director would call action, and *maybe* we were quiet. There was at least one scene where we didn't quiet down until just before the first line of dialogue. This sounds unforgivably chaotic, but it wasn't. For us, it was a way of working. The energy we had off camera carried straight through into the dialogue, without a break.

There were many things that made the show work: the writing; the skill of the actors and directors; the power of knowing that real people lived through these stories. But this feeling of being a group, sometimes an apparently disruptive group, and the connectedness, the energy, that came from it, was vital. It transformed us; it kept us fresh and glad to be there. I had never been as comfortable working with actors since the days I had acted with the person I knew best—my father.

After a few seasons on *M*A*S*H*, I heard that my father had been asked to do an episode with us. I could see the excitement in his face, and I felt the same excitement. We hadn't acted together for a long time. He was playing a surgeon with a drinking problem, and the script called for a confrontation about his drinking at the end of the show. Just before we shot the scene, I found him sitting alone in the Swamp going over his lines, and I asked if he wanted to run the scene with me. He said sure and we started trading lines, but halfway through, I stopped.

"What?" he said.

"Maybe if you did it like this . . . ," I said, and I gave him a different reading. This wasn't one of the shows I was directing. I was stepping in where I shouldn't have, but he let me.

"Okay," he said, smiling. "You're directing me, huh?"

"No, no," I said. "It's just an idea." But I *was* directing him. I was still doing it. I still wouldn't let up on him. I couldn't figure out why I had this rivalry with him. Maybe I wanted to play Oedipus for more reasons than I knew.

No matter what progress I made in my work, no matter how smart I thought I was, in many ways I was still an adolescent boy with a father I needed to best. When was I going to accept where I came from and who I was? He had been both my inspiration and the one I locked horns with. Acting with him could be like floating on air—but coming offstage could be a hard landing.

The summer after Arlene and I were married, I worked with him in a tour of summer-stock theaters. When we played a scene head-to-head, our eyes locked and we were each playing with someone we knew as well as you can know anyone. We tossed the ball back and forth freely and casually. We were playmates.

But then we'd walk offstage and we were father and son again. I was rebellious, and he was controlling. We'd get into our cars to travel to the next town, and he'd want me to follow behind him for the whole two-hundred-mile trip. Silently, I'd get in my car and slam the door. "I'm a married man," I would say to Arlene, "and he's afraid I can't find my way to Cleveland." I would throw the car in gear and follow him grudgingly—relishing the grudge.

When we worked together on *M*A*S*H* for the second time, I finally dealt with my feelings about this. I wrote a show for him in which his character, Borelli, is so controlling that it drives Hawkeye crazy. It gave us a chance to play out the tensions between us as other people. I wrote a scene for my brother, Tony, that let him lose his patience at the squabbling between the two surgeons we played; so there were three generations of us hashing it out. My father loved it. He even had an idea for the resolution of the story. "What do you think of this?" he said, his eyes glowing. "Hawkeye and Borelli are both hurt when the aid station is shelled. They have to do surgery, and one of them can only use his right hand and the other can only use his left. They each become the other's hand."

I didn't tell him, but the idea sounded corny to me, too much like the neat ending of a Tin Pan Alley song or a burlesque sketch. But for once I didn't hold myself above him; I decided not to be so precious about my elevated taste, and I wrote his ending into the script.

It wasn't until we were actually shooting the scene, sewing a stitch with one hand each—two men having to work together in spite of themselves—that I realized what my father had given us to play. Like the two characters, we were working hand in hand—and it had taken a few wounds to get us there. It was as though the scene were a wish on his part and a gentle nudge to us both, delivered through the medium of play. I felt his shoulder against mine; my father's arms entwined with mine. We tossed the scene back and forth between us, and over our masks our eyes locked and we were playmates again.

A few years later, he went into the hospital for a quadruple bypass. As I sat in a small waiting room, it was taking him a long time to come out of the anesthesia. I went into the ICU and spoke to him, hoping he could understand me. His surgeon was beside me, watching me talk to my father's sleeping body. "He's very deep," he said.

I didn't understand what this meant, and I went on talking reassuringly to my father. "You'll be fine, Dad."

The doctor said again, "He's very deep." Then I realized he was telling me my father was in a coma. I was angry at the euphemism. Why hadn't anyone said the word *coma*?

My father stayed comatose for days. When he woke up, he couldn't walk and he couldn't speak or read. He'd had a stroke on the operating table.

This was someone who loved language. The day I was born, he wrote a poem that was published in a New York newspaper. In it, he compared the death of King George V eight days earlier to the birth of his new son: one life passing, another taking its place. All his life, he was always at work writing something—a screenplay, a lyric, a novel.

And now he couldn't speak.

We got him into a rehabilitation center, but his brain was no longer wired the way it had been. Now he rolled wildly in bed, tearing at the sheets with his teeth like a trapped animal. He was unable to tolerate therapy for more than a few minutes at a time, and unless he could last for fifteen minutes, they said, they would have to release him. "He's plateaued," they told me. Plateaued. Where did they get these fucking euphemisms? I began to work with him, improvising bits of therapy. Because he was comfortable with me, he could last for fifteen minutes with my version of the therapy, so I worked with him every day, trying to get him to tolerate a slightly longer session. He was aphasic and it was hard for him to speak, so I tried to *trick* him into speaking. As we walked slowly down a corridor, I pointed out the window and said, "Dad, quick . . . what's that?"

"Tree!" he said.

"What's *that*?"

"House!"

If he thought about a word and *tried* to say it, he couldn't; he could say the word only if he didn't try. It was a kind of caring without caring. After a few weeks of this, he was able to tolerate therapy for a full half hour, and they let him stay in rehab.

After a few months, he could move slowly and talk haltingly. But he was another person. When I visited, he stood at attention in the doorway, like a little boy playing soldier. And once he asked me, one syllable at a time, if I could write a movie for the two of us to act in. I told him I was working on it.

About two years later, he went into a decline and never came out.

I wanted to speak at his funeral; I wanted to put into words who he had been—as a father and as an actor—but I didn't know if I could. Some of the best things about him couldn't be put in words: the performer's energy, the willingness to please, the frank gladness at contact with the audience. And how could I put into words the rude ambivalence I felt toward him, the way I had held myself above him for so long, in spite of his unconditional acceptance of me, the gentleness of his manner? None of that could be said in words.

I got up in the chapel, walked to the front of the room, and looked at the people who had come to remember him. I said a few simple things about his kindness, the sweetness of the man, and then I just dropped the words and I *did* him. I walked over to the side of the chapel and showed the people who had gathered to remember him how he used to make his entrance onto the vaudeville stage: the banana curve, the hand on his rib cage. And as I did this, my ambivalence evaporated. They smiled and chuckled in recognition, and he was there for a moment. For a moment, the performer and the actor came together in me, without conflict or judgment. I didn't just accept him, I *was* him. It brought him back. I could see him, smell him, love him; I could accept him as he was. And I could accept how much of him was in me. In my imagination, he was in the room with me. And for a moment so was Hecuba.

chapter 15

FAMOUS WOMEN
I HAVE KISSED

I notice I haven't mentioned many famous people in this book yet. Except for Beetlepuss Lewis and Bela Lugosi, there are few inside stories about the rich and famous. And damn little sex, too. A book of this kind is expected to have something hot in it, so I've tried to recall some of the famous women I have kissed. I'm sure there are more, but certainly that list would include Jacqueline Bisset, Carol Burnett, Ellen Burstyn, Blythe Danner, Jane Fonda,* Teri Garr, Veronica Hamel, Barbara Harris, Madeline Kahn, Shelley Long, Rita Moreno, Michelle Pfeiffer, Diana Sands, Meryl Streep, Loretta Swit, Marlo Thomas, and Cicely Tyson.

Jane Fonda gets an asterisk because at the last minute, even though the script called for a kiss, she would only shake hands. We were playing a good-bye scene in *California Suite* between two people who had recently divorced, so I understood her not wanting to kiss the guy. I did kiss all the others, on the lips and with fervor. I kissed Veronica Hamel while we were half-naked in a shower stall in an apartment in Toronto.

Arlene came home early, looked in at us, and said, "Alan, what time are we having dinner?" We were shooting a scene from a movie at the time, and there was a full crew crowded into the bathroom with us, but I think this shows Arlene's complete sangfroid about movie kisses.

They were all movie kisses, but a movie kiss, even though you're thinking about other things at the time—like *Which one of us talks first when this is over?*—is still a kiss. And Arlene always took this part of my work in stride.

What I can't completely understand is most other people's fascination with what the famous among us do with their lips and the rest of their bodies. Why do ordinary people become the target of this curiosity simply by virtue of the fact that other people recognize their names and faces but know almost nothing else about them? Why do we care what they think, what they wear, what they eat?

What I can't understand, in other words, is fame. It would have been good if I had understood it better when it happened to me, because I found it hard to adjust to.

After *M*A*S*H* was on the air for a few months, my life shifted. People started pulling me by the arm and pointing at me. "Hey, Ray, look at *this.*" I was "this." A beefy guy in a restaurant called me over to his table, and then, as he shook my hand, he involuntarily pulled me to him so hard that I fell across the table. I began to realize that some people are not in their right minds when they meet famous people. I wasn't when I met Liv Ullmann. I said hello and started thumping, heart first, like a rabbit. We were standing in the parking lot behind a Chinese restaurant, and a friend introduced us. The exhaust fan of the kitchen was blowing the combined smells of fried oil and chicken fat over us, but I sensed we were in a field of waving grain, awash with the aroma of new-mown hay, as I watched her face for signs of the characters she had played. Gradually, as we talked, I came to my senses. *She's an actor,* I thought. *Like you. She's a* person, *just like you.*

I came to see how it can happen to all of us. Each of us has someone we've seen on a screen in a darkened room—a screen we scan, possibly, with the same part of our brain we use for dreaming—and when that person magically steps out of our dreams and into reality, we can become disoriented. We're not much different from the four-year-old boy who came up to me in a restaurant and stared at me for a full minute and then said, "How did you get out of the TV?"

Even some adults seemed to think that because I was on their television screen, I truly had special powers. I began receiving letters from people on the verge of suicide, asking me for help—help they felt for some reason I was qualified to give them. I wanted to answer these letters before the people carried out their acts of despair, but after I struggled with what I should say in answer to the first letter I received, I realized I had taken a week. That was too long. At a certain point, even the right words might be useless. I couldn't take that long with every letter. Finally, I wrote a draft of a note that could be tailored to anyone who wrote me in desperation, and I checked it with a friend who was a psychoanalyst. In each letter, I included the number of the local suicide prevention clinic. I tried to make the letter seem personal and genuine, hoping they wouldn't choose a permanent solution to a temporary problem, but each time I sent out one of these letters, and there were a number of them, I felt strange. *This is what getting famous does to you,* I thought. *You wind up sending suicidal people form letters.* It was an attempt to reach them before it was too late, but I felt as though I were writing the kind of letter they were getting in the same batch of mail that said, "You may already have won a million dollars."

I was trying to be famous and ordinary at the same time, and it was difficult to accomplish. I had never really wanted to be famous. Everyone is supposed to want to be rich and famous, but as a boy I never knew what *rich* was, and the first view I had of *famous* made me leery. I was walking down Hollywood Boulevard late one night with my parents when I was eight years old and a young girl about sixteen came up behind us, punched my father in the back, and screamed, "You son of a bitch!" then ran off down the street. We were all shaken. My parents explained to me that some people don't know how to react to people they've seen on the screen and that I shouldn't let it make me afraid. Being afraid of a person like that, though, seemed like a good idea.

I had always wondered why people wanted to be rich *and* famous. If you could be rich and anonymous, that would be fun. To be famous and not rich, the way we were, was the least fun. It takes time and effort to be famous, and if they offer you fame without the money, don't take it. It's a scam.

Finding myself the object of sudden and intense attention was disorienting. I knew, of course, that signing on for a television show was going to involve getting better known, but I thought I could handle it. I simply didn't know what it involved. Now people were pulling at me, yanking at my clothing, grabbing me, putting their hands on me in places I had reserved for other occasions. Sometimes they were hostile, demanding I smile or cross the street to where *they* were standing.

The first time I saw someone in my bedroom in the middle of the night, glaring at me, I started screaming. The next time, screaming was difficult because I woke up only after he had gotten onto the bed and was choking me. He came every night, at about the same time, and each time I jumped up in bed, screaming. These night terrors began about the time the show first climbed in popularity, and they lasted for months.

Sometimes the threat wasn't imaginary. I got a call on the set one day from the FBI. Two agents were asking to meet with me. The next day at lunchtime, I sat with them in my dressing room. They were polite men in sport coats, assigned to the show business unit of the local FBI office. *The show business unit? There's a show business unit of the FBI?* I thought this was pretty amusing until they told me in a matter-of-fact way why they were there. Nothing to worry about, probably, but a young woman had escaped from a mental hospital in Florida and she was thought to be headed for California, where she was going to get revenge on Alan Alda and Clint Eastwood. It seems we had both abducted her in a car in Los Angeles a couple of years earlier and had driven her around town for a while before doing something unspeakable to her, and she was coming after me with a handgun. I thanked the agents, and we put a guard on the door at Stage Nine for a while. I don't know what Clint Eastwood did about it, but I noticed he ducked out of sight for a while by becoming mayor of Carmel or someplace.

I began to be self-conscious about going out in public. But I loved big, ordinary events like street fairs. There was a street fair on Ninth Avenue in Manhattan I really wanted to go to with Arlene and the girls. There were going to be stands selling Italian sausages and sfogliatelle. I couldn't stay away. I pasted crepe hair on my face and gave myself a beard. I put on a fedora and glasses and went to the fair. We stayed out for hours. Too many hours. Pushing it a little, we went to dinner at Mamma Leone's. Unhappily, I still didn't know how to glue fake hair to my face, and as I ate dinner, the hairs started separating from my skin and the beard got longer and longer. By the time dessert came, I looked like a Hasidic rabbi playing Howard Hughes. I went into the men's room and stared at myself in the mirror. There was this strange man in a fedora, with a straggly beard down to his *pupik*. This was not how I had expected to look at this point in my life.

A man came over to the sink and silently washed his hands. Then he dried them, without looking at me. Before he left, he came up behind me and spoke quietly: "Nice disguise."

When I got home, I threw out the crepe hair. If I was going to deal with the changes in my life, I would have to rearrange things *inside* my head.

chapter 16

THE DEVIL IS IN
THE BEDROOM

In a way, it was her madness that was killing my mother.

She never left her house, never saw a doctor. She wouldn't cook because she'd seen the devil in the kitchen, so she would send out for pizza and try to live on that. She wouldn't sleep in her bed because she also saw the devil in the bedroom, so she slept on the sagging couch in the living room. Finally, her body gave out and one of her organs started to fail. I met an ambulance at her house and rushed her to the hospital.

I was with her as two doctors came into the hospital room to examine her. She watched them come in, then turned to me and whispered something I couldn't understand. I asked her to repeat it.

"I can't let them touch me," she whispered a little louder.

"Why not?"

"They're devils."

There was a pause. "Are you sure?"

"Yes. I can tell. Take me home."

I was crestfallen. I had just rushed her to the hospital to save her life. I couldn't let her go home without being examined. Somehow I had to get past her paranoia without letting her think I was a devil, too.

"You know what?" I said. "I'm not going to disagree with you. I'm not going to deny your reality." I actually said it in this awkwardly formal way. "But I think I know what you can do about this."

"Really?" she said. "What?"

She looked up at me with the trusting face of a child. Unfortunately, I had no idea what I was going to say. How could I find the words to ask her to let a devil examine her?

I decided to just keep moving my mouth and see what came out. I reached into the dark.

"Well, I think this would work, if you're willing to try it. . . ."

"What?"

"Even though you know they're devils . . . if you act *as if* they're doctors, I think they'll be able to help you."

"Really?" she said.

"Yes," I said. "I really think so."

"Okay," she said, "I'll try it." And she let them treat her.

So that night my mother was given another couple of years to live by Konstantin Stanislavski.

But then too many parts of her body began to fail. And her dementia got worse. They put her on Haldol, one of the drugs our silence had helped her escape when she was younger, and now she did turn into the zombie she might have become then. She curled up, fetal and glassy-eyed, and drool came from her mouth. Her speech was slurred, and it was difficult to understand her. She called me in New York and asked in a faint voice when I was coming out again to California. "Not for three weeks," I said. She said something I didn't understand.

"I'm sorry, what?"

"I can't last that long," she said.

Sure you can, I told her. But she knew better, and a week later I got a call that she had died.

At the funeral, I stood by her casket and spoke about her, not as authentically as I'd have liked. I said she had led a troubled life and had suffered. I tried for compassion, but the conflicts in my feelings came through. As I finished speaking, I said, "So long, Mom," and patted the casket. I was only dimly aware at the time of how strangely theatrical this gesture was, indicating emotion without really feeling it. The casket, the least garish one I could find, was made of a crappy-looking burnished metal, and when I patted it there was a hollow, tinny sound, the same sound my words had. The words were meant to express feeling, but they didn't. They just expressed ambivalence. Our daughter Elizabeth, my pomposity detector, told me later how weirdly funny it was to see me tapping on her casket as if I were trying to see if anyone was home.

A week later, I went to her house alone to clean it out. I sat on the floor of her locked storage room and sorted through dozens of shoe boxes and paper bags filled with memorabilia and mail-order junk. I was sorting through my feelings as much as through her belongings. There was the sterling silverware, never used. The gold flatware, never used. Hummel statues and plastic Kewpie dolls. The remnants of a life that was almost lived. Then I opened a box and saw an envelope. Inside it was a key. There was one last inner sanctum to look in: the safe-deposit box, where she kept her most secret treasures.

In Burbank, I walked down blazing white sidewalks with no one else on them, the hot sun bouncing off everything around me, dizzying me.

As a boy in Paris, I had steeped myself in the existentialists. The first line of *The Stranger* by Camus was in my head now; it had always been my favorite first line: "Maman died today. Or yesterday maybe, I don't know."

I pushed my way through the heavy desert air of the San Fernando Valley. Camus was saying, ". . . today, with the sun bearing down, making the whole landscape shimmer with heat, it was inhuman and oppressive." I walked from my car to the building on the corner and pushed open the brass door beneath the giant gold leaf emblem of the

Bank of America. I showed a tall, thin woman my mother's key. The woman got a matching key and took me down to the vault. We unlocked the drawer, first with the bank's key, then with my mother's. And then she stepped out of the room so I could open the box in privacy.

I lifted the lid, wondering what my mother had hidden away all these years.

Now, in my memory, I'm in the vault again and I lift the lid, but this time I see what's in the box in a way I couldn't see it then. Then I could see only the artifacts of a damaged mind. Now I see that as damaged as she was, there were things she treasured. And the person who is still somewhere deep in my brain, the remains of the woman who was my mother, can move me now by what she chose to keep deep down in her own vault.

The box was nearly empty; there were just a few simple things that an eight-year-old might keep in her special drawer. A bracelet. A letter. And at the bottom, an old photograph: a picture of me when I was a boy.

In her childish handwriting, on the scalloped edge of the picture, it said: "My beloved Allie."

chapter 17

MR. SMITH GOES
ON AND ON

People were screaming at me. I was standing at the podium in the Illinois State Legislature, thanking the legislators for asking me to speak. They hadn't really asked me to speak. I was in the Capitol looking for support for the Equal Rights Amendment, and the president of the senate had asked if I wanted to say a few words. As I walked to the podium, our ERA political consultant had said, "Don't make a speech about the ERA." But that's what I was going around the country doing, and I had been brought here by her to get support for it. They had just passed a measure in Illinois that would help the Equal Rights Amendment enormously around the entire country, and I thanked them for their vote. I hadn't meant to make an actual speech, but I went on for a few rousing sentences, and the more I warmed to the subject, the more restless the legislators became. It didn't occur to me that since the measure had just squeaked through, almost half of the people in the room were opposed to it. They didn't just disagree with the ERA, they hated it. And it became clear that they hated me for mentioning it. Catcalls started, then booing and whistling. Then yelling and screaming. Like an idiot, I kept talking. The political consultant who had brought me there crawled on her hands and knees to a place behind the podium where she could pull on my pants leg. I looked down and saw her looking up at me with an urgent expression on her face. "Let's get out of here," she said.

I thanked them for their kind attention, a gesture that went unheard in the din of hoots. We had to walk through the chamber to get out, and people were coming up to me, denouncing me angrily. I wondered how the measure had managed to pass at all in this group of people. A short, thin man in his eighties squared off in front of me. He spoke rapidly, in a voice pitched with fury.

"I was in World War One," he said, a little bit of white showing at the corner of his mouth. "Do you know what war is like? Have you seen it? I have. I've seen what mustard gas can do to you. Blistered lungs, blindness, agonizing death. You want women going through that?"

I told him I didn't; I didn't want men going through it, either. I could understand his feelings. But I could also understand the feelings of the women who said they wanted full citizenship and the responsibilities that went with it. He walked away in disgust.

The consultant and I fought our way to the car and got in. She started the motor and we drove for a while in silence. "It was not a good idea to mention the ERA in there," she said.

"Right," I said. We were quiet for the rest of the trip.

This all began when the phone rang one night in the kitchen of our house in New Jersey and an old acquaintance asked me if I would help out with the campaign for the Equal Rights Amendment. "It was ratified in state after state," he said, "and now it's running into trouble." I said I'd do what I could to help. That began ten years of campaigning. When I wasn't in front of the camera or writing a script, I was writing a speech or traveling from town to town talking in meeting halls and churches and lobbying state legislators in their homes and in their hallways. I'd fly to Oklahoma or Florida or Louisiana and drive for a hundred miles, then get out and go into a town hall where hundreds of people were waiting. Once, I had to get from a city in the Southwest to a rally a thousand miles away. Someone arranged for a private flight. There was just barely room in the small plane for me and the woman who was piloting it. We strapped ourselves in, and as she started the engine she said, "Well, this will be your test as a feminist, won't it."

"Why is that?" I asked.

"I've only been flying for two weeks," she said, and then we took off into a thunderstorm, lightning flashing all around us. The takeoff alone made such a strong impression on me that I used it as the basis for a scene in the movie I wrote a couple of years later called *The Seduction of Joe Tynan*. And the impression I got of politicking during those years found its way into a good deal of *Joe Tynan*.

I met too many people in state legislatures who didn't seem especially inspired by the founding fathers, if they'd ever heard of them.

There was enough pointless horse trading and outright lying to depress even someone fresh out of Hollywood. One assemblyman said he would vote for the ERA if his town's high school band could march in the inaugural parade. The president of the senate in Florida promised me he would not only vote for ratification of the amendment, but do everything in his power to round up the votes for it to pass. A few weeks later, he was reading from the Bible on the floor of the senate and preaching that God was against the ERA.

A woman in Illinois told me about an encounter with a legislator who had refused time after time to vote for it, saying it just didn't matter to his constituents. After she had made every argument she was capable of, he finally said, "All right. I'll vote for it if you come up to my hotel room this afternoon and give me a hand job." And he wasn't joking. Something like voting for the Fourteenth Amendment in exchange for a couple of good slaves.

"Why are *you* working so hard for equality for women?" I was asked, a little suspiciously sometimes. In fact, I was asked this so many times, I began to realize I didn't know myself what the answer was. At first, I tried flip answers. "I come from a long line of women," I said. Or,

"Well, I'm from a mixed marriage. My father was a man, and my mother was a woman." But these jokes didn't explain it. Why was I spending so much energy on it, even willing to get some people mad at me?

Partly, it was that I knew it could be helpful if a man spoke out in public about these things, and I kept going out, trying to help. And there's no doubt that I loved getting up in front of audiences and making speeches. There certainly was that. I could hear the nun behind me chuckling again. But mostly, I think, it made me angry that we were refusing to guarantee half our citizens equality under the law.

Finally, though, with all the efforts of hundreds of thousands of people, the amendment lost. These few words never made it into the Constitution: *Equality of rights under the law shall not be denied or abridged by the United States or by any state on account of sex.*

I retreated from this brush with politics having learned a couple of things and having changed a little. One of the things I learned is what most people know going in: It's all appearances. If you think you might lose, you don't say so. If you think your best argument won't fly with this crowd, you don't make it. In the course of stumping around the country, I had learned how to talk like this, and I didn't like how I sounded. As the time limit on ratification was approaching, I was standing in front of a crowd, making one last effort to rouse them to action. Someone in the audience called out to me. "If it fails, will you keep working?" she asked. "Will you help reintroduce it? Will you keep fighting?" I said I would, even though I knew I had run out of steam. I sounded like the people I had written about in *Joe Tynan*.

I went home and thought about the time I was spending trying to be an amateur politician, and I wondered how much more I might contribute if I spent that time where I had a better chance of knowing what I was doing.

But it seemed to me that a kind of time limit was approaching for *M*A*S*H,* too. I thought we were running out of fresh ideas. Other people on the show thought so, too, and rather than lose respect for what we were doing, we talked about ending it.

Ending my fabulous political career was easy. Ending *M*A*S*H* was going to be a little harder. There's an old aphorism in vaudeville: Getting onstage is easy—just toss out your hat and follow it on—getting off is the hard part. Writing a good exit wouldn't be easy, and neither would *making* the exit.

It had been life-changing work for all of us, and the show was still at the height of its popularity, but we decided to let go of it before the audience did. And if we *had* waited until they'd lost interest, we'd have missed a closing night that was one of the most extraordinary any of us had ever known.

chapter 18

DIPPING A TOE IN NATURE

The night the series ended, all of us who had worked together on the show went to the studio and watched the last episode projected on a big screen. The last reel ended for us just as the rest of the country began to see the program on their television screens. We had been affected by the good-byes in the story and the good-byes that were implicit in our lives. There hadn't been much laughter during the screening. Quietly, we got into our cars and headed for Koutoubia, a Moroccan restaurant a few miles away, to celebrate.

On the way, I had an eerie feeling as I looked out the window. Something was strange, but I didn't get it right away. Then I turned to Loretta. "Lorette, look at the streets. They're empty."

At an hour when people were usually on their way out for the evening, the streets were completely quiet. We were quiet, too, for a minute as it sank in. Then someone said, "They're home, watching."

No one really knows how many people were watching that night. They counted the TV sets that were tuned in, as they always did, but many of those sets were watched by large gatherings. In at least one town, people crowded together at the city hall to watch. About half the people in the country—125 million of them—were seeing the same program at the same time.

The next day, we read in *The New York Times* that the city's water supply was strained at every commercial break because so many hundreds of thousands of toilets were flushed at the same time; it was an honor we'd never hoped for.

Someone from WQXR, the classical music station in New York, said a record number of people were calling in to ask for the name of the piece they'd heard on the show. I had used the Mozart clarinet quintet in the final story, partly because of its sentimental connection to Arlene. She had played it the night we met. The station manager said that more people heard it that night than all the people who had heard it since Mozart wrote it. Unfortunately for Mozart, the story called for it to be played on Chinese instruments, so they heard it in a way he never could have imagined.

Even though I had been instrumental in ending the show, I felt the finality of its ending more strongly than I had thought I would. We all felt emotional about leaving one another. Late one night, we had sneaked over to a patch of dirt next to the commissary and buried a medical chest with a red cross painted on it. The chest contained a memento from each of the actors, something connected to his or her character: dog tags, a rosary, a surgical clamp. It was a kind of time capsule, and we left a note in the box explaining to whoever found it years in the future who we were and how much meaning these souvenirs had for us. The sentimentality of this gesture was undercut somewhat by the financial activities of Twentieth Century–Fox. A couple of months later, they decided to saw the commissary in half and sell the land under one of the halves to a company that wanted to erect a high-rise office building. A construction worker dug up the box and called us, asking what he should do with it. We had thought the box wouldn't be found for a hundred years or so, and we thought when it *was* found, it would be regarded as some kind of treasure. "I found your box," he said. "You want it?"

"No," I said. "It's yours."

"Well, I mean, don't you want it? What should I do with it?"

"Keep it." *Keep the damn thing,* I thought but didn't say. Having your time capsule opened while you're still alive is not a good idea.

I had the time now to work on other projects. But I didn't expect the sadness I'd feel not having that familiar place to work every day and the familiar faces to share it with. I got such a case of sadness that I had to keep reminding myself that it had been my idea to end it in the first place.

One day, I opened a letter like many I'd received before, this one asking if I'd like to host a science program on television. This usually meant reading a narration. But my eye was caught by the title of the show: *Scientific American Frontiers.* I had been reading almost every issue of *Scientific American* for about thirty years. This was tempting.

"Do-it," Arlene said. "Just do it. You'll love it."

I was writing and directing movies, and I was supposed to leave myself free to work on them. But if I didn't do what interested me, whatever it was, I'd be keeping score according to someone else's rules. How long was I going to wait to keep score by my rules?

I talked on the phone with Graham Chedd, one of the producers of the show. I asked him if he thought I'd actually be able to interview the scientists and not just read a narration. The thought of spending whole days talking with scientists got me excited.

Graham and his partner, John Angier, decided to take a chance, and they pretty much shoved me out in front of the camera and let me ask questions. At first, I had a tendency to prepare for the interview by reading everything I could that the scientist had written. This served two purposes. It kept me from feeling ignorant, and it gave me a chance to look smart. Both of these were mistakes. One day, after interviewing Carl Sagan for a couple of hours, I felt immensely satisfied, having prepared myself so well that I could have an actual conversation about astrophysics with a real astronomer. John invited me to have a cup of coffee before I talked with the next scientist. It's no good to gloat about things like this, and I tried to prepare myself to take it in stride when he told me how great it had gone. Instead, he looked up from his coffee and said in a very direct way that I had been showing off. And he was surprised that I would do that. Why hadn't I just asked questions as if I didn't know the answers and let Sagan be the smart one?

My ears burned with anger at John. *Showing off?* What was he talking about? I was trying to be *prepared.*

I smarted for a day or so, and then it finally sank in. All the preparation I was doing was making me ask questions that I thought revealed a knowledge of the scientists' work, but it only got in their way. My questions were based on assumptions that often boxed them in. After that, I began to go into interviews with little or no preparation, which forced me to ask truly basic questions, questions I would have avoided before as dumb, but which let the scientists explain their experiments from the ground up. I could see a change in the scientists' faces as they answered my questions now that I was willing to look as dumb as I actually was.

What came out of this were shows in which you saw a real conversation between us. Most scientists are good teachers, and they often have a love of life and a good sense of humor, and all of that would come out in a true, relaxed exchange. The audience would be able to see in the scientist a vibrant person playing with ideas, instead of someone locked in lecture mode. And if we were lucky, a moment would come while we were on camera in which I finally understood a difficult concept, and the scientist's excitement, as well as mine, would be palpable. We hoped for moments like these, because the moment of revelation would be an event and not just an explanation. It would be real television.

All of this was good. The only hitch was that the producers of the show were trying to kill me.

It was better television if I took part in the scientists' experiments. And the most visual experiments took place in dangerous locations.

We did a story on the Leaning Tower of Pisa. As we walked into the tower, the custodian of the tower was telling me that it was still tipping over a little more every year, and unless one of their theories worked to stop it, it wouldn't just tip over, the pressure on the middle of the structure would make it explode. As he talked, we passed a sign that read, NO ONE PERMITTED BEYOND THIS POINT. As we started up the steps of the tower, I said, "Are people allowed up here?"

"Oh, no, not anymore," he said. "But in your case, we made an exception."

When we got to the top, we walked out on a ledge where a wind was whipping at us furiously. When I interviewed him, we had to chain ourselves to a wire that ran around the building to keep from being blown off. And in this case, given that I had been dumb enough to go up there, asking dumb questions was easy.

A week later, we did a story about Mount Vesuvius. Graham said, "We just have to climb to the top. Should only take a half hour or so."

I said, "Graham, I don't think we should climb to the top of Mount Vesuvius."

"Really?" he said. "Why not?" You could always tell there was trouble when his voice had this innocent tone.

I said, "The reason we should not climb to the top of Mount Vesuvius is that the story we're doing is about how the volcano is way overdue to erupt and it could blow at any second."

"No, no," he said, smiling. "The scientist up there has all this monitoring equipment. She knows exactly what's going on."

So I climbed to the top of Vesuvius and sat next to the scientist. As we talked, I kept looking past her down into the mouth of the volcano. There was a grassy patch of ground sitting on its cap, dotted with steaming jets of gases. Vesuvius is not considered an inactive volcano, and it didn't *look* inactive. She was telling me that if it blew, a million people in the area would have no way to escape in time because there was only one road out. We would have even less time. We were sitting three feet from the thing.

"But I hear you have all this monitoring equipment," I said. "How much do you learn from that?"

"Oh, not too much," she said. "We really don't know when it'll blow."

I became strangely incurious about volcanoes, and before long we were trotting down the mountain again.

A couple of years later, off the coast of Hawaii, we were doing a story about sharks. When a shark attacks a human, the people in the area often go out in boats hunting for the shark and kill the largest shark they can find. But out on the water, the scientist explained to me that by tracking sharks with radios, we've learned that sharks have routes they travel that cover hundreds or thousands of miles, and by the time people are out looking for revenge, a shark is most likely long gone. Large sharks prey on small sharks, and by killing whatever large sharks they find, people only increase the number of small sharks, which prey on fish; this ends up hurting the fishing industry and doing nothing about the shark that caused it all. A fascinating story, but to tell it on camera, someone had to help catch a large shark and then stick a transmitter in its belly. Graham seemed to think I was ideal for this.

I watched the scientists for a while and decided they knew what they were doing, so I agreed to get in the boat with them. Somehow, they got a shark on the end of a line and hauled him over to the boat. We were in a twelve-foot rowboat, and we had maybe an eight-foot shark. I helped them flip him on his back, and he immediately went to sleep and stopped thrashing around. This was good, because the skin of a shark has the same structure as his teeth. You can use it as sandpaper. If you brush against it in the wrong direction, you can lacerate your hand, which I did. Then someone handed me a kitchen knife and said, "Just make a slit in his belly and we'll put a transmitter in there."

I looked at the knife, and then at the shark, sleeping peacefully but lashed to a boat he could sink with one bite. "You don't think he'll mind?" I said.

I made the slit, slipped in the radio, and sewed him up. They turned him over and he swam away, with a fast boat behind him tracking his route. What was wrong with me? I'm not a brave person; I'm cautious. I don't even like bugs.

I had always been terrified of tarantulas. When I was ten I found one in the swimming pool, and in a frenzy of fear I smashed it repeatedly with the end of a stick until its hairs floated eerily to the surface. Before the series had run its course, I would let a tarantula the size of a small grapefruit walk across my hand. I could feel the pads on his feet and could sense the life of a fellow creature in him, something I could never do when I recoiled in fear from these animals.

For all the anxiety I had about doing the show—and I actually had some real anxiety—I loved the program because it gave me a look at nature I would never have had in any other way. What I hadn't expected, though, was the look it would give me into my own brain. In Marilyn Albert's lab in Boston, her assistants slid me into the claustrophobic tube of a functional magnetic resonance imaging machine. I was told to try to remember pictures flashed on a screen. In the other room, Marilyn watched a seahorse-shaped region of my brain, called the hippocampus, flashing on and off as I worked on storing the images. About a half hour later, they slid me back out and I went into the room where Marilyn was looking at images of my brain on her monitor. "How did I do?" I asked.

She turned in her chair and smiled. "You have a plump hippocampus!" she said. I had never received that compliment before, and I couldn't tell if it was what she told all the boys, but I grinned with pride anyway.

In older people, she told me, especially if they don't exercise their brains with puzzles and learning new things, the hippocampus gets less and less active. The hippocampus is crucial in laying down memory. Your ability to recall memories already stored can stay the same, while your ability to make new memories can diminish, and this is why there's a tendency to remember what happened to you when you were twelve but not what you had for breakfast. "It's really a case of use it or lose it," she said.

I hadn't lost it, and I was feeling pretty good about my plump hippocampus. Then I met Daniel Schacter.

Schacter, a professor of psychology at Harvard, and I were walking in a Boston park. As we moved down serpentine paths beside a lake, we chatted about the intricate web of paths in the brain that gives us memories. He mentioned casually that even a healthy memory is an unreliable aid for autobiography. And then, to show me what he meant, he actually made me remember some things I had never seen.

We sat on a bench and for ten minutes we watched a couple having a picnic. It wasn't a real picnic, but a scene he had staged for our science show. After a while I left, and without my knowing, he restaged the picnic and took photographs. The pictures were of some activities I had actually seen and some that I hadn't but that *could* take place at a picnic. Two days later, he showed me the photographs, and I could see immediately that the man and woman in the photos were doing some things they hadn't done while I was watching.

But a while later, he showed me the pictures a second time.

Again, I was certain I knew which pictures were of things I had seen and which had been staged for the camera after I'd gone. But as certain as I was, I was dead wrong about 15 percent of the time. He'd made me feel sure I had seen in person what I had seen only in photographs. I had the memory, but I couldn't remember the *source* of the memory. This was a shock.

I wondered how much of what I remembered of the Eden of my childhood was real. Was I actually remembering my past the way it happened? Was I remembering it at *all*?

I'd always been surprised at how far back my memories go and the detailed scenes I'd been able to call up. I felt I had the raw material for understanding my beginnings. But now I began to wonder.

There are images I'm certain I remember correctly: the stripper tossing her clothes at my feet in the wings; standing with my face in the chorus girls' silk garments; crouching in the safe and peeking through the slits in the wood; waking up on the seats of the train, the impression of the cane basket weave still on my cheek.

But I was also this certain of my memories of Daniel Schacter's picnic—memories that turned out to be false. Come to think of it, how could I have a memory of the basket weave on my cheek? I couldn't have seen my cheek at the time. I remember my mother rubbing my face, but I also think I see the pink impression on my skin. Somehow I'm seeing myself in this memory from a point outside myself, as if I were in a movie.

I wondered how much of my childhood really happened, and this shook me up a little.

I was learning things on *Scientific American Frontiers* that made me question my most dearly held assumptions, but the biggest shift in my thinking came from talking to Kári Stefánsson in Iceland.

I hadn't been in Reykjavík since the polar flight with my mother when she thought I wanted to throw her out of the plane. All I saw then was a shed in the snow where we refueled. When I went back with *Scientific American Frontiers,* I saw a modern country where researchers were extending the reach of science. Kári has a company that combs through the human genome looking for genes that are associated with certain diseases, and he uses a quirk of the Icelandic population to make his work go faster. The quirk is that among the world's populations, the Icelandic people have been isolated for so long that almost all of them can trace their genetic inheritance back to a few people who settled there a thousand years ago. As a result, when a gene is associated with a disease, it is much easier to identify. And one of the first genes Kári tracked down was neuregulin 1, which is implicated in schizophrenia.

He told me about this when I interviewed him, but I didn't really hear it. It was painful for me to think about my mother's illness, and I was still shielding myself then from knowing more about her disease. A few years later, I decided I needed to talk with him again. I was reading about his work on the Web, and I learned that neuregulin 1, the gene associated with schizophrenia that he'd identified, signals brain cells to receive several types of neurotransmitters, the chemicals that carry messages between nerve cells. He was suggesting that a defect in neuregulin 1 might lead to a growing number of badly formed synapses in the brain.

I wanted to understand this now. I wanted to know exactly what my mother had gone through. I got in touch with Kári, knowing that if he had the time, he could help me understand at least the biology of her illness.

But Kári is a sensitive man as well as a scientist, and he drew me into the emotional side of his research almost immediately.

"I think I may understand how you feel about your mother's illness," Kári said. "My oldest brother is a chronic schizophrenic, and he's been sick since he was seventeen." It was why the genetic link to schizophrenia was the first one he set out to find. Kári told me his brother was two years older than him.

"Did you look up to him?"

"He was my hero when I was a little kid. He was the best athlete in the family. He taught me to appreciate literature. He held my hand when I was learning to cross the street in front of our house. And I watched him disintegrate before my eyes."

Now, when Kári visits his brother in the hospital where he's confined, it depresses him. "Partly because he's ill and partly because I'm so close to him." As he talked, I could see why my mother had depressed me, why I had avoided talking with her, even thinking about her, for so long. I was too much like her. I was afraid I'd become her.

"You see in your own behavior a reflection of the disease of your loved one," Kári said. "The abnormality of schizophrenic behavior is simply an exaggeration of what is found in the 'normal.' Only it's persistent."

Not long after I talked with Kári, I picked up a copy of *Nature* and read something that brought me the rest of the way: "During REM sleep, there is . . . selective activation of the amygdala and other parts of the limbic system." The amygdala, the part of the brain that is so important in registering emotions and is crucial in laying down long-lasting memories, is also active in dreaming.

> This is relevant for our understanding of the heightened emotion—especially the feelings of anxiety, anger and elation—that so commonly dictate the development of the dream plot.... An abnormal sensitivity to dopamine is thought to mediate psychosis and its unmodulated action in REM may contribute to the madness of dreams.

The madness of dreams.

I remembered a dream I had had thirty years ago but is still vivid to me.

> I'm walking in Atlantic City. I turn a corner and out on the ocean I see two large cruise ships lying on their sides. I have a feeling of dread. I walk quickly, anxiously, until I find an entrance to a tunnel. Underground, I open a door and there are twelve people around a table. We eat and drink some wine. We're all strangers, but there's a feeling of fellowship, all of us having made it to safety. We introduce ourselves around the table. The last person to introduce himself is a man with a bald head. "Well," he says, "I'm known by many names." Instantly, I pitch forward, my head thudding the table in death.

I woke up after this dream with a pounding heart. I knew I was alive, but in the twilight between sleep and waking, the dream was still real. I saw him say it again, "I am known by many names," and he almost had me once more.

Now, not only did I know what it was *like* to be her, I realized that I actually go through a version of her madness every night when I dream—especially when my dreams stir me with fear and anxiety. She must have felt that same sense of helplessness, except that eventually I would wake up to a world that seemed right again, but she never would.

chapter 19

IN THE ZONE OF EROGENY

Raquel Welch, whom I've met but never kissed, once called the brain an erogenous zone. It is. But I've had to learn how to woo the thing.

Starting with a gray cloud of brain cells that was subject to storms and flash floods, I had to learn to make my own internal weather. I had to learn to act on my anger when I chose to and be suspicious only when I ought to. I'd wanted to write since I was eight, but I had to learn to organize my mind so that the pleasure of putting words next to one another and playing with sound and meaning could become a more structured, higher-level game. It meant so much to me to be accepted as a writer the night I won an Emmy for writing an episode of M*A*S*H that I actually did a cartwheel in the aisle on the way to the stage to receive it. But at first, simply getting the words to come out of my head was the achievement. It took three years to write the screenplay for *The Seduction of Joe Tynan* because I couldn't get a scene down on paper when it didn't want to come out. When it was ready, I'd give myself over to it, no matter where I was. So a lot of it was written on planes and in the backseats of taxis.

With the screenplay for *The Four Seasons,* I holed up in a room in our house and would come out only for dinner at the end of a long day. After six weeks, all I had was sixteen pages and a tortured look on my face. Arlene said, "Your eyes are spinning. It's like you're not here. Why don't you go off for a couple of weeks by yourself? Maybe you need a break. I know I do."

I borrowed a friend's house by a lake, and on the way there I stopped off and bought enough food to last about ten days. My plan was to turn off the phone and write day and night, stopping only to eat and sleep.

My brain had been stuck in revision hell, and the reason I had only sixteen pages was that I kept making changes every time I wrote a line. Norman Lear told me once about a way of working that had saved him from severe writer's block, and I was going to use it at the lake. I dictated the scenes into a tape recorder and disciplined myself never to go back to change or even listen to what I had said earlier. I was working from an outline, so it became a kind of controlled improvisation, but it poured out. If I got stuck while I was sitting in a chair looking out over the water, I moved to another room or walked in the woods. When I got stuck there, I took out the rowboat and sat in the middle of the lake, talking to myself as if I were the characters in the movie. At the end of the tenth day, the food ran out and I had finished the first draft of the screenplay. Later, reading the transcript of what I had dictated, I was surprised at how many useful things I had come up with, things that I couldn't even remember saying. I reworked the script many times before we shot it, but most of that draft from the lake house wound up in the picture.

As I got older, I noticed there was a lot more I needed to work on. I had always been a little anxious—uncomfortable in a crowded room, even reluctant to answer the telephone, since I might have to chat, which made my heart rate go up. It wasn't until I learned to ask questions on *Scientific American Frontiers* that I overcame stage fright at cocktail parties.

Actual stage fright hit me once when I was doing a play in London. I was playing the Stage Manager in *Our Town,* a part in which for most of the evening you talk directly to the audience. There are almost no cues from the other actors to prompt you, and the danger of forgetting your lines hangs over you all evening. As a young actor, I never gave a thought to learning lines. After two rehearsals, I could put down the script and play the scene without missing a word. But onstage in London one afternoon, as I spoke to the audience, I heard a voice in my head that spoke in a taunting tone. This was disturbing, because it was clearly my own voice. *What makes you think you'll remember the next line?* it said. I tried to ignore the voice and said my next line. *Well, sure, you got that line,* the voice said. *What makes you think you'll remember the* next *one?* I could feel rivulets of sweat running down my body. This attack lasted for about a minute, with the voice challenging me on every line. No one watching knew what was happening, but I understood, standing there in my drenched shirt, that I was now, officially, an anxious person.

I found, too, that I could easily move into a blue mood without much provocation. Early in my life, this was masked by an ebullience that spilled over onto everything I did, but after about forty years together, Arlene said to me, "You know what? You're not laughing anymore. Everything seems negative to you." Our friend Steve Cohen, a doctor, suggested gently to me during a walk down a country road that I might talk to his brother-in-law, Sandy, an expert in pharmacology. I hated the idea of taking pills, but I went to see him.

"What seems to be the problem?" Sandy asked.

"Well," I said, "my wife tells me I don't laugh anymore." I wondered if there was a pill for that. After a few questions that probed a little deeper, he said he thought I did have a problem and that he could try me out on Zoloft. I said sure, and it worked. He had warned me it might not kick in for a week or two. But he hadn't known how susceptible I was to suggestion. I had been the star subject in the hypnosis study in the Bronx. I was Mr. Placebo. After the very first pill I was laughing again, back in the erogenous zone. A good thing, too. In a couple of years I would be headed for the experience of my life, and it was one that needed a pretty good sense of humor.

chapter 20

DOWN IN CHILE

The best things come last. You spend hours with someone, and then as you say good-bye, one of you says something casually that puts your heart up where your head was. It happened when we said good-bye to *M**A*S**H,* and as the series of science shows was coming to an end, it happened again. I finally got in touch with the inner and outer reaches of the universe.

8:50 P.M. SATURDAY

The Andromeda Galaxy is in front of me, and to my right are some nice spiral galaxies and a couple of supernovas. I'm staring at photographs on the wall of a white room eight thousand feet in the sky.

I'm just outside of La Serena, Chile—in a giant observatory that glows in the night like a white knob on top of a mountain called Cerro Tololo. I'm here to interview astronomers about dark energy in the universe. I'm not aware yet that there is a bit of dark energy bubbling inside me.

I'm sitting on a blue leatherette bench in the waiting room while the crew lights the observatory's control room for the last shot of the day. I hear a gurgle in my stomach and feel one of those very slight cramps that signal you may or may not be in for a night of urgency. But it's only one gurgle. It could go away.

Maybe this is the afterglow of that hot pepper sauce I had at lunch yesterday at the observatory up on Las Campanas. Everybody warned me against it. When I got some of it on my fingers, my astronomer friend, Alan Dressler, took me into the men's room and washed my hands so I wouldn't get any of it in my eyes and blind myself.

Now my stomach is gurgling again. And this time the cramps are sharper. I'm pretty sure the discomfort will go away. On the other hand, my belly is getting larger. It's actually swelled to almost twice its normal size. I undo the top button of my pants and pull my sweater over the open zipper. I decide not to tell the crew I'm not feeling well. I must think it's a minor problem, because I love to tell people I'm in pain. I'm macho only when I can get credit for it.

9:00 P.M. SATURDAY

The observatory's control room is all computers and keyboards. The astronomers, Nick Suntzeff and Chris Smith, are taking me through the process of locking the telescope on to a patch of sky and taking two-minute exposures, hoping to catch that moment when a star begins exploding eight billion or so light-years away.

My stomach is very much distended now. It's pushing the top of my pants farther apart, but it's hidden under my sweater and the pain isn't that bad yet. I joke with them as they explain to me what they're doing. They tell me that tonight is the beginning of a new run of observations that will pinpoint the exact locations of supernovas so the Hubble and other telescopes can look at them with greater resolution. By examining a supernova's red shift, they can tell how fast its galaxy is moving away from all other galaxies. All of which will throw light on the ultimate fate of the universe. Contrary to what everyone thought until recently, the expansion of the universe is not slowing down. It's speeding up. What is the dark energy pushing it apart? Will it keep spinning away from itself, faster and faster, forever?

After about twenty minutes, we're done with the interview. Peter Hoving, the cameraman, closes in for a tight shot of my face. If you look at the tape of this shot, you can see my wan, slightly green face as the energy drains out of it. "I can't do this anymore," I say to the camera. "I'll be in the toilet."

9:30 P.M. SATURDAY

I'm facedown on the blue leatherette bench in the waiting room. Now I'm really sick. I'm ER sick. The pains are coming in waves. They form my own private universe, and the expansion of my universe is not slowing down, it's accelerating. The final fate of my insides is as much a mystery as the final fate of the cosmos in the other room.

In a case like this, you read the faces of the people looking at you as you writhe to figure out how bad it is. Graham Chedd looks concerned. In the past, I've kidded him about his casually putting me next to sharks and volcanoes and wild bears. Now, as he morphs in and out with the blue vinyl of the bench, he doesn't look casual. Reassuring me, he says, "We don't have to go back to La Serena tonight. We can stay here and go down in the morning when you feel better."

I lower myself back down, and the blue vinyl fills my field of vision. *Stay here? Here is what's killing me.* I want my natural habitat: a hotel lobby. Room service. Cable.

"I have to get off the mountain," I say, lifting up my head. "Maybe I have altitude sickness." We did a story once on altitude sickness, so of course that's what I think I have.

I get another wave and sink back into blue vinyl. Days later, on the Internet, I'll read a formal description of what's going on.

The Merck Manual, Sec. 3, Ch. 25

Mechanical Intestinal Obstruction: Complete arrest or serious impairment of the passage of intestinal contents caused by a mechanical blockage.... In strangulating obstruction, arterial and venous flow of a bowel segment are cut off.... Severe intestinal distention is self-perpetuating and progressive, intensifying the peristaltic and secretory derangements and increasing the risks of dehydration, ischemia, necrosis, perforation, peritonitis, and death.

None of the people around me has quite the turn of phrase possessed by the folks at Merck. But their huddled muttering produces a decision.

They call for the medic. Because of a history of mining accidents, Chile by law requires a medic and ambulance to be standing by in remote mountain locations like this. A few minutes later, the medic is palpating my belly and looking as uncertain as Graham.

Merck: ... if cramps become severe and steady, strangulation probably has occurred.

The cramps are severe and steady. And I'm feeling the strangulation. Someone has his hand inside my belly and is squeezing it like a pink Spalding.

Merck: The bowel becomes edematous and infarcted, leading to gangrene and perforation.... Strangulating obstruction can progress to gangrene in as little as 6 hours.

Thank you, Mr. Merck. You can shut up now.

10:00 P.M. SATURDAY

They take me a couple of hundred yards down the mountain road to the clinic. We stopped here when we arrived earlier in the day. I said hello to the medic and stuck my arm out the window of the car to shake his hand. Now he's trying to stick a needle into the artery of that arm, but he's having trouble jamming it in. He wants to check my blood oxygen.

I have the sudden, grateful urge to throw up. Grateful, because I cling to the hope that if only I can get the badness out of my system, I'll be all right. I make a vomitory announcement and lean over the side of the gurney.

Merck: Vomiting starts early with small-bowel obstruction.

It certainly does. But of course there's no relief. It's getting worse. It hadn't occurred to me it could get *worse.*

The medic and I both think it might be appendicitis. He calls down to La Serena, maybe the fourth largest city in Chile, and tells them to have a doctor standing by who can do an appendectomy.

11:00 P.M. SATURDAY

I'm packed into the ambulance for the trip down the mountain. But we sit there.

They can't get the ambulance started.

The motor turns over, again and again, without success. Someone gets out and tinkers under the hood. Finally, the motor rumbles and we start the hour-and-a-half descent down bumpy mountain roads. With every peristaltic thrust, I moan. About halfway down, Nick Suntzeff, the astronomer, reassures me that we're getting onto a stretch of smooth road now, but it makes no difference. The pain gets worse, and I can tell by Nick's involuntary wince that my moans are getting louder.

1:00 A.M. SUNDAY

Ceilings are skimming by overhead as they wheel me down corridors of a clinic. We're in La Serena. I go in and out of consciousness, but I never take a break from the screaming. The show must go on.

Later, I pieced together much of the rest of this night and the days that followed.

We were met by Dr. Nelson Zepeda. Not only could he do an appendectomy, he's a fully qualified colorectal surgeon. As we met, I was all moans, but he couldn't give me morphine until he knew what was wrong with me.

Quickly, he arranged for X rays and ultrasound. He had a CAT scan machine, but no one could find a radiologist. It didn't matter. He knew what was wrong. I didn't have appendicitis, and it wasn't the hot peppers at lunch; I had intestinal blockage. Some of my bowel was poking through a band or loop that had grown on the side of my omentum. The omentum is an apron of tough material that lies over the gut, protecting it and defending it against injury. In this case, like a corrupt police force, it wasn't trying to protect and defend; it was causing the harm. The small intestine had poked through the loop on the omentum, and its blood supply was choked off. Peristalsis kept pushing it through. With each passing minute, more and more of me was dead and dying. He had to operate as soon as possible.

But this clinic wasn't as well equipped as the public hospital across town. So we headed for that hospital.

Back down the hallways, ceilings going by overhead. Bumping across the sidewalk, listing precariously as I was lifted into the ambulance. The ride. Out of the ambulance, listing as they lift. Another bumpy sidewalk. (*Another* bumpy sidewalk?) More ceilings flashing by overhead, but this time the ceilings and walls were older, dimmer, dirtier. In spite of the dinginess, though, this was where the equipment was better. At one point here, I finally got some morphine.

1:30 A.M. SUNDAY

The pressure on Graham was enormous. He had to weigh everything he saw and heard and then get through to Arlene, five thousand miles away in New York, and then to me, five thousand light-years away on planet Morphine, and help us decide whether or not to go ahead with an operation. What did he make of the dingy, dirty hallways, the dimly lit emergency room?

The man on the table next to me had gunshot wounds. A guy across the room had knife wounds. We later learned that the knife wounds were self-inflicted while he was in the custody of the police, forcing the police to bring him to the hospital. He'd arranged with his girlfriend to wait outside the hospital, and at one point in the evening when no one was looking, maybe when everyone's attention was turned to the actor from North America, he slipped out of the hospital, met his girlfriend . . . and escaped. There are eight million stories in La Serena.

Graham, who has seen countless surgeries in thirty years of producing science documentaries, asked to take a look at the operating room. Dr. Zepeda, in his modest way, invited him in, and Graham could tell immediately that it was, in fact, very well equipped.

Graham got Arlene on the phone and gently, but not wasting time, told her I needed an emergency operation. She agreed and, surprisingly free of panic, she called the airlines and started arranging a flight down to Chile. Then she put in a call to Sally and Steve Cohen, close friends and both doctors, to see what they could tell her about what little she knew of my condition. She realized she didn't even know the name of the hospital or the surgeon. She was wondering: *Into whose hands are they putting my husband's life?* Steve got on the Internet and then on the telephone, and within fifteen minutes he'd managed to track down the surgeon in La Serena.

In a hurried call, Steve asked Dr. Zepeda a few pointed questions. They both knew there wasn't a lot of time. Every few minutes, more and more of my bowel was getting sucked through the loop on my omentum, where, given enough time, it would burst.

Steve: "Does he have peritonitis?"

Zepeda: "Not yet."

After a few more exchanges, Steve called Arlene and told her the guy knew what he was doing.

Steve and Sally both wanted to fly down to La Serena with Arlene. But Steve had to appear as an expert witness in court, so Sally and Arlene got ready to fly down together.

3:45 A.M. SUNDAY

They tugged at me and drew me out of my morphine stupor. "Alan? . . . Here's what's happening to you. You have a blockage in your intestine and you need surgery as soon as possible. We have to make a decision. This is Dr. Zepeda."

For the first time, I held the gaze of the man who would soon hold my life and several feet of my intestines in his hands. He was young, but he had the gentleness and presence of an older man. He smiled with mature warmth, and behind his rimless spectacles were intelligent and completely confident eyes.

"Here are your options," he said in halting English. "You could be operated on here in La Serena. . . . This is a well-equipped hospital. Or, you could fly to Santiago, where the hospitals are bigger."

Graham leaned in and said, "It's a two-hour flight, though, to Santiago. And we'd have to charter a plane, which would take some time. We could try it, but there's a problem with that. The airport here in La Serena is totally fogged in."

In a matter-of-fact way, just laying out my options for me, Dr. Zepeda said, "You could try to fly to Santiago. But if you wait for the fog to lift, you may not make it."

Well, that was pretty straightforward. *You may not make it.* In my own morphine-induced fog, those words became instantly engraved on my brain. No one had ever said to me before, "In a few hours you may be dead." It's true—it *does* concentrate the mind.

"Let's do it here," I said. And I could see on their faces that giving me the final decision was really just a courteous formality.

Interestingly, I wasn't afraid. It must have been Zepeda's quiet confidence and Graham's gentle, rational manner that let me simply accept as the next logical step that this man whom I'd never seen before would now take a sharp knife, cut open my belly, and permanently rearrange my insides. And I was never the kind of person who would kiss on a first date.

"The blood supply to some of your small intestine has been choked off and it's dying," he said. "I have to go in and resect the bad part and then sew the good parts back together."

"Oh," I said, "you're going to do an end-to-end anastomosis."

He was stunned. "Yes," he said. "How do you *know* that?"

"I did many of them on *M*A*S*H.*"

It's true. I did them on extras and day players alike. And although all I operated on was a piece of foam rubber, I could picture exactly what I was supposed to be doing.

There was a short pause, and then he laughed. Through my haze, I smiled. My real illness, it seems, is my compulsion to amuse. Apparently, you can offer to disembowel me, but I'll still see if I can make you laugh.

He went away again to get ready for the operation, and after about thirty seconds his phrase came back to me.

You may not make it.

I called over to Graham. "Graham, I need to tell you some stuff." I noticed that I said this with no emotion. I was just taking care of business. "If I don't wake up, I want you to tell this to Arlene and my daughters and my grandchildren—"

"Wait a minute," he said, "I'd better get a piece of paper."

I came up with a couple of sentences, and he wrote them down. I tried to say the unsayable in fifty words or less. A minute later, unsure that I had said enough to Arlene, I called him back and said a little more. I wanted to say more to my daughters and my grandchildren, too, but time was up.

4:00 A.M. SUNDAY

They started the anesthesia, and I went gladly into the good night.

Graham and Nick sat and waited on wooden chairs in a hallway lit by one dim bulb. The hospital was silent, empty.

5:10 A.M. SUNDAY

After an hour and ten minutes, Dr. Zepeda came out of the operating room. Graham got up and asked how it was going. "It's all done," Zepeda said. "He's all sewn up."

A while later they were wheeling me, semiconscious, out of the recovery room. Graham dialed Arlene and held his cell phone to my ear. Neither of us can remember what we said to each other. But I can remember the sound of her voice and the peace I felt hearing it. It was the first sound I heard as my life began again. We were back in Eden, starting over.

NIGHT AND DAY—SUNDAY

I woke up in my hospital room. Nurses were changing IV bags over my head. Every few minutes, it seemed, they were waking me up to take my blood pressure and stick a thermometer in my armpit, when all I wanted was to sleep.

But my dreams were worse. I was making a movie with a famous actor. In each dream, it was a different actor and a different movie. But each time I had to stop shooting to go do something on the other side of town. I never made it back to the set, where I knew I was needed. I was frustrated. I kept getting drawn farther and farther away from my obligations.

I woke up to see the night nurse hovering over me. Sometimes she was replacing my IV bottle. Sometimes she was taking my blood pressure. This time she was just looking at me enigmatically: a silent, beautiful Indian face, staring down at me, like a serene angel of death. When she left I reached back into the dream, looking for another few minutes of sleep. But then, it wasn't the famous movie star I saw. This time Rush Limbaugh was sitting across from me, glaring at me. Somehow I had disappointed him. He was angry with me. He called me hurtful names. He seemed to think I was weak, useless. Why was he mad at me? *Rush, don't be angry with me. I'm an entertainer like you. I think you're funny.* He glared at me, hate in his eyes. He wanted to kill me with his glare.

I woke up to daylight, and Nick and his wife, Jerushka, were there.

Nick had brought me a plaque signed by all the astronomers at the observatory, making me a member of the Brotherhood of Observational Cosmologists. I asked them to prop it up on a shelf where I could see it.

Jerushka, Nick's striking, ebullient Croatian wife, had brought me flowers and a large plastic bag from a store. She held up the bag triumphantly. It was full of toilet paper. I wondered why a bag of toilet paper was a triumph. Then Graham came over to the bed and proudly showed me a stack of towels he'd stolen from the hotel. Why was Graham stealing towels? The hospital towels would be fine. Then someone explained it to me: There *are* no towels in the hospital. You have to bring your own. You have to bring your own toilet paper, too. Not only that: Graham had been sent out to buy antibiotics for me at a pharmacy. Dr. Zepeda had told him he'd get a better grade of medicine if he bought it himself. I was beginning to get a feel for the little realities that marked the difference between have and have-not.

After a long night of sweaty sleep, my pajamas were wet rags. Jerushka took them home to have them laundered for me. Meanwhile, the day nurse tried to help me into a pair of hospital pajamas, but none of them fit. *Chilenos* are all much smaller than me. I squeezed into a top, but the only bottoms I could fit into were skimpy shorts. I was cold in them, and I felt ridiculous. As I crossed the room in my Chilean *gatkes,* I remembered a radio joke from my childhood in the forties. My father and Jack Carson were at the microphone in a live broadcast, doing lines by Jack Douglas, who was legendary for writing weird jokes.

- Once, my plane crashed in the jungle and I walked half-naked across South America. I wrote a book about it.
- Really? What's it called?
- *From the Indies to the Andes in My Undies.*

All my life I'd remembered this stupid joke. Now I was living it.

I moved slowly across the room and sat on the bed. I lifted my legs as a counterbalance and lowered myself sideways onto the lumpy mattress. I crawled back into sleep, and there was Rush Limbaugh again, glaring at me. *What does he want from me?*

I had trouble staying asleep. First of all, they'd put me in the maternity ward, and all night long I heard newborn babies crying. That wasn't so terrible. I like the sound of babies. But they'd also provided me with a night nurse who, when she wasn't hovering over me, staring down like the angel of death, was sitting in her chair right next to my bed, snoring. She didn't snore like an angel, either; she snored like a fully grown moose.

10:00 A.M. MONDAY

I woke up surprisingly refreshed. Dr. Zepeda had told the nurses to let me rest, not to wake me even to take my vital signs. For the first time I was given a little food. Crackers, a fresh cheese called *quesella,* some generic red Jell-O, and a glass of fat-free milk. It all tasted fantastic.

I drifted off to sleep and then opened my eyes when I heard a noise at the door. Arlene was coming into the room. I could feel a grin spread across my face. She knelt beside the bed, took my hand, and cried quietly.

10:00 A.M. TUESDAY

Sally and Arlene were worried about the countless people coming in to see me, all of them either shaking my hand or kissing me. When you say hello to a woman in Chile, you kiss her on the cheek whether you know her or not. If you don't kiss, you risk offending her. And then there were the dingy surroundings. Nick hinted that the private clinic where they first brought me might be more comfortable, and within a couple of hours I was on my way there.

3:00 P.M. TUESDAY

On a gurney again, moving down the halls, through the doors of the old hospital and out onto the pockmarked sidewalk, *kidda-clunk, kidda-clunk.* While they worked on prying open the doors of the ambulance, I looked up at the eaves of the building. Directly above my head, three pigeons were sitting on the drainpipe, facing the other way, their fat bottoms poised for a direct hit.

Ah, gravity.

Get the ambulance open, guys. Do not fiddle with it. Open the door.

3:30 P.M. TUESDAY

The new room was gorgeous. Clean. I met my nurses. The night nurse, Jocelyn, I was certain, would not snore. And the day nurse, Tatiana, was full of life and eager to teach me Spanish. It was essential that I learn a little because no one, at least no one who hung around here very long, spoke English.

Nick arranged for people from the observatory to come over and translate for us. Elaine, a Scottish-Chilean woman who worked at the observatory and spoke perfect English, took Arlene shopping. They bought me a down pillow to replace the hospital pillow, and I instantly understood why people long ago chose to sleep on feathers instead of potatoes.

Tatiana helped me translate articles in the Chilean press about my illness. It seemed to be big news down there. Spanish-speaking journalists were calling the hospital room from Bolivia and Miami. I had apparently reached the point in my life where I was getting more attention by getting sick than by acting.

8:00 P.M. TUESDAY

Exhausted, Arlene went to sleep on the bed next to mine, but I stayed awake. For the first time, I had enough energy to watch television. And to my surprise, I found myself passionately involved in the World Series. I was surprised because during my childhood, my father's ear was perpetually filled with the music of Mel Allen's exuberant vocal cords, and my rebellion was pointedly to ignore baseball entirely. The game I watched that night in the hospital was perhaps the fifth or sixth I'd seen in my entire life. And I loved it. I had apparently come back to life as a completely different person.

Not knowing whom I was supposed to root for, I found myself intimately caught up in the fortunes of Hideki Matsui. Every time he came to bat, he fascinated me. Even when the pitcher nearly killed him with a fastball close to the head, his expression never changed. He became my hero because his concentration was inspiring. Also, he didn't spit. *What is it with the spitting?* And why does the video director constantly cut to a tight close-up just as a wet one slurps out? Or do they all spit so copiously that you can't cut to anyone without capturing a Niagara of jaw juice?

Anyway, I was fascinated with Hideki. I wanted him to get on base. But he kept hitting these quasi home runs, ideal trajectories that were perfect right up to the moment a guy on the other team, almost always the same guy, stepped in casually and caught the ball. Beautiful parabolas ending in the glove of death. *Gravity, Hideki, gravity. You can't forget that you're hitting into curved space.*

Hideki walked away hitless, heroically not changing his expression, and not spitting. I fell asleep. Two hours later, I woke up to the sound of the vital signs alarm going off. I'd rolled over on my side and pulled the needle out of my arm. They stuck it back in, and I began training myself to sleep without turning. I called on the concentration of my new spiritual guide, Hideki Matsui.

7:00 A.M. WEDNESDAY

I woke up refreshed. Tatiana helped me out of bed and walked me to *el baño,* where she helped me take a shower. I was grateful for her tact as I undressed, revealing as little of myself as possible. Actors are shy exhibitionists. I once bolted across a Paris hotel room because the maid delivering breakfast was coming through the door without knocking and was liable to see me in my pajamas.

I stood with my back to Tatiana while she held the shower head, and we chatted in broken English and tattered Spanish. I was beginning to believe that I would actually learn to speak some Spanish before I left. I've always thought you could learn to get around in any language if you concentrated on about thirty well-chosen verbs, a couple of dozen nouns, a few pleasantries, and some basic sense of word order.

So a few minutes later, I was sitting up in bed, drawing diagrams for a revolutionary new language system that would enable anyone to learn any language in a week. My old pattern was intact. I don't just get flooded with ideas, I get flooded with systems. Mike Nichols diagnosed this for me one day when we were in rehearsal for *The Apple Tree.* There was a moment in the play where my character was supposed to recall something from the past, and Mike didn't think I was convincing.

"Recall something right now," he said. "Actually remember something. What were you thinking when you got out of your car this morning in the parking lot?"

"That's easy. I was thinking, Should I take my jacket with me or leave it in the car? It's warm. I probably won't wear my jacket today. But should I bring my jacket all the way into New York from New Jersey if

I don't wear it? That seems pointless. What should I do in the future? Is there a good jacket policy I can derive from this?"

There was silence in the dark auditorium. Then Mike said, "You're insane."

Yes, but look at how much I get done. It was only ten-thirty in the morning, and already I had a basic language system laid out. It used a version of a memory aid that was popular in the Renaissance: an imaginary mansion where memories can be stored and enable you to remember a string of hundreds of words. Then I incorporated an element from my friend Harry Lorayne's Memory Power System. So of course, if he liked this idea, Harry and I could go into business together. In fact, he and I could make an infomercial together. And then—wait—our friend Mel Brooks could join us on the infomercial. To Mel's amazement, we'd have him speaking Hungarian, a language he'd never heard before, in seven days. Was I manic? That description didn't come close. Galaxies were exploding in my neural networks. I was alive, and like a newborn star, I was cooking with gas.

Alan Dressler came down from Las Campanas after a night of observing. He sat on a bed across from me and genially launched into what he knew would cheer me up. "I've been thinking about your question," he said, "about curved space."

I'd been bothering all the astronomers I'd met on this show with the same question. What does Einstein mean when he says gravity is curved space? How can you picture such a thing? And not only that— gravity is supposed to be curved *space-time.* Even if you could picture how space might be curved, how do you curve time? I've decided that before I leave Chile, I'll get the answer. This is impossible, of course. Even Einstein couldn't picture it, except in two dimensions. He suggested we imagine a mattress or a rubber sheet that's been stretched on a frame, with a bowling ball on it. The bowling ball makes a depression. If you roll a baseball across the sheet, it will curve in toward the heavier ball. Curved space.

Alan Dressler knew this image didn't make it clear to me, so he said, "This morning I remembered an image that's always appealed to me. Curved space is like stepping onto a moving merry-go-round. You expect to move in a straight line, but a force, in this case the Coriolis effect, makes your path curve."

It's an image that lets you come in at another angle and *feel* the pull. But I still wished for something more tangible, more vivid. We chatted for a while, mostly about being glad to be alive, then Alan left and Nick arrived. Generously, he sat on the other bed and talked for a half hour with me about supernovas and dark energy. He knew how curious I was about his work, and he laid out a feast for me.

I was haunted by desire in Chile, and the object of my lust was curved space-time.

The astronomers had all chuckled at me, and one after another, they'd said almost the identical words to me: "You feel bad because you think you're the one person in six billion who can't picture the fourth dimension?" But I thought they *could* picture it. My friend, the mathematician Steve Strogatz, said once that as a boy, while charting the motion of a pendulum, he realized that "there could be order in the universe and that, more to the point, you couldn't see it unless you knew math." I suspected that through the language of math they have a glimmer of nature that I can't have. But somehow it can't be translated into *my* language.

THURSDAY

Tatiana helped me out of bed and walked with me down the hospital corridors, teaching me Spanish as we walked. It reminded me of walking down the hospital corridor with my father, trying to get him to blurt out words in English.

A charming, lithe man with a ponytail and a face and voice exactly like those of Ricardo Montalban came to the room and taught me to breathe with one arm draped over my head. This would prevent pneumonia, he said. Until Ricardo Montalban told me this, it didn't occur to me there were still ways to die from the operation. I wrapped my arm over my head and breathed as deeply as I could.

Every day, three times a day, Nelson Zepeda visited me to see how I was doing and stayed for fifteen or twenty minutes. There was a lot of laughing, and Nelson's wife, Tita, also a doctor, taught me how to laugh without pulling my stitches. You cross your arms over your belly and grab your sides. Tita speaks excellent English. She learned it one year as an exchange student in the United States, where she graduated from high school in Oshkosh, Wisconsin. Chile is a narrow strip of a country cut off from the world on all four sides by the Andes, the desert, the ocean, and Antarctic ice, yet Nelson studied surgery in Japan and Tita graduated from a high school in Oshkosh.

FRIDAY

Nelson said I could be released. We packed up the towels to return them to the hotel. The press was waiting in front of the hospital, and I couldn't resist a chance to perform. As I dressed, I figured out a little speech in Spanish, my new first language.

On the sidewalk, I launched into my speech, a blend of corn and sincerity:

> Yo nací en Norteamérica, y yo renací en Chile. Ahora, soy medio norteamericano y medio chileno.

This, of course, got big smiles.

> I was born in North America, and I was reborn in Chile. Now, I'm half North American and half Chilean.

I pulled Nelson over to me and kissed him on the head. Then, not knowing when to quit, I took questions and attempted answers in Spanish, which came out in a sort of Italian.

SATURDAY

Tatiana and Jocelyn came with us to the hotel.

I spent hours chatting with Tatiana in Spanish. It took hours because we could spend fifteen minutes on one sentence before I knew what she meant. She told me about her father, who worked for a large Chilean company, and about the company town on top of a mountain where she was born. Later, she pointed excitedly to a picture of the town in a book of photographs of Chile. There wasn't anything green on the entire mountain. It was barren. A lonely road wound to the top of an ashen plateau, where the housing was sited in neat rows.

"There aren't any trees," I said.

"No," she said simply, admiring the picture of her birthplace. "It's arid."

Tatiana asked about my family, and I tried to tell her, but I was still suffering from the aftereffects of the operation. I had lost some of my memory.

"I have three daughters," I told her. "There's Eve . . . Elizabeth . . ."

"And the third?"

"I can't remember . . . the anesthesia."

"Anastasia?"

MONDAY

As a surprise, our daughters Eve and Elizabeth flew down with our niece Beverly to help us make the trip home. I was feeling pretty good, so they spent a day shopping and sightseeing, and it was good to hear their laughter.

When they heard I had dictated my last words to Graham, they wanted to know what I'd said. Elizabeth particularly wanted to know if I left everything to her. But the anesthesia and the stress of that night had obliterated all of it. Finally, I got an e-mail from Graham:

The alleged last words of Alan Alda, as scrawled by GC at 3:30AM October 19 outside the O.R. at La Serena Hospital, Chile:

"I'm thinking of Arlene, Eve, Elizabeth, and Beatrice. My heart is full of love for them and all my grandchildren, and I have complete confidence if anything goes wrong that they will mourn for me and then carry on with their happy lives and take care of each other."

A few minutes later, just before being wheeled into the OR, you added this, for Arlene:

"I love you with all my heart and know that you have the strength, wisdom, and creativity to keep the family . . ." (At this point you faltered, and either you didn't complete the thought or I failed to hear what you said.)

So we still didn't know what I said. Maybe I *did* leave it all to Elizabeth.

We joked about last words, but reading Graham's letter, I choked up.

Nelson took out some of my stitches and ran a slide show on my computer of photographs of the operation. There was the necrotic ileum, and there was the anastomosis. I was surprised that I wasn't repelled by these pictures. Even the full three feet of dead intestine curled up like a huge worm on the operating table looked no more threatening than dead leaves in the backyard.

Then he handed me my dead intestine in a plastic bag, so I could give it to my doctor in the States for tests. This got us to wondering about how I'd explain this package in customs.

"Do you have a permit to take this out of the country?"
"No, no, I came in with it."

As I hugged Nelson and Nick and said good-bye, I choked up for the second time.

TUESDAY

After we were up in the air, as Nelson had warned me it would, my stomach became distended and I had to leave my trousers undone at the top. Every time I headed for the bathroom, Eve reminded me to hold on to my pants so they wouldn't fall down. Arlene said she was happy for me that if my pants did fall down, I'd finally have a legitimate reason to say I was going from the Andes to the Indies in my Undies. This got me talking at length about rhythm and sound in the construction of a joke. Why did Jack Douglas say "from the Indies to the Andes" and not the other way around? Is it funnier to go from the Indies to the Andes than from the Andes to the Indies? Arlene heard my rush of words and decided I was high. She wondered what would come next and asked Sally when I'd be able to go back on Zoloft.

Was I high? I was high.

I looked down from forty thousand feet at the Amazon. At first it looked like a fat, brown, curving snake glinting in the sun. But then it became obvious what it really was. How could anyone miss it? The Amazon is a giant ileum. It carries nutrients and waste downriver through loops and folds and, pulled by gravity, it experiences a kind of curvature of space.

And then the *real* reality of the green jungle below me percolated to the surface. If I had become sick flying over this stretch of the Amazon instead of on Cerro Tololo, I would have been four or five hours from any good-size city, no matter in which direction they might have diverted the flight. And that would have been it.

After thirteen hours, we landed. I was waiting for the luggage to be collected, my head propped up on my lucky pillow. Abruptly, I opened my eyes and called out, "Who's got my guts?"

Elizabeth held up the red biohazard bag. "I've got them. Relax."

I put my head back on the pillow. It was under control.

WEDNESDAY

We were back in our New York apartment, fifty-one floors above the city, our little *pied au ciel*. Arlene had developed a slightly fearful concern for me, as if I were now disaster prone. She went out for milk but immediately called upstairs from the lobby. On the way down, she'd noticed something wrong with the elevator. "Don't take the elevator on the left," she said. "It has a wobble. The one on the right is the one without the wobble, but the one on the left is no good. Don't take it."

"Wait a minute," I said. "Do you realize who you're talking to? I had anesthesia. How can I remember this? The shaft on the left has the wobble with a bobble, but the site on the right is the flue that is true?"

"Don't take the elevator. Please." She hung up.

FRIDAY

I was restless. I got caught up in hypomanic projects around the apartment. I rewired the phone so it reached my easy chair. I set up a wireless network so I could go online without leaving the chair. I hid more wiring under the rug so I could charge my laptop at the chair. All this so I could get some rest in the easy chair.

We have a French grandfather clock from about 1840 that had gained five minutes a day since we bought it. I decided to fix it. I remembered that Steve Strogatz had told me it's not the weight of the pendulum, it's the length that affects the timing of its swing. So I went down to the hardware store and bought a nut and bolt to lengthen the pendulum. This made it *slow* by a minute a day, so I shortened it a little. Then, a few hours later . . . bingo, it was keeping perfect time, right to the second.

I was thrilled. I was not just measuring time, I was measuring gravity. Gravity, time, space . . . I ruled them now. I just couldn't picture them. But this was better. I was like the dog with his nose out the window of a car: The neighborhood smelled glorious to me, even if I couldn't show you where it was on a map.

Fiddling with the pendulum, I felt as if I'd touched gravity itself. I'd put my hand inside its belly and felt its beat. I'd gone to Chile with the wrong question, but I'd come back with an answer.

I still wanted to see what Nick sees, what all the physicists and astronomers see, and maybe among them I'd find a Tatiana who would teach me their language. But now I wanted more than to see these things; I wanted to taste them, too.

I'd never before felt this ecstasy at the taste of being alive. Everything was in vivid colors now. Smells were pungent. The ordinary was extraordinary. The experience in Chile had pressed my reset button.

My euphoria had a touch of sadness, because I knew it would go away before long and I'd miss it. Arlene saw a more dangerous pattern forming: Man, glad to be alive, gets hypomanic; floats above the clouds; crashes to earth. On the phone, I told Steve Cohen how good I was feeling. "I hope you have a soft landing," he said. I saw their point, but how can you be just *moderately* glad to be alive?

It was morning. I was in the living room of our New York apartment, overlooking the city. The grandfather clock was ticking softly. The pale early sun painted itself across the floor and gilded the town's eastern walls while I read *The New York Times*. I felt a rush of emotion. I looked up from the paper and said to Arlene, "This is one of those mornings when I'm filled with happiness. *Filled* with it. And I'm brimming with love for you. Brimming. It's overflowing." I waited for an answer, and I didn't have to wait long.

"Right," she said. "I talked to Sally. You can start your Zoloft again anytime now."

We burst out laughing. I grabbed my sides and pressed my arms against my stitches.

I was coming in for a landing.

Up in Manhattan.

chapter 21

GOLDEN TIME

On a movie set, after the crew has worked twelve straight hours, they go into overtime pay in which every hour is worth two. It's called golden time. After Chile, I was on golden time. It was clear to me that everything I did was something I couldn't have done if I'd checked out in La Serena. Now, at last, there was no pressure to succeed. There was nothing I needed to prove to anyone. There was only the chance to have another day and to have some kind of fun with it; trivial fun or deep fun, they were both good. I still wanted to get better at what I knew how to do, but that was just another kind of fun.

There *was* one thing I needed to prove to myself: that I could still remember a play. The Bay Street Theatre in Sag Harbor, near where we lived, sent me a brilliant play by Charles Mee. It was essentially a two-character piece, and it would mean learning an enormous number of words. I worked hard on it so I wouldn't be standing there on opening night wondering what to say next. I used the memory tricks I'd learned from Harry Lorayne and a few I'd invented myself.

The biggest challenge in the script was a complicated speech that went on for two pages and needed to be spoken at a fast clip. That was okay. I could do that. But I also had to remember it while I watched the actress in the play, a voluptuous young woman named Nicole Leach, as she kept changing her dress, repeatedly stripping down to her French underwear.

I was transported back to the Hudson Theater of my childhood. Only now I wasn't in the wings, I was out onstage, and I had to watch Nicole while I kept talking as though I knew what I was talking about. Whether I accomplished this or not wouldn't make much difference, of course. As a friend said when he came backstage, "Well, you don't have to worry about knowing your lines in that speech. Nobody's paying any attention to *you*."

Sort of the position my father was in when he sang the opening number.

But I hadn't lost my memory. It was stronger than before.

Even better, I was enjoying the pure pleasure of acting; it was the doing of it that was fun. It didn't matter if it was for a few hundred people in a small theater in Sag Harbor or for millions of people, running for president on *The West Wing*. Now, events that once would have jolted me into a grinding anxiety only amused me. I was nominated for an Academy Award for Martin Scorsese's movie *The Aviator,* and the pressure started immediately.

Camera crews would be waiting when I came out of a building. Gifts started arriving, a new form of promotion called Oscar swag— suitcases full of the stuff. There was a cell phone designed especially for the nominees; a specially designed watch; a trip to China. There were also eighty pounds of face cream; a gift certificate for Botox along with a free visit to a plastic surgeon. How much more imagination Hollywood has than Stockholm, where winners have to be content with a grubby truckload of cash.

As silly as it can get, the attention focused on the nominees can make you nervous. It feels as if you're being sent to the Olympics. Earlier, all this would have thrown me: *What will I say if I win; how will I look if I lose?* Now, instead of fretting, I went back to my old acquaintance, probabilities, and I figured out my chances. Online, I looked up the odds that were being given on all the nominees by bookies in London and Las Vegas. None of them gave me a chance over Morgan Freeman. *That's fine,* I thought. *He's one of our greatest actors who's been nominated three times before and never won.* He was due. I could relax, which was good, because every honor comes with a dose of reality. The morning of the ceremony we had no milk in the house, so I went to the market to buy some. I was putting my shopping basket back in a pile near the door as a woman walked in briskly and saw me stacking the baskets. She looked me up and down and said just a little brusquely, "Do you have parsley?"

I pointed to the back of the store, and she brushed past me without a thank-you. You can tell a lot about people by the way they treat the help.

Living on golden time doesn't mean things come easily. Just because you get the day for free doesn't mean you don't have to work at it. I found this out a month later when I started rehearsals for a revival of *Glengarry Glen Ross* on Broadway. David Mamet's dialogue is so beautifully abstracted from everyday speech that if you leave out a syllable, you throw the whole scene off. And there are times when there are seven people onstage at once, all of whom have to speak in such a precise rhythm that the words are dizzying to learn. And because the story is told in truncated fragments of dialogue, you don't really know what is happening in the scene until everyone has mastered the exact words and rhythms. But, of course, you can't really get the rhythm right until you know what the words mean. This may be why William Macy, who has acted in a lot of Mamet, told me that any actor who tries to memorize a Mamet play eventually wants to commit suicide.

Three years earlier, I had acted on Broadway in *QED,* a play by Peter Parnell about the physicist Richard Feynman. In that play I was alone onstage for almost two hours, often speaking in the language of quantum mechanics, and that was easier to understand than these tough-talking guys from Chicago. We spent six years getting QED ready. With Glengarry, we'd have three weeks.

After two weeks of rehearsal, I felt like an amateur. I was still struggling to understand what I was saying or even remember it. The disjunctive way the dialogue jumps from thought to thought captures real speech, but you have to find out why it's jumping like that. As the evening of our first performance with an audience approached, I began talking about my appointment with Dr. Kevorkian.

I was sitting up until three in the morning one night, trying to understand it so I could learn it, or learn it so I could understand it; I'd have been happy with either way. For a break, I turned on the television set. An Abbott and Costello movie was playing, and I watched the old familiar routines. After a while, I locked on the screen. I was hearing something I hadn't expected. I was hearing something very similar to Mamet's rhythms. Instead of the lighthearted nonsense of Bud and Lou, of course, Mamet had the scathing, corrosive bile of Ricky and Shelly. But the rhythms were similar. These were rhythms I knew from my childhood—first listening to them in the wings, then performing them at the Hollywood Canteen. I picked up the script. When I saw the dialogue in these rhythms, it suddenly fell into place, as if I had cracked the Germans' Enigma code. The phrases that had seemed to shoot off in all directions now had a thrust that went like an arrow to the heart of what the character wanted.

Our whole company had to cope with the language, and everyone found the solution in his own way, but we had been in a foxhole together and we became a loyal team. We watched out for one another; we took the stage when it was ours and gave it back when it belonged to the other guy.

The first audience shocked us with their response. It was a bombastic evening—one of those nights where you wake up from the recurring dream of rehearsal to realize that you're alive in a world you've created wholly out of imagination. On the other side of the membrane of your imaginary universe, people are whooping with laughter at your human frailties.

In one scene that night, I looked across a desk at Liev Schreiber, who was brilliantly playing Ricky Roma, and I saw a look in his eyes that I had seen somewhere before. I held his look. We were exchanging an awareness of what was happening, an acknowledgment of what a pleasure it was to be playing this scene and to know it was working. It was the same look my father and I used to exchange. Liev was young enough to be my son, and yet—through the comradeship of the theater—there, sitting across from me, was my father. I was glad to see him again.

chapter 22

SIMPLE, AFTER ALL

So, it turned out not to be all that difficult.

I found a way of caring without caring, and it let me take chances, and when the chances I took didn't work out, it let me shrug off the mistakes and blind alleys as fun little diversions. True, things I didn't know were precious when they were here are gone now. My parents have faded to that same distant place where the trains that clattered over the railroad tracks went, where the comics laughing late into the night went, and the chorus girls combing my hair—and where my first taste of *any* part of life—have gone. They've gone to that place where the harder I try to pull them back, the more they recede and the less real they seem.

And I wonder . . . is that it? Things come and go, they blow past me like a breeze across a field, and there's nothing I can do about it?

Maybe that's so. Maybe God is the ultimate bully who teases us with life, then pulls it out of reach. Maybe there's nothing I can do but let life curl up and disappear like an old photograph.

Or maybe I *can* get it back. Maybe imagination gets it back. Perhaps *play* lets it breathe again. Someday, if in a moment of despair that voice speaks to me out of the whirlwind and says, "I will question *you* and you will answer *me*. Can *you* bring forth the creatures of the earth? And when their days are over, can *you* bring them back to life?" I'll say *yes*.

Yes, I can.

It *is* kind of simple. Except that it can't be put into words. And now that I've had my odd childhood, and become an actor, now that they invite me places to tell them what I think, to tell them what I've learned, what can I tell them?

"Perhaps you might say a few words to our students that they can carry with them all their lives?"

I look out at the kids. What can I say that would do them any good, if they don't discover it for themselves?

Look, I want to tell them, *do what you want.*

Just live. Laugh a little.

But if you have to hear some advice, if you must have advice . . . whatever you do, for God's sake, don't stuff your dog.

afterword

Hanging from a tree at a hotel in the West Indies is a birdcage like none other I've ever seen. Its door is always open. The birds fly in, peck at some seeds in a dish, and then fly out again. The first time I passed it, I stopped and watched the activity in the large iron cage for a long while. I was grateful to whoever had thought of this wonderful thing, this defiance of prisons, this rejection of holding life in place; a cage that let life fly in and out as it pleased.

We had come down to the tropics for a winter vacation. This book had come out in hardcover five months earlier, and the effort to get it launched and to finish up work on *The West Wing*, which was coming to an end, left us needing to get away. Flying to this island was a change for us. The enormous success of *M*A*S*H* had allowed us to begin taking winter vacations in the first place. And for thirty years we went to the same island in the Caribbean. Now we were trying something new, and we were seeing things with a fresh eye.

Like the birds flying in and out of the cage, a lot of changes have popped in and out of my life in the months since this book came out. Some of the insights that came with those changes stayed with me, and some, like the birds, flew right out again. One jolting experience, and one that could happen only once, was my reaction to my first sight of the book itself. The moment a first-time author hefts his own book can be an arresting moment.

Lillian Ross, the legendary writer for *The New Yorker,* had come to interview me in my dressing room at the Jacobs Theatre while I was finishing up the Broadway run of *Glengarry Glen Ross.* During the interview, a large envelope arrived from the publisher with the first copy of my book in it. She watched me open the envelope and take out the book, and as soon as she realized I was seeing it for the first time, she started scribbling a note on her small pad. "You'll take that home and read it," she said. "You'll want to see your words in print."

"I don't think so," I said, oozing a cool professionalism. "I read them hundreds of times while I was rewriting them."

"You haven't read them in a book yet. You'll want to see how they look on the page. Every writer does."

I smiled. But when I got home, I cracked open the book and started reading. It was like a drug. Words I had puzzled over, penciled out, and penciled in again were now set in type. Other people soon would be holding a book just like this, reading these same words. It was like the excitement I'd feel decades earlier when I'd sit down at airtime to watch a new episode of *M*A*S*H,* knowing that other people were watching it at that same moment. It was like performing for a kind of virtual live audience. Soon I'd become used to the sight of the book and holding it in my hands, and that first moment would be only a pungent memory.

When *Glengarry* closed I began a long tour around the country designed to make sure there would not be a living person over the age of six who didn't know I'd written this book. One of the first reviews came from my granddaughter Livvie, who was eight. She'd seen the book on her mother's desk and opened it. She read the first line ("My mother didn't try to stab my father until I was six . . .") and closed the book abruptly. "Well, *that's* weird," she said.

Most authors seem to hate going around the country talking about their books. I loved it. I went everywhere I could, and as the writer Alexander King used to say, I covered America with the slime of my amiability. I'd get up in front of hundreds of people in theaters, gymnasiums, or bookstores and tell stories about my life. It was like doing a one-man play. In fact, some of the material from the book had come from a one-man show I'd written ten years earlier. I'd written it so I could have something to perform whenever I felt like getting onstage again. Now I was doing it every few nights, and when I came offstage I'd sit down and sign books—sometimes hundreds of them. This was a nice way for a new author to spend his time.

And I learned some new tricks, like how to sign books really fast. I became absorbed in this new skill, as though I were in training to become some kind of penmanship athlete. I think sometimes that my life has been a string of obsessions. It's how I get things done. Generally I tend toward indolence, but by working myself into a frenzy, I can get every last bit off the bone. And as with most other things, I couldn't resist taking book signing to an extreme.

I flew to a giant warehouse in Tennessee to meet the salespeople and sign a huge pile of books. I had never seen a place like this. There were acres of stacked books and miles of conveyor belts carrying books past robotic arms that would flip out and knock them down chutes into shipping boxes. My handlers sat me down in a room with dozens of boxes of books, which I had to sign (as many as I could) before they rushed me to the airport. There were six people helping me—getting the books out of boxes, shoving them toward me, and getting them back into the boxes. I was doing all right, but after the first hundred books, my morbid infatuation with systems began to lick at my soul and I started reorganizing everyone. I moved the six people to different positions around me so I could shave a few seconds off each motion I made. I put one person in front of me so that each book would come straight at me and I'd be starting the first letter of my name before the book even stopped moving. Then I'd pull the book off to my left before I finished my signature so that the tail of the last letter was still going down on paper while the book was zipping off toward the box.

This was the kind of systematizing from which writing the book was supposed to have emancipated me. But I was deep in competition mode. Without looking up from the books flying past me, I asked if anyone had ever signed faster. They told me Jimmy Carter had signed faster but that his signature wasn't that legible. I gloated, of course. But my competitive mania got the job done. When I was finished, I'd signed fifteen hundred books in two hours.

I had to slow down a little when I got to the bookstore signings so I could say hello and shake hands with the people who'd been waiting in line. The champion at this, they told me, was Bill Clinton. "Well, yes," I said, "but how legible was his handwriting?" Actually, they said, it wasn't bad. I didn't bring up his name again.

I did get stopped in my tracks, though, and the system flew out the window one night when a woman came up to me with a book in hand and carrying a manila envelope. She told me she was a fourth cousin of mine and had some family pictures to give me.

I thanked her and opened the envelope quickly, trying to keep the signing machine going. I yanked the photographs out of the envelope, but as soon as I saw the picture on top of the pile, time stopped. The people waiting in line faded out of my vision, and I was back more than sixty years in La Tuna Canyon.

She had given me a photograph of my father with his arms around my dog Rhapsody. The real, living dog. It was the first time I'd seen an image of Rhapsody since he'd been stuffed. Both my father and the dog had a youthful innocence in the picture that I hadn't remembered. The image I had retained of the dog was the miserable stuffed thing on the blue velvet with the ferocious face, and I was surprised by how power-fully the taxidermist's version of my dog had blotted out my memory of this little animal I had loved so much. In the picture he seemed sweet, hardly older than a puppy, with soft eyes and a gentle mouth. He was an animal you could love and who could love you back. But that image had been wiped out almost completely by my memory of the stuffed dog. In fact, that's how I tended to refer to him now: as "the dog." But when I saw the picture, I knew immediately that this was the Rhapsody I had given my heart to. As I looked at the yellowed photo, the two images jumped back and forth in my head: the caricature of a stuffed dog and the vague memory of the living animal, as if they were vying for dominance. *This is your dog,* one said. *No,* this *is your dog,* said the other. I was holding in my hand the sad proof of how a memory can be completely erased and replaced by another.

It's surprised me as I've traveled from town to town how often people have asked me with real interest about what happened to the stuffed dog. I have no idea what happened to it. I was so disappointed in how he looked when he came back from the taxidermist that I had no sentimental attachment to the thing at all. As time went on, I became far more interested in what the stuffed dog had come to stand for: hanging on to the past, standing in place, and not moving on. Getting him out of my sight and out of my head would have been fine with me. I guess he's in someone's garage right now. Although with all the publicity he's had, he's probably on eBay. Wherever the stuffed version is now, I hope some little boy or girl is looking at it and wondering, *Why would anybody stuff a dog?* It's the kind of question that can lead to all kinds of other interesting questions.

I was traveling around, telling stories that were mostly about this search of mine to learn how to let go of the past and face uncertainty, and right in the middle of it all, I got a chance to test my progress. John Wells and the other producers of *The West Wing* were kind in letting me sandwich in the traveling I was doing with the shooting of the show, but at one point I came off the road and was given the chance to look uncertainty right in the eye. Jimmy Smits and I were playing presidential candidates, and we had ten days to get ready for a one-hour live debate.

A debate. Live. There would be no scenes in which people got into personal, emotional issues. There would be no scenes at all: just two guys on a stage, arguing political philosophies and policies. It would be scripted, but we would do one live performance that would go out to the East Coast, then another live performance for the West Coast, with the central time zone getting a delayed tape of the East Coast show. With two performances, we had two chances for things to go wrong. It brought me back to my early days as a young actor, when I had loved improvising. It was terrifying, but fun, to be thrown out onstage and to have to come up with a sketch out of thin air. Even on Broadway in those days, I would look forward to an actor's forgetting a line or actually forgetting to come onstage. It was a chance to make up the play as I went along. Later, on *M*A*S*H,* one of my favorite episodes was "The Interview," which was the only show we did that was almost completely improvised. And I had fun in the three movies I had done with Woody Allen, because unlike most writer-directors, he actually encouraged the actors to mess around with the words. The debate wouldn't be improvised; it was going to be written, and the arguments were probably going to be dense, so every word would count. But because it was live, we might still be flirting with the terror that we would suddenly not know what we were saying or that we would skip ahead to the end and suddenly have nothing to say for the last ten minutes of the show.

I waited for the script with real anticipation. For maybe the first time, I began to hope that a show I was in might have some small impact on the country. On *M*A*S*H,* I had only hoped we could produce something of quality—I can't remember ever wanting to influence people's political thinking. In fact, I thought of that kind of thing as propaganda, which I felt was the enemy of art, and still do. In the live debate, I didn't want to change anybody's mind about the way they voted, but I did hope that in a small way it might help change how we all thought about political debate. If one episode of television could make even a minute contribution, I hoped it would be to show a genuine argument—where people actually listened to and answered one another. I was playing Arnold Vinick, the Republican, and I hoped Vinick's arguments would be as sharp and convincing as possible. I wanted this partly because every actor identifies with his character and I wanted to win the debate, but also because I wanted us to show what it might be like if each person actually tried to present a reasonable case instead of mere contempt for the opponent. When the script came in, we were all excited to see that Lawrence O'Donnell had written exactly that.

Just before the first performance of the debate, Jimmy and I met backstage for a supportive hug and then ran back to our starting places. We heard the countdown before going on the air live, and then we dove in. The studio audience reacted as if they were at a real debate. They became part of the show. We managed not to lose our place in the script, and we had enough control over what we were saying to be able to toss in interruptions once in a while that were spontaneous. The second studio audience, for the West Coast show, was even more volatile, applauding and reacting so loudly to one of Jimmy's speeches that I had to quiet them down so I could get in a topper. It was exhilarating. It had the feel of improvisation, yet I didn't feel terror. I wasn't shaking with fear the way I had long ago in Illinois, when only finding a cockroach in my pocket could bring me to my senses. I knew there were millions of people watching, but I heard a voice in me say, *You've done this before. You can do it again.* The situation couldn't have been more uncertain, and I couldn't have been more comfortable with it. I was feeling as though I were getting somewhere with this search I was on.

But the changes weren't finished coming yet.

A few months later I turned seventy, a change that, as I insisted to my friends, was only symbolic. But maybe I protested too much. The day before my birthday, the book was about to be published in England and I was being interviewed in a restaurant in New York by a British journalist who asked me about receiving awards. Which one had meant the most to me? I said I guessed it was probably the Emmy that I got for writing, since that's when I did a cartwheel in the aisle on the way to collect it.

"Ah yes," he said, smiling. "The cartwheel. That was something. Do you wish you could still do a cartwheel?"

"I still can," I said, amazed at the question. "What makes you think I can't do a cartwheel?" I hadn't actually done one since I was frolicking on the grass with my grandchildren a couple of years earlier, but I was annoyed that anyone would keep score of my physical abilities according to an arbitrary number system.

A week later, with family and friends, we celebrated my seventieth birthday at a mountain retreat overlooking the Catskills. At the party, the stirring music of a klezmer band filled the room, and people started to dance spontaneously. We moved in a circle, and then we snaked through the room between tables, around pillars, collecting people along the way. As we danced, I felt an almost uncontrollable urge to do a cartwheel. *Wait a minute,* I thought as I kept dancing. *What would that accomplish? You want to do a cartwheel or just prove you can? Trying to prove you can makes you old, not young. The number 70 is more than symbolic if you have to do a cartwheel to prove it's only symbolic. And everybody who sees you do it will know that. You won't be a vigorous, youthful figure; you'll be a pathetic old man.* All this was taking place in my head while dancing and clapping my hands. I decided not to go for any acrobatics. It would look as if I were trying too hard.

But a month later we flew to the West Indies for our family vacation. I was watching my grandchildren play on the beach, and I couldn't bear not knowing any longer. I stood up and said, "Let's do some cartwheels." The kids love cartwheels, and they started turning them like wagon wheels. For my part, I did just one. As my hands hit the sand, time went into slow motion, as it had many times before in my life in bone-threatening crises. My feet swung over my head, making an arc in the air, and I could hear my muscles communicating with one another. *What's this? What's he doing? He's trying to kill us.* Meanwhile, I was thinking: *Get the leg that's pointing at the sky on the ground before the other one gets there. Then make the other leg hit the ground before you do.*

I made it back on my feet without tearing a muscle or slamming onto the sand. I had done a cartwheel that wasn't entirely graceful, but then my cartwheels never had been. I thought about doing a few more, but I decided against it. That would be showing off. That would be pathetic.

The book was an account of how I'd come to terms with fading powers and the present drawing back into the past, but possibly I hadn't learned to twist and turn with change as adroitly as I'd thought I could.

Even before the cartwheel, as we were getting ready to fly down to the West Indies, another change was occurring halfway around the world that would give me a chance to find out how well I could deal now with the passing of time. I got a call from Reuters. A reporter wanted to interview me about a shift in military medicine: The last MASH unit left in the world was about to be decommissioned. I had thought of MASH units as something that would always be there. Now, what had sparked an enormous part of my life was going to disappear. I doubted that I had anything quotable to say about it, but I called the reporter back to see if he could tell me what would become of the whole concept of MASH units. I wondered how the army would deliver emergency services now, and I asked him a dozen questions. He tried his best to answer, but eventually he said, "I don't really know that much about this. My beat is entertainment." He did say that the last MASH unit left had been stationed in Germany and had been flown to Pakistan to help with relief efforts after the 2005 earthquake there. And now, even as we spoke, the Americans were handing over the unit to the Pakistanis so that they could continue the relief work. I was glad to know that helping people in distress, the heart of MASH, would go on. He asked if I had any thoughts about the changeover from America to Pakistan. I thought for a second.

"Well," I said, "I just hope that the army leaves their phone number on the desk, in case bin Laden drops in for a checkup."

I had managed to avoid talking about my feelings, but then another call came in. *Nightline* was asking me on the show to talk about how I felt about the end of the MASH era. I said thanks, but I didn't think I had anything much to say, and I turned it down. I didn't want to focus on myself or on the past. But the next day, as we were flying down to the West Indies, my feelings started to surface. I realized I should have gone on the program. It wouldn't have been to talk about myself at all or about any of us who had made the television series. It would have been about the people who had lived through all those decades in real MASH units. I could have thanked them—not just for keeping alive thousands of wounded, but also for keeping alive that amazing human impulse we have at times to put ourselves in the line of fire to save another person's life: someone we don't know, someone who may never know we were even there. They gave us a look at the finest part of ourselves. Their devotion was, in fact, the finest kind.

And, of course, they *had* affected me, and in a very personal way. Without the chance to play at living their lives, I'd never have got to where I did in my own life. Without them, I wouldn't be on a plane to the West Indies; I wouldn't have had the chance to grow as an actor or as a director or writer. I probably wouldn't have written this book. Even the night in Chile when Dr. Zepeda saved my life had an echo of *M*A*S*H*. The end-to-end anastomosis he did on me was the first operation I had learned about when we began the series. And he had watched the show while he was in high school. We had both come to that night from a fictional background, and now we were doing the real thing.

But from here on, MASH units would exist only in history books, in the novel by Dr. Hornsberger, in the movie by Robert Altman, and in our television series. People who had been through a real MASH experience would have their memories of it, but even those memories would be affected, and changed, perhaps, by the books, the movie, and the TV show. We had tried to keep the series as true as we could to the lives they had lived and still meet the demands of a weekly half-hour comedy. But now *we* were the representation of a life that had totally passed. Were we like the stuffed dog that was a lifeless caricature, or were we like the photo my fourth cousin handed me that brought back Rhapsody so vividly and warmly? I hope what we did was like the iron cage with the open door, letting life fly in for a moment.

Sometimes on a trail in the woods, you hold out your hand and offer it to a small bird, hoping it will sit there for a moment. And if you're lucky and artful, it does. But just for a moment, and then it flies off again. There's no formula that can capture it; it's a kind of art. And art is many things. It's work and intelligence and intuition, and sometimes it's thinking with your body as well as your brain. But it's also play—play that's at once intelligent and innocent, both controlled and abandoned.

Freud said that life is all about being able to love and to work. And I think it *is* about those things. But it's also about play. Play can bring back the past, but even if it doesn't, play is now; play is fun. More than ever, I have the feeling that all of what we do that counts is just love and work and play.

And for me, because it makes the other two even better, the best of these is play.

At least that's how it seems today, here in the shade of this palm tree.

—ALAN ALDA
West Indies, 2006

Robert Alda and Rhapsody

ALAN ALDA played Hawkeye Pierce for eleven years in the television series *M*A*S*H* and has acted in, written, and directed many feature films. He has starred often on Broadway, and his avid interest in science has led to his hosting PBS's *Scientific American Frontiers* for eleven years. He was nominated for an Academy Award in 2005 and has been nominated for thirty-two (and has won five) Emmy Awards. He is married to the children's book author and photographer Arlene Alda. They have three grown children and seven grandchildren.

ABOUT THE TYPE

This book was set in Requiem, a typeface designed by the Hoefler Type Foundry. It is a typeface inspired by inscriptional capitals in Ludovico Vicentino degli Arrighi's 1523 writing manual, *Il modo de temperare le penne*. An original lowercase, a set of figures, and an italic in the "chancery" style that Arrighi helped popularize were created to make this adaptation of a classical design into a complete font family.